20TH-CENTURY COMPOSERS
Sergey Prokofiev

Sergey Prokofiev

by Daniel Jaffé

Φ

Phaidon Press Limited
Regent's Wharf
All Saints Street
London N1 9PA

Phaidon Press Inc.
180 Varick Street
New York, NY 10014

www.phaidon.com

First published 1998
Reprinted 2008
© 1998 Phaidon Press Limited

ISBN 978 0 7148 4774 0

A CIP catalogue record for this book is
available from the British Library

Cover illustration by Jean-Jacques Sempé
Designed by HDR Design
Printed in Singapore

Frontispiece, Prokofiev strikes
a lonely pose in a New York
street: with the turn of the
1930s, after almost ten years
touring Europe and America,
Prokofiev felt increasingly
homesick and restive with
Western audiences.

Contents

Preface

Prokofiev is paradoxically one of the best loved yet one of the least
known of twentieth-century composers. In my late teens I heard by
chance a radio broadcast of Itzhak Perlman playing a wonderfully
lyrical concerto with some of the most bewitching sounds I had ever
heard from an orchestra. (It was the BBC Symphony Orchestra,
celebrating their fiftieth anniversary, conducted by Gennady
Rozhdestvensky, then their chief conductor.) I was utterly astonished
when it was announced afterwards that this was Prokofiev's First
Violin Concerto; such ethereal scoring and delicious lyricism (rather
than mere melodiousness) seemed unlikely from a composer I had
associated with rather grandiose, heavy-weight orchestration and
bluff humour. It is as if one knew a man with a distinct public
persona – jovial and mischievous – who then, in a particularly
confiding or private moment, dropped his mask and revealed his true
self as a tender-hearted, sensitive person, capable of a radiant poetry.

Prokofiev is full of such surprises. In the midst of aggressively
colourful music within his opera *The Love for Three Oranges* comes an
oasis of impassioned lyricism with the appearance of the three
princesses; then there is the extraordinary simplicity with which
Prokofiev in his First Violin Sonata creates an utterly beautiful and
poignant moment – just a piano playing a series of gently chiming
chords and a violin playing a rapid scale up and down its entire
compass; and who would have expected of him those long-breathed
melodies of such aching nostalgia within that bleak masterpiece, the
Sixth Symphony?

Despite Prokofiev's enduring popularity and the respect his music
has earned from both musicians (such as Sviatoslav Richter, Gennady
Rozhdestvensky, Mstislav Rostropovich, Edward Downes and Valery
Gergiev) and composers (Britten, Poulenc, Walton, Roussel and
Stravinsky among them), certain critics and most musicologists are
inclined to dismiss him as superficial, lacking the intellectual or
revolutionary qualities to be found in such composers as Stravinsky,

Is H. to S. revealing of himself? add to conclusion too.

Debussy or Schoenberg. This is surely to miss the point. Prokofiev may have lacked the technical finesse of a Berg or a Britten, but was arguably a far more creative and inventive composer. Certainly he was one of the most extraordinarily prolific of the twentieth century – which may account for the reluctance on the part of writers to assess his output, and why they have parroted the 'naughty boy of music' line, a cliché founded on a handful of his better-known works. But above all, his music, at its best, speaks with power, directness and truth in ways more protean, possibly, than any other composer this century.

I spent several years in my late teens and early twenties looking for informative and readable books on Prokofiev. Alas, for English-language readers little was available in the 1980s and 1990s. Prokofiev himself made two attempts at an autobiography: the first, *Notes from Childhood*, written from 1937, is an enormously detailed and revealing portrayal of his early life, based both on his memories and his extensive collection of diaries and letters. Given its length and detail, it is hardly surprising that it remained unfinished at his death in 1953 (he had covered only as far as 1909). An abridged version of *Notes from Childhood* was published in English as *Prokofiev by Prokofiev* in 1979. A second and much less detailed biography was begun in 1941 to a commission from the journal *Soviet Music*: this traces events up to his return to Russia in 1937. Both autobiographies are out of print.

Almost every English-language biography, including this one, has been indebted to Harlow Robinson's heavily researched (if not altogether reliable) biography, which revealed more about Prokofiev's character than perhaps anything else since the publication of *Notes from Childhood*. My own debt, however, is greatest to those who knew Prokofiev, above all his son Oleg, who gave of his time to talk to me about his father, offer advice and who generously loaned his treasure trove of family photographs and his own telling portraits of his father which are reproduced in this book. Special thanks are also due to the following: Ian McDonald, who first suggested I should write this book; Noëlle Mann at the Prokofiev Archive, Goldsmiths College, London, who gave me access to the papers of the late Christopher Palmer and of Lina Prokofieva, the composer's first wife; picture researcher Deirdre O'Day who discovered some rare photographs of my subject; Mstislav Rostropovich, who talked revealingly about Prokofiev's final years; and Roger Sears, Ingalo Thomson and Daniel

Cunningham of Phaidon Press for their editorial support. Others who have directly helped are the conductors Valery Gergiev and Theodore Kuchar, David Gutman, Norman Lebrecht, Robert Matthew Walker, Edwin Stacey, Frith Trezevant, Grainne Jones and Dierdre Ferenghi. Needless to say, responsibility for opionions and for any errors of fact within the present volume lies with the author. Finally a big thank you to my colleagues at *Classic CD* magazine who have not only tolerated but encouraged my work on this book.

A note is necessary regarding dates mentioned in the text. Until February 1918 Russia followed the Julian (Old Style) calendar, which in the nineteenth century ran twelve days behind the Gregorian (New Style) calendar in use in Western Europe; by the twentieth century it was thirteen days behind. At midnight, 31 January 1918 the Soviet government switched to the New Style calendar, declaring the next day 14 February. All dates given in this text are according to local usage: thus, when Prokofiev is in Western Europe, all dates are according to the New Style calendar, whereas dates relating to Russian events and performances up to January 1918 follow the Old Style.

Daniel Jaffé
Bath/South Wraxall, 1997

Preface to First Reprint

Since the original publication of this book, much in the way of scholarship and further publication on the life and work of Prokofiev has taken place. In 2003, the year marking the fiftieth anniversary of the composer's death, Prokofiev's voluminous and detailed diaries, which he had kept – with occasional breaks – from 1907 until 1936, were released. They have been published in Russian by his family (up to the year 1933), and Anthony Phillips is in the process of making an excellent translation into English (see Further Reading, p226). While the general form and scope of my original text remains the same, I have taken the opportunity to make some amendments and corrections in the light of these publications.

Bristol, 2007

I

The one-year-old Prokofiev
with his parents, Maria
Grigoryevna and Sergey
Alexeyevich, in the orchard at
Sontsovka, 1892

*My mother loved music, and my father
respected it. No doubt he, too, loved it, but on a
philosophical level, as a manifestation of culture,
as a flight of the human spirit ... My mother's
attitude toward it was much more practical ...
It can hardly be said that she had musical
talents ... But she had three musical virtues:
persistence, love, and taste.*

Sergey Prokofiev, *Notes from Childhood*

The Russian Wunderkind 1891–1914

Sergey Sergeyevich Prokofiev was born on 11 April 1891 (23 April New Style) at Sontsovka, a Ukrainian estate managed by his father. His mother, Maria, had an impoverished background: her father, a serf until the emancipation of 1861, had had a succession of jobs but – through both ill-luck and lack of formal qualifications – had often found it hard to support his family. The fun-loving and witty Maria had courted and married Sergey Alexeyevich Prokofiev against considerable opposition from his family. A graduate from the Petrovsko-Razumovskaya Agricultural Academy near Moscow, he was intelligent and well-read. When Maria first met him, he had seemed serious and forbidding, but for all his reserve he was a kind, even tender-hearted, man. Sergey Alexeyevich had been running his own small property, but with little success due to poor soil and the necessary expenditure on machinery. Facing the possibility of having to support a family, he accepted an offer from a fellow Academy graduate, Dmitry Sontsov, to run the extensive Sontsovka estate in the Ukraine.

It was into this isolated, rural community that his son was born – two girls had earlier died in infancy. Sontsovka, almost 1500 kilometres south of Moscow, could only be reached from the nearest railway station by horse and carriage along twenty-five kilometres of rough and often rutted rural roads. Maria Prokofieva did not relish the bleakness of Sontsovka's winters, and usually abandoned husband and estate during these months to stay with her aristocratic St Petersburg relations, the Rayevskys. Even when her new-born son became ill with dysentery, she refused to change this routine, revealing an almost ruthless determination which her son would inherit. (Her apparent *sang-froid* was perhaps natural to women of her generation, to whom infant mortality was an everyday reality.) The infant Sergey did recover, however, and Maria, overjoyed at his survival, was from that winter onwards to devote herself whole-heartedly to his health and well-being.

From infancy Prokofiev heard his mother play the piano, mostly Beethoven and Chopin; as a result, he became 'genuinely scornful of light music'. While his father took care to educate Sergey in Russian language and literature, it was Maria's love of music and piano playing which most profoundly captured his imagination. While still a very young child Prokofiev attempted to join in while Maria practised: 'I would try to find room for myself at the keyboard. Since she was using the middle register for her exercises, Mother would sometimes let me use the two upper octaves, on which I would tap out my childish experiments. The noise was rather frightful, but my mother knew what she was doing, for before long I was sitting down at the piano by myself, trying to pick out some tune.'

Aged five Prokofiev composed his first piece for piano, an *Indian Galop* so named after overhearing grown-up talk about a famine in India. Maria put it down on paper, quite a task for someone who had never before written down music, and the result is a charming, perky little tune with an alternating two-note accompaniment. Intrigued by the process of writing music on paper, Sergey was soon trying it out for himself. By his seventh birthday he had composed several pieces including a March for four hands. Maria encouraged this interest in music and began teaching him the piano.

Sergey's sole companions were the children of the household servants. He later recalled the girls with particular affection, volunteering rather less about his male companions: 'They all called me *barchuk* ('young master') and addressed me with the formal *vy*. I called them by their first names and used the familiar *ty*. They had strict orders to behave properly towards me, the *barchuk*, and not do "anything stupid".' Sergey's son, Oleg, has since pointed out that *barchuk* is in fact a pejorative expression, meaning 'the boy who plays the lord'. No malice may have been intended by the nickname, but it certainly encapsulated a situation where the estate boys had no option but to comply with the wishes of the estate manager's son.

Prokofiev was not a robust child, but he was tremendously energetic. As he grew older he relished organizing the estate children in such games as cops and robbers, explorers and naval battles waged on stilts. His lively imagination made him a popular companion; according to a family friend, when the teenage Prokofiev later went away to study 'the others missed him, since without him they didn't have anything to do. They often came to the house to ask if he was coming back soon. When the summer holidays drew near, they were especially excited, and they would greet him with unfeigned delight.'

This popularity nurtured a spontaneous charm in Prokofiev that in adult life was to be such an attractive feature. On the other hand, his expectation of getting his own way, as the estate manager's son, led to a certain ungraciousness in dealing with his peers – the merest disagreement or frustration could make him abusive and petulant. Maria indulged her son's energetic activities although she worried that he would drive himself into a fever and, as his musical skill manifested itself, that he might injure his hands. Prokofiev enjoyed teasing his mother, which may have sparked the 'rebellious' streak that later affected his behaviour towards those in authority.

In January 1900, to celebrate the new century, the Prokofievs took their eight-year-old son to Moscow, which was more than two days' travel from Sontsovka. They went to the opera at the Solodovnikov Theatre to see Gounod's *Faust* and Borodin's *Prince Igor*, and to the Bolshoi for Tchaikovsky's ballet *Sleeping Beauty*. *Faust* particularly impressed Sergey, and he was very taken with the character of Mephistopheles – 'a lovely Devil,' he noted, 'but naked and without a tail.' Back at home he started making up his own plays, which 'inevitably included a duel – the result of Faust's duel with Valentin'. He also began composing his own opera, *The Giant*, fashioning its plot piecemeal from the various plays he improvised with friends.

When the score was completed, his mother checked it for obvious mistakes before passing it to the French governess to make a neat

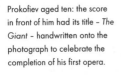

Prokofiev aged ten: the score in front of him had its title – *The Giant* – handwritten onto the photograph to celebrate the completion of his first opera.

copy. *The Giant* was first performed that summer at his uncle Rayevsky's house on the Pokrovskoye estate. On the first evening of their stay Maria, worried about Sergey's nervousness, insisted it be performed without further ado; the family participants only staged its first act, which was all they had managed to learn. It went down very well, and Prokofiev was encouraged to start work on a second opera later that year. *Desert Islands*, which told the typically boyish story of a storm and shipwreck, was a weightier work, 'each scene almost as long as the whole of *The Giant*'. Though Prokofiev had a better grasp of basic notation, the new opera proved too ambitious an undertaking for the nine-year-old: he had failed to think the story through and after eighteen months abandoned it with only the overture and first act completed.

Prokofiev's parents recognized his talent, and organized a trip to St Petersburg for more opera, then to Moscow where – through family friends – he was introduced to Sergey Taneyev, a highly respected composer and professor at the Moscow Conservatory. Taneyev invited Prokofiev to play the overture to *Desert Islands*, then examined the score to *The Giant*. Impressed by what he heard and saw, he recommended that Prokofiev take lessons in compositional theory, emphasizing the need to learn correct harmony before acquiring bad habits. He also offered to find a suitable conservatory graduate – 'a genuine composer' – who would come to Sontsovka for the summer to give Sergey tuition in composition and piano.

In the summer of 1902 a four-horse carriage set off to collect Reinhold Moritsevich Glière from the railway station and delivered him, clutching a violin case, to Sontsovka. Glière quickly won his young pupil's heart by his willingness to play croquet, chess, even taking up a challenge to a duel with dart pistols. He also made a point of watching Prokofiev and his young friends at play, considering their make-believe scenarios useful training for a budding opera composer. Glière taught Sergey harmony, 'song' form (the fundamental musical structure in which the opening theme returns to end a piece after a contrasting middle section; for some time afterwards Prokofiev called his short piano compositions 'songs') and some rudiments of orchestration. While working on a Beethoven sonata, for instance, Glière would point out various passages and chords suggesting how they might be suitably orchestrated – before widespread use could be

Reinhold Moritsevich Glière (1875–1956), the young composer who came to teach Prokofiev compositional theory at Sontsovka, in the summer of 1902

made of gramophone recordings, Glière could only appeal to
Prokofiev's imagination.

It was not long before Sergey demanded to have a go at writing a
symphony and, with Glière's assistance, a symphony was completed
by November. That month he and his mother visited Taneyev in
Moscow. With Sergey, Taneyev played through the four-hand
arrangement of his new symphony, then said, 'Bravo! Bravo! But the
harmonic treatment is a bit simple. Mostly just … heh, heh … I, IV,
and V progressions.' This stung Prokofiev into harmonic
experimentation, which was something of a mixed blessing. He
discovered individual sonorities which were pleasing to him and gave
a distinctive flavour to his music, but two years later, when beginning
his studies at the St Petersburg Conservatory, he was frustrated by his
teachers' insistence on orthodox harmonic procedure when his own,
distinctive style was already emerging. His very precocity meant he
would find it hard, almost impossible, to benefit from their teaching.
For a long time afterwards, his compositions suffered from the lack of
the kind of discipline acquired by those who have learnt their craft
more slowly but surely.

Glière spent one further summer at Sontsovka, setting Sergey the
task of composing a one-act opera on Pushkin's *Feast in Time of
Plague*. He was approaching the age of thirteen, and his parents
needed to make arrangements for his high-school education. Moscow,
the nearest city, seemed the most realistic possibility, but Maria, not
wishing her son to board, was attracted to the idea of finding a
Moscow apartment where both she and Sergey could live during term-
time. Sergey's father was dismayed at the prospect of losing wife and
son for the better part of each year: Sergey was woken one night by a
stormy discussion from his parents' bedroom and was distressed to
overhear his father saying, 'In that case there's nothing for me to do
but shoot myself.'

Despite her hopes, Maria's investigation into high school places in
Moscow was discouraging. Early in 1904, after two fruitless trips, she
and Sergey went to visit relations in St Petersburg. Here, Maria fell
suddenly ill; the exact nature of her illness is unknown, but the
situation was serious enough for her husband to be summoned
without delay. Maria's health improved, by which time she had
thought further about Sergey's future, and had become convinced of
the advantages of moving to St Petersburg: her sister, Tanya, knew

many people in the city – including one of Russia's leading composers Alexander Glazunov, a former pupil and now a close friend of the legendary Rimsky-Korsakov (one of the nationalist composers of the group known as the *kuchka* or 'Mighty Five') – and could introduce Maria to more privileged circles than would be possible in Moscow. This time her husband readily acceded, unwilling to argue with his wife when she had come so close to death.

Prokofiev was granted an interview with Glazunov, then professor at the St Petersburg Conservatory. As Maria did not appear to be planning a musical career for her son, there was little at stake over this meeting, so it is perhaps unsurprising that Prokofiev could not recall much about it. He remembered only that Glazunov praised his *Feast in Time of Plague* before turning to speak to his mother. Yet just over a week later Glazunov came to see Maria, urging her to send her son to the Conservatory. Bemused by this turn of events, she provocatively asked whether Sergey would not be better off preparing to be an engineer or an architect, giving him a more reliable career. To this Glazunov countered: 'If someone of his talent doesn't go to the Conservatory, then who should?' Reiterating his belief in Sergey's ability, Glazunov assured her that should he be proved wrong, the Conservatory provided enough academic studies to enable the boy to pursue an alternative career.

After careful thought, Maria took Glazunov's advice. In September Prokofiev was presented for examination by the Conservatory's board of professors, who included Glazunov and Rimsky-Korsakov. (The latter was impressed when Prokofiev came before the board bearing no less than two folders, one containing compositions written that year, the other older works.) Prokofiev was examined in sight-reading a Mozart sonata, in recognizing intervals and was asked to play part of his new opera *Undine* – a work started earlier that summer at the suggestion of a literary amateur, Maria Grigorevna Kilshtett, an acquaintance of the Rayevskys. Prokofiev's abilities impressed the board, and the examiners assigned him to take the prestigious composition course run by Rimsky-Korsakov and Anatol Lyadov.

Life at the Conservatory, however, was quite different from the nurturing world of Sontsovka. Thrown among many other students, Sergey found himself the youngest of those studying composition, some of whom were as much as fifteen years older than him: he was a boy among men. Furthermore, the Conservatory's rigid, even spartan

С. Петербургъ — St. Pétersbourg   Консерваторія — Le conservatoire

'That horrible musical prison': Stravinsky's description of the St Petersburg Conservatory, where Prokofiev studied from 1904 until 1914

c.f. Moscow on return.

atmosphere was difficult for even relatively mature composers (Igor Stravinsky, who was at this time in his early twenties and studying privately with Rimsky-Korsakov, later called it 'that horrible musical prison'). In addition, Prokofiev's ability in compositional theory soured relations with the adult students. Some were clearly embarrassed to share classes with a child, let alone be often bested by him. Matters did not improve when Prokofiev, possibly out of boredom, began to keep statistics on the errors made by students in his class.

Moreover, Prokofiev was ill-matched to his composition tutor, Lyadov. Though highly talented, Lyadov was notoriously indolent and incapable of sustained work. (Years later, by failing to make progress on a ballet for the impresario Sergey Diaghilev, Lyadov would present Stravinsky with his first big break – *The Firebird*, Stravinsky's most popular ballet, was the result.) Prokofiev, highly strung and industrious, could hardly have been more different from his teacher, whom he found distasteful: 'I can still see him – the corpulent figure, the swollen eyelids, the bloated face, the short arms with the hands stuffed deep into his trouser pockets – as he swayed on the tips of his high shoes with prunella uppers, waiting for his student to go away and leave him in peace.'

Maria felt her son was receiving insufficient encouragement from his teachers: 'No one at the Conservatory cares about talent. Mediocrity is easier to deal with, and less trouble.' Her resentful attitude to the Conservatory's treatment of her son could only, unfortunately, have reinforced in him a degree of contempt for his teachers. Fortunately for Sergey, though, Maria arranged extra tuition over the summer from Mikhail Chernov, a Conservatory graduate who came recommended by Glazunov.

Maria was also discovering that being in St Petersburg did not automatically grant her entry to a glamorous social life: 'We are still living a very isolated life,' she wrote to her husband. 'You'd think we weren't in the city at all. No one comes to see us, and we don't go to see anyone.' From being a woman of consequence in their Ukrainian estate, she was now reduced to a provincial. Their only regular contacts were their well-connected relations, the Rayevskys, and one or two of their acquaintances.

Three of Prokofiev's Conservatory professors: (left to right) Nikolay Rimsky-Korsakov, Anatol Lyadov and Alexander Glazunov; although all were accomplished composers, they disapproved of the latest musical innovations which Prokofiev was to relish.

In many respects the Rayevskys, courtiers to the royal family, were typical St Petersburgers. The wide boulevards and neo-classical, Italianate-style façades of Petersburg (so named by the locals) reflect the aspiration of its founder, Tsar Peter the Great – that the city should match the great European capitals. The city, long despised for being western and un-Russian – Gogol and Dostoyevsky were just two

writers who portrayed St Petersburg as stiff, cold and unnatural, inhabited by courtiers and petty bureaucrats – enjoyed a renaissance of appreciation at the turn of the century, largely due to the artist and writer Alexander Benois. In *Mir iskusstva* ('World of Art') – the short-lived but influential art magazine he co-founded with Diaghilev in 1898 – Benois revealed the glories of St Petersburg, arousing pride not only in the capital but also in Russian culture. He inspired many cultural figures, in particular the young Diaghilev, to promote all that was best in contemporary Russian art, thus heralding a flowering of the arts in what became known as the 'Silver Age'.

Early in January 1905, when on their way back to St Petersburg after their winter holiday, Maria and Sergey stopped off to see Glière in Moscow. There they heard news of strikes and demonstrations in the capital. On Sunday 9 January, a peaceful procession of workers had come to the Winter Palace to present a petition. The Tsar's troops, ill-trained to cope with crowds and roused by rumours that the Palace was to be besieged, opened fire on the demonstrators at point-blank range. Forty people were killed outright. The massacre

'Bloody Sunday', 1905: the infamous moment when the Tsar's troops guarding the Winter Palace opened fire on a peaceful procession, so precipitating the 1905 Revolution

sparked an uprising of outraged workers that was bloodily put down the same day: at least 200 people were killed and many hundreds more injured. The shock waves that swept through Russia by what became known as 'Bloody Sunday' caused irreparable damage to the Tsar's reputation among both the educated classes and the workers; for many months thereafter Russia was in a state of near anarchy.

Maria and Sergey arrived in St Petersburg on 12 January to find the city in uneasy quiet. 'You often run into Cossack patrols from two to five men,' Sergey wrote to his father, 'and all the storefronts and shop windows are boarded up.' It was not long before discontent stirred again: the railways went on strike, and store windows were smashed and raided. It became dangerous to go out at night and Maria would not allow her son to leave the apartment by himself.

On 4 February, Grand Duke Sergey, second cousin and brother-in-law of the Tsar, was shot by terrorists. As a direct result, a large number of Conservatory students went on strike. Matters came to a head on 16 March as mounted police surrounded the Conservatory and arrested more than a hundred student protesters. When the director, A.R. Bernhard, ordered all those detained to be expelled, a group of teachers sent him a letter demanding his resignation. Within a week, Rimsky-Korsakov was dismissed from the faculty for his criticism to the press of the directorate's handling of the strike; Glazunov and Lyadov, aghast at the dismissal, both gave public notice of their resignation.

Two days later Glazunov directed a performance of Rimsky-Korsakov's *Kashchei the Immortal*. The composer was given an ovation as he entered, and the occasion soon turned into a public demonstration, someone even crying, 'Down with autocracy!' The police were called in; they lowered the safety curtain then dispersed the audience. Thereafter Rimsky-Korsakov was kept under police surveillance, his works banned from performance by the governor general. The Conservatory building was closed for six months.

During that time Prokofiev took lessons from both Lyadov and his piano teacher, Alexander Winkler, at their homes. Although he had signed a student letter of protest against the Conservatory's directorate, Prokofiev was too young and politically naïve to be fully involved in the student protests: furthermore, he took his lead from his mother, whose attitude was that he should study and 'not become involved in unfathomable matters', reminding him that they had left his father in

Sontsovka in order for him to study in St Petersburg. By the Easter
holiday it was clear that the Conservatory would not reopen for some
time, and Lyadov advised Prokofiev not to bother returning for the
summer term. So ended Prokofiev's first year at the Conservatory.

In the five months preceding the following school year he was
coached thoroughly by his parents for his academic exams. He made
friends over the summer with the new local vet, Vasily Mitrofanovich
Morolev, a keen amateur musician and chess player, whom Prokofiev
liked immediately as his 'talk was larded with witticisms'. (Prokofiev
eventually dedicated his first designated opus, the Piano Sonata in F
minor, to him.) But even in this apparent haven there were
revolutionary stirrings:

> On 29 June ... an anonymous letter was nailed to the fence of the big
> orchard. It was addressed to my father and ... stated that it was high time
> for the landowners and their managers to get out of Sontsovka before they
> were dealt with in the appropriate manner. My father was alarmed and
> called a small meeting of peasants. ... I believe it was all rather peaceable,
> since the letter was apparently of outside origin and indifference still
> prevailed in the age-old core of the Sontsovka peasantry ... But in August,
> when the mown hay had been piled into high stacks which were often
> several kilometres distant from Sontsovka, fires began to break out. The
> peasants were burning out the landowners. Usually this happened around
> midnight, when I was asleep. I would be awakened by the sounding of the
> alarm, and in the dark southern night the bright glow of flames could be
> seen on the horizon.

Partly to distract Sergey from these disturbing events, his father drew
up a reading list of 'grown-up literature' for him. Back in St
Petersburg, Sergey joined a local library and, following his father's list,
read Tolstoy's *War and Peace*, Thackeray's *Vanity Fair*, Goncharov's
The Frigate Pallas and a selection of Ostrovsky's plays. Prokofiev
started to give ratings to the books he read, in the manner of school
marks. *War and Peace* was awarded his highest score.

The increasingly disastrous war with Japan, which broke out in
1904, had forced the Tsarist government to sue for peace, signing the
Treaty of Portsmouth on 5 September. Russia's humiliating defeat,
following the recent memory of 'Bloody Sunday', stirred popular

outrage. The Tsarist government's attempts to calm the people with promises of a new representative parliament ironically brought the political crisis to a head. In the hope of mollifying students, a measure was passed on 27 August making universities no-go areas for police and allowing students to hold assemblies. Far from defusing the situation, students and radicals used their inviolable university platform to incite the workers. Towards the end of September a wave of strikes over wages erupted, which soon became politicized. By the end of October, Russia was paralysed by a general strike, which lasted ten days: cities were left without communications, food and medical supplies; there was no electricity and water; and all railways, apart from the St Petersburg–Moscow line, came to a standstill. The Tsar had no alternative but to make political concessions; on 17 October he signed the so-called October manifesto in which he promised to create a Duma – a parliament with administrative powers, elected by a wide but limited suffrage. This manifesto was joyously received and with the St Petersburg soviet's vote to end the strike, workers returned to their posts. A return to normal life, however, took some time. Right-wing thugs – as part of a backlash – attacked those, particularly students, whom they believed responsible for the Tsar's humiliation: in practice this meant anyone who looked either intellectual or Jewish. Conservatory classes would not revert to normal until the spring of 1906, when Glazunov was appointed director.

The new academic year allowed Prokofiev's class to start counterpoint without taking any examination in harmony beforehand. Unfortunately, Rimsky-Korsakov – who usually taught the counterpoint class – wished to spend more time on his own compositions, and now only gave classes in orchestration. Prokofiev's year found themselves still under Lyadov, who continued to hold his classes in a desultory, grumbling manner. Rimsky-Korsakov's orchestration course was to prove disappointing. Prokofiev admired him greatly as a composer: he was to perform his teacher's Piano Concerto well into maturity, and shared in the general excitement of the première of his *Invisible City of Kitezh* on 7 February 1907. But Rimsky-Korsakov's renown as a great orchestrator led to heavily overcrowded and impersonal classes. Prokofiev found it hard to pay attention while the master, seated at the piano, looked through the scores of one student after another, and after two years he 'barely passed' his exam.

Rimsky-Korsakov did not conceal his dislike of much that was considered avant-garde in music. Though a former member of the radical *kuchka* that had forged a distinctive Russian national style, he had since refined this style into an idiom that, by the turn of the century, was itself conservative. (This conventional 'national' style, ironically, failed to embrace the innovations of Modest Mussorgsky, the most significant member, historically, of the *kuchka*. Mussorgsky's insistence on writing music true to Russian speech inflection and expression, coupled with an instinctive and sensitive approach to harmony, had created an utterly unique style. His music profoundly influenced the works of a number of leading turn-of-the-century composers, most notably Debussy.) And while Rimsky greatly admired and was influenced by Wagner, he seems to have disliked any composer who attempted to surpass Wagner's harmonic audacity. Prokofiev saw his professor at a rehearsal of Skryabin's Third Symphony, *The Divine Poem*. He looked 'as if an electric current had been sent through his seat. He kept jumping up and waving his hands, or shrugging his shoulders, or jabbing his finger at the score …' Prokofiev himself, well primed by an earlier exposure to Wagner's operas, was fascinated by the work.

He received most encouragement that year not from any of his professors but from a new student who joined Lyadov's counterpoint classes: Nikolay Myaskovsky. Ten years older than Prokofiev, Myaskovsky 'showed up at the Conservatory in the uniform of a lieutenant […] with a big yellow portfolio under his arm'. In marked contrast to the sometimes insolent Sergey, he was reserved, polite and taciturn. Their friendship was instigated by Myaskovsky, who was looking for a duet partner to play Beethoven's Ninth Symphony in a four-hand arrangement. Prokofiev suggested that they have a go at it at his mother's flat. So began a regular pastime of reading through piano scores of works they wanted to study: as well as Beethoven's symphonies, they played Rimsky-Korsakov's *Scheherazade*, Glazunov's Fifth, Sixth and Seventh Symphonies and Wagner's *Faust* overture.

One work they played several times was Max Reger's Serenade. When Reger had conducted this in St Petersburg, in December 1906, Prokofiev was intrigued by the way in which the work 'juxtaposed distant tonalities with such ease that one would think they were the tonic and dominant'. He later developed this trait in his own writing, most memorably in the Gavotte of his 'Classical' Symphony. The rich, chromatic lyricism of the Seranade's third movement also seems to have made a deep impression: its influence would be evident almost thirty years later in the love music of his ballet *Romeo and Juliet.*

Almost as important to Prokofiev's development was Nikolay Tcherepnin, who taught him conducting from the spring of 1907. Although Prokofiev had taken his course in score reading the previous year, it was now that Tcherepnin, who was to conduct the first Paris seasons of Diaghilev's Ballets Russes in 1909, became something of a mentor. He provided the intellectual stimulation and enthusiasm for the latest developments in music that Prokofiev sorely missed from his other teachers. Tcherepnin was initially not so successful in teaching him baton technique; despite extra coaching from a fellow student, Kankarovich, Prokofiev remained stiff and a little awkward on the podium, though he eventually gained enough confidence to conduct several premieres of his own music.

Over the summer of 1907, Prokofiev began to correspond regularly with Myaskovsky and another student, Boris Zakharov, exchanging and commenting on each other's compositions. Prokofiev's first package to Myaskovsky included a piece which he tentatively called *Carnival.* Its galloping, dotted rhythm theme became the third main idea in his First Piano Concerto, composed four years later. It was typical of Prokofiev then and for a long time afterwards to think in terms of individual, well defined themes rather than planning a work's

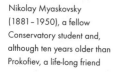

Nikolay Myaskovsky (1881–1950), a fellow Conservatory student and, although ten years older than Prokofiev, a life-long friend

overall scale and direction. He wrote to Myaskovsky on 26 June: 'I am still writing the last part of Act IV of *Undine*, which I gave you in May.' He had presented the first act of *Undine* when being interviewed for entry into the conservatory. Although he had since encountered Wagner's *Ring* cycle and had been impressed by the lush harmonies and orchestration of Skryabin's *Divine Poem*, and despite the extraordinary rapidity with which his style was now evolving, Prokofiev still persisted in adding to this decidedly juvenile work, apparently quite unconcerned with resulting incongruities of style.

In the next school year Prokofiev, now sixteen, had to return to the Conservatory's academic classes by order of the inspector (although his parents' tuition had been effective enough for him to gain five As and four Bs in his latest examinations). After almost three years of being exclusively among adults, he was to rejoin pupils his own age, including girls – seventeen of them attending the classes, almost double the number of boys. He became friendly with some of the girls, and one, Leonida Glagoleva, became the object of an infatuation. Slender, tall and dark, her austere behaviour 'cloaked a temperament that was really quite fantastic'. We know very little more about her, though in his autobiography Prokofiev hints that her relations with men were teasing, even cruel. Their relationship did not last beyond his graduation, but the impression she made on him is clear from his later operas – *Maddalena* and *The Gambler* – centred around dark-haired, capricious and even emotionally unbalanced women. A more enduring friendship was formed with Vera Alpers, who 'loved to talk about music'. While Prokofiev regarded her as just a friend, she developed something of a crush on him and felt quite jealous of his interest in other girls.

Early in 1908 Prokofiev, aged seventeen, was taken by Chernov to meet the organizers of the St Petersburg Evenings of Contemporary Music. This series of concerts had been set up in 1901 by leaders of the 'World of Art' movement, including the music critic Vyacheslav Karatïgin (himself a graduate from the Conservatory), Alfred Nurok and Walter Nuvel. The concerts had become something of a focal point for St Petersburg's musical avant garde; new works by German and French composers were performed as well as those by young Russians such as Stravinsky. Prokofiev played the series organizers a number of his piano pieces, including those later collected in the sets

Opp. 3 and 4. In the music's blend of piquant chords, unexpected harmonic progressions and idiomatic pianism, Karatïgin perceptively recognized 'a compound of Reger, Mussorgsky, and Grieg' and became one of Prokofiev's most consistent champions. Nurok, equally excited by what he had heard, invited Prokofiev to discuss possible collaboration on a drama, but Prokofiev – though flattered by the attention – was not interested in the proposed pantomime.

He passed his spring exams and in June travelled with his mother and Aunt Tanya to the Black Sea coast, where they stayed with an old school friend of Maria's, Olga Smetskaya, whose husband owned an estate in Sukhumi. The hills around the house had been planted with many exotic plants including Australian eucalyptus, South American palms, agaves and cacti. Prokofiev relished his three-week stay: 'The south, the June night, the dark sea, the marvellous scent of the southern trees and plants, and the brightly lit port – all this was delicious.' He was to return several times to Sukhumi and he wrote some of his finest early works there.

During his journey back to Sontsovka, Prokofiev was distressed to read of Rimsky-Korsakov's death earlier that month. He planned a piece in his former teacher's honour incorporating a theme from *Tale of Tsar Saltan* 'as though characterizing the man himself'. Though nothing came of this plan, more piano pieces, including the dazzlingly virtuoso *Suggestion diabolique*, were composed that summer. He also worked at a challenge he and Myaskovsky had set each other: to write a symphony.

To avoid upsetting Glazunov, Prokofiev deliberately chose to compose his symphony in a conservative style, avoiding the harmonic daring of his post-Skryabin style. Even so, when the work was completed the following year, Glazunov only agreed to arrange a closed rehearsal of it after considerable pressure. After its play-through Prokofiev's mother asked Glazunov for his opinion of her son's work, to which he replied: 'What can I tell you? It's written with verve, but there's a bit too much dissonance in places, and the orchestration is rather pale.'

Glazunov has often been represented, not unjustly, as having hindered Prokofiev's latter student career, though he extended many kindnesses to the young composer: when Wagner's *Ring* was being rehearsed at the Mariinsky Theatre in 1908, for example, Glazunov

readily gave permission for Prokofiev to borrow a precious full score of
Das Rheingold from the Conservatory Library, usually only available
for loan to Rimsky-Korsakov and himself. In any case, Prokofiev
concurred with Glazunov over the failure of his symphony. After two
play-throughs he withdrew the work, reusing its first movement nine
years later as part of his Fourth Piano Sonata.

In the autumn Prokofiev played the works he had written over the
summer to the organizers of Evenings of Contemporary Music. They
did not care for the symphony, but were enthralled by his piano pieces
and offered him a concert. This would be his first public appearance,
and he had to seek formal permission from the Conservatory in order
to participate. A few weeks before this concert, Prokofiev gave a recital
at the Conservatory, playing Chopin, Brahms and a C minor Étude
by Rubinstein. In preparing this last work, full of staccato chords, he
decided not to use the usual wrist staccato but 'played the chords with
an absolutely stiff wrist'. Despite this unorthodox technique, his
recital impressed the Conservatory's top piano professor, Anna
Esipova, and convinced his friend Boris Zakharov – a favourite of
Esipova's – that it was time for Prokofiev to change teachers. Using his
utmost charm, Zakharov persuaded Esipova to take on Prokofiev,
provided that Winkler gave his permission. Such was Prokofiev's
regard for Winkler that he felt as if he were 'playing Judas' when
asking permission to transfer early the following year.

On 18 December 1908 Prokofiev made his début with Evenings of
Contemporary Music, playing several piano pieces including *Suggestion
diabolique*. The St Petersburg audience, seeing a young Conservatory
student produce music of such 'wild, unbridled fantasy' (as described by
the critic of the newspaper *Slovo* ('Word')), were astonished and excited.
Several reviews appeared in the papers, most of them – evidently
bemused by the young talent – using such faddish words as 'modernist'
and 'decadent'. Encouraged by this reaction, Prokofiev from then on
made his piano works in particular not just vehicles for daring harmonic
experiments, but conscious attempts to bedazzle and shock.

This début marked a significant first step in his public recognition,
but it would be a mistake to assume that it represented Prokofiev's
coming of age. 'After he finished playing,' Vera Alpers recalled, 'he
joined his mother in the audience and sat next to her with his head
resting on her shoulder.' More importantly, the seventeen-year-old

had not developed a stylistic consistency nor, his greatest weakness for some time, the ability to structure large-scale forms. Only days later, Prokofiev spoke with Tcherepnin about Tchaikovsky's opera *Cherevichki* ('The Slippers'), after a story by Gogol. Tcherepnin told him how Rimsky-Korsakov had hesitated to set the same story as an opera before Tchaikovsky's death, whereupon he started his own version entitled *Christmas Eve*. Although Rimsky-Korsakov's music for the fantastic scenes was more striking, the lyrical scenes of Tchaikovsky's opera seemed most successful. To Prokofiev's suggestion that Tchaikovsky's lyrical music might be combined with the fantastic music by Rimsky-Korsakov to create 'a marvellous opera from beginning to end', Tcherepnin smiled indulgently and replied, 'I don't think the two halves would fit together.'

On 19 March 1909 Evenings of Contemporary Music presented the first performance of Mussorgsky's *The Marriage*, in a version prepared by Rimsky-Korsakov. Prokofiev certainly attended this: such was his devotion to the opera that years later he was able to play whole scenes at the piano from memory. Inspired by Dargomïzhsky's *The Stone Guest*, *The Marriage* was one of Mussorgsky's earliest experiments in translating speech patterns and their melodic contours into music. The result is spare, with abrupt changes of direction, driven almost entirely by highly expressive vocal lines. Its method – expressing Gogol's text minutely from moment to moment – would have appealed strongly to Prokofiev, matching as it did his own piecemeal method of composition.

Prokofiev returned to composing opera. Immediately to hand was the libretto of *Feast in Time of Plague*, set six years earlier under Glière's supervision. His original final scene, following Glière's suggestion, had used liturgical organ harmonies to support the priest's final harangue. But now, 'looking at what I had composed so long before, I felt that the priest was no easy-going churchman in gorgeous garb but a medieval prelate who foamed at the mouth as he railed against the feasting sinners.' Prokofiev rewrote the scene with many dissonant harmonies and a highly charged vocal line quite divorced from conventional sung melody. Inevitably, when he presented this as part of his qualifying exam, his professors were scandalized. He nevertheless graduated from the compositional course, receiving the official designation of 'free artist'. Prokofiev, who had become quite a dandy, persuaded his mother to finance his own distinctive wardrobe to celebrate his graduation: the purchases were a grey suit, coloured shirts, ties, cuff links and yellow shoes.

Shortly before graduating, Prokofiev met a student one year younger than himself, Maximilian Schmidthoff. Highly intelligent, Schmidthoff was a cynic who shared Prokofiev's taste in intellectual banter. The two boys and Vera Alpers became something of a threesome, often going on walks during which Schmidthoff – or Max, as he became known – and Sergey exchanged opinions on music and philosophy. Encouraged by Max, Prokofiev broached Schopenhauer, whose writings he would return to several times over the next two decades. Schopenhauer's theory – that experienced matter is ultimately the expression of will, as in the will to live, and that the most direct expression of the will is music – was to have a profound influence on his development as a composer. Max became a close friend – perhaps the closest Prokofiev ever had.

That summer, when not whiling away his time reading Dostoyevsky, he completed four Études for piano; he also made progress on a Sinfonietta (inspired by studying scores by the Classical masters, and by Rimsky's work of the same name which he had heard earlier that year.) A 'Grande' piano sonata composed six years earlier was revised to create his first published piano sonata. The work, which is similar in style to Skryabin's early works, gained the approval of his new piano teacher, Anna Esipova.

Little need be said about Prokofiev's postgraduate tuition in his last five years at the Conservatory. He briefly studied composition with Lyadov (who terminated the lessons, pleading ill-health), was a brilliant but unruly piano student under Anna Esipova, and continued his fruitful studies with Tcherepnin. Possibly his mind was not fully engaged with his studies due to family matters. In February 1910 his father, while in St Petersburg, suddenly fell ill and had to be hospitalized. That month Prokofiev, regardless, visited Skryabin at his 'fashionable Petersburg quarters', bringing his own piano arrangement of the first part of the *Divine Poem*. Inspired by this encounter, Prokofiev started a tone poem in homage to his hero, one of Russia's greatest instrumental colourists: he dedicated the work, *Dreams*, 'to the author who began with *Rêverie*', referring to Skryabin's early orchestral work. *Dreams* is a deceptively simple piece built almost entirely on scalic figures, made interesting by the juxtaposition of different keys and, above all, by richly evocative orchestration. The low, velvety strings and the glowing horn and clarinet colours give testimony to both Tcherepnin's effective instruction and the profound influence the rich colours of *Divine Poem* had on Prokofiev's music.

Prokofiev's father, after undergoing two operations, was diagnosed as having liver cancer, effectively a distressingly painful death sentence. Maria and Sergey, for the first time since moving to St Petersburg, remained in the city that summer to be with him; he died two weeks after his sixty-fourth birthday on 23 July 1910. The Sontsovka estate now had to be surrendered, and a month was spent there straightening out business affairs and planning a permanent move to St Petersburg. Notwithstanding the grief Prokofiev expressed in his diary over his father's death, he presented a stoic front. Even so, the emotional strain may have played a part in his increasingly fragile relationship with Zakharov, leading to a temporary rupture in their friendship which Prokofiev replaced with the chic attractions of the dandified Max. Years later he wrote to Max's sister, Ekaterina, 'At that time I was not always myself, but half-Max. His influence on me was enormous.'

In August Prokofiev began work on a new tone poem, *Autumnal Sketch*. As he pointed out later, it bears the influence of Rachmaninov, in particular his *Isle of the Dead* (performed in Moscow the previous year) and his Second Symphony, which had had its première in St Petersburg early in 1908. When the piece was finished, Prokofiev wrote to Myaskovsky, 'I don't know if you'll like it or not, but then it's the sort of piece that doesn't have any pretensions about trying to please anyone.' It was a work he evidently cared for: he revised it twice – in 1915, then in 1934 when living in Paris. *Autumnal Sketch* shares some characteristics with *Dreams*, including the use of scalic themes and a slow-paced, ruminative character; but this time, except for its impassioned and – for Prokofiev – extraordinarily lush string writing at the climax, the orchestration gives more emphasis to plangent oboe, tenebrous bass clarinet and the icy effect of strings playing *sul ponticello* with their bows close to the bridge of their instruments. Despite his use of such vivid orchestral colours, Prokofiev protested at the work's perceived pictorial representation: 'The critics wrote about gentle rain and falling leaves, and they quoted poems. Not one of them realised, though, that it reflects an internal world, not external. This kind of "autumn" can come in spring and in summer.' Written in direct response to his father's illness and death, the work was – if not written in his memory – at least a much needed outlet for Prokofiev's feelings.

Prokofiev and his mother now had to make ends meet. The Rayevskys helped them to keep the luxurious apartment they had moved into late in 1909, but Prokofiev had to consider what part he ought to play in supporting himself and his mother. He was nineteen.

In September, mother and son again stayed at the Sukhumi villa. The setting seems to have inspired Prokofiev, for he began his first truly successful composition for orchestra: his First Piano Concerto. At the end of the month he returned to St Petersburg and battled to get himself published, first putting sets of piano pieces in order, then sending aggressive letters to Jürgenson and Koussevitzky (the conductor, virtuoso double bass player and early champion of Skryabin who had used his wife's family fortune to set up Russian Music Publishers). When these failed to produce the desired result, Prokofiev, as he told Myaskovsky, sold his 'bicycle and a photograph' so that he could afford to publish his music himself.

Serge Koussevitzky (1874–1951), who was to champion Prokofiev's music as publisher and conductor, began his career as a double-bass soloist.

If he was yet to see his music in print, his fame as pianist and composer was at least growing. He continued to appear at Evenings of Contemporary Music, giving the first complete performance of his four Études in December; each was greeted with applause, and his performance so pleased the organizers that they asked him to give the Russian première of Schoenberg's *Klavierstücke*, Op. 11. On 28 March 1911, Prokofiev introduced Schoenberg's music to Russia for the first time. In the meantime the ever-loyal Myaskovsky, while in Moscow for performances of his own music, had persuaded the conductor Konstantin Saradzhev to perform *Dreams* and *Autumnal Sketch* in his open-air summer concerts held in Sokolniki Park, and to programme for the following summer Prokofiev's Piano Concerto, yet to be completed. Myaskovsky also began to write laudatory reviews of Prokofiev's music in the Moscow weekly journal *Muzyka*, run by the critic-editor Vladimir Derzhanovsky. Judging by his voluminous correspondence with such composers as Stravinsky, Myaskovsky and – eventually – Prokofiev himself, Derzhanovsky was a well-respected, intelligent and kindly man who actively promoted contemporary music, largely through his influential journal which, out of necessity, he managed to run on a shoe-string.

That summer Prokofiev began a new one-act opera, *Maddalena*, which took him three months to compose, mostly in Sukhumi. Two years conducting the student orchestra had given him confidence in his knowledge of orchestration; his scoring of the opera was, he told Myaskovsky, like 'a jewel, a chocolate with expensive liqueur inside'. Student conductors were closely associated with the Conservatory opera group which, besides standard repertoire, occasionally staged operas by Conservatory pupils, and he hoped *Maddalena* might be produced by the Conservatory. It was deemed too difficult for student performers, however, and had to be shelved. Recognizably by the same composer who wrote *Autumnal Sketch* and the Sinfonietta, its opening – restrained, richly orchestrated and mildly chromatic – is remarkably similar in style to Stravinsky's early orchestral works, such as *The Firebird* and *The Nightingale*. The work's immediate provenance, though, is Rachmaninov and – perhaps surprisingly given Prokofiev's earlier dismissal of his music as 'all that scratching' – Richard Strauss. Maddalena is a child of Strauss's Salome, singing siren-like above the increasingly violent, angst-ridden orchestral accompaniment. The music of *Maddalena* strikingly foreshadows Prokofiev's later, highly ambitious opera, *The Fiery Angel*: even the serpentine cello and bass lines that meander beneath the off-stage chorus of gondoliers in the first scene reappear again, disquieteningly yet seductively, in the final act of the later work.

Wonderful though much of the music is, it is hardly great opera. Even allowing for its expressionistic style, a comparison of *Maddalena* with *Salome*, not to mention such later masterpieces as Berg's *Wozzeck*, reveals caricatures rather than characters: it is impossible to feel much outrage at the fate of the two hapless men who, in jealous pique, kill each other over the *femme fatale*. The story likewise foreshadows the later *Fiery Angel*. Prokofiev was not alone in favouring plots about men in thrall to dangerously capricious women, but that this should have been his abiding interest well into the next decade perhaps reveals how damaging Leonida Glagoleva's relationship with the naïve young composer had been.

In May 1911 the St Petersburg musicologist Alexander Ossovsky came to Prokofiev's aid, writing to Jürgenson that 'this courageous young composer' with his 'superb technique' was ripe for a great career; publishing Prokofiev would not represent a risk, he said, since his music 'ought to make its own way and find a market'. This finally persuaded the reluctant publisher to add Prokofiev to his list of composers. By February 1912 Prokofiev's First Piano Sonata and Op. 3 piano pieces had been published and the Études were at proofing stage. Prokofiev started composing his Second Piano Sonata, and a ferocious Toccata.

Perhaps the most important work completed during that period was his first Piano Concerto. Originally conceived as a concertino, the concerto, like his first sonata, is an extended single-movement sonata form rather than a multi-movement work. Here Prokofiev, rarely credited with formal innovation, adds welcome contrast with a slow, dreamy *andante assai* interlude – where violins float a languid, wistful theme over pulsating lower strings – before announcing the development section with a cadenza. The work could be seen as a charming, utterly unself-conscious self-portrait: its energetic and breezy opening pokes gentle fun at grandiose openings such as that of Tchaikovsky's First Piano Concerto. Then, typically of Prokofiev's lighter humour, the piano launches into an étude-style passage in the 'prosaic' key of C major before getting 'back on the rails' with a fanfare-like theme (the *Carnival* Prokofiev had sent to Myaskovsky in 1907). In the course of this, the soloist revels in ostentatious display with rapid hand leaps and glissandos. At the concerto's poetic heart, with its potent suggestions of the tropical, lazy evenings Prokofiev enjoyed at Sukhumi where he had started the work, sentimentality is avoided through the charming insouciance of the clarinet's lightly ironic but charming trilling, and the sardonic, 'off-key' imitation of the piano melody by the brass.

By late March Prokofiev's work-load combined with the freezing, damp climate of St Petersburg had taken their toll, and he came down with pleurisy. On his recovery he went to Essentuki in the Causcasus to spend six weeks learning his concerto: 'They say the hall in Moscow is bursting with people,' wrote Prokofiev, '– up to six thousand listeners – and since it will be my first appearance with an orchestra I'll have to know it cold.' The first performance on 25 July was a tremendous public success. With characteristic restraint, Prokofiev noted afterwards, 'there were many curtain calls and three encores: the 'Gavotte' [from Op. 12] and the fourth Étude of Op. 2 twice. I didn't have anything else prepared. I am satisfied. It was not difficult to play with an orchestra – it was even extremely pleasant.' Most of the critics were rather less enthusiastic. The *Petersburg Gazette* declared Prokofiev 'ripe for the straightjacket', while Leonid Sabaneyev of *Golas Moskvy* ('Voice of Moscow') claimed that the concerto 'hardly deserves to be called music. In his search for "novelty", a quality that he lacks in the inner depths of his nature, the composer had definitely overreached himself.' A more perceptive review came from *Russkiye Vedomosti* ('Russian Newspaper'), which said of Prokofiev's playing: 'Beneath his fingers the piano does not sing and vibrate. It speaks in the stern and precise tone of a percussion instrument … the tone of the old-fashioned harpsichord. But it was … the convincing freedom of his playing and the clear-cut rhythm that won the composer such enthusiastic applause from the audience.'

After the concerto's second performance in Pavlosk on 3 August, Prokofiev travelled to join his mother at her favourite resort at Kislovodsk in the Causcasus. It was there that by 28 August he had completed his Second Piano Sonata. More than twice the length of his first, this work sets out to shock by seeming to unfold conventionally, if impetuously, in its first few bars before suddenly and unnervingly seizing up on a jarring, insistently knocking dissonance. Yet in the course of the movement Prokofiev demonstrates a convincing relationship between these and other contrasting ideas through the skilful development and transformation of his themes.

From the sonata's quirky character and its harmonies, it seems that Prokofiev had heard Stravinsky's ballet *Petrushka*, composed the previous year: the distinctive 'Petrushka chord' (combining C major and F sharp chords) is hinted at in the middle section of the finale, although the sonata has rather more mockery and less pathos than Stravinsky's work. What is most remarkable is how much of Prokofiev's 'mature' style here reaches full definition: the second movement scherzo is recognizably by the same hand that wrote the scherzo of the Fifth Symphony more than thirty years later; the slow movement has something of the wistful lyricism of the Sonata No. 6 (1940); and the sparkling finale looks forward to the style of *The Love for Three Oranges* (1919) and the finale of the Fifth Symphony.

On 26 April 1913, shortly after his twenty-second birthday, Prokofiev received a note sent by Max from Terioki, outside St

Petersburg on the Finnish Gulf: 'Dear Seryozha, I'm writing to tell you the latest news – I have shot myself. Don't get too upset but take it with indifference, for in truth it doesn't deserve anything more than that. Farewell. Max. The reasons are unimportant.'

Prokofiev learnt about those reasons from the Schmidthoffs: Max, for all his extravagant lifestyle, was impecunious, and he had chosen to end his life rather than face the humiliation of exposure. Grief-stricken, Prokofiev dedicated four pieces to Max Schmidthoff's memory: the newly completed Second Piano Sonata; the 'Allemande' of the Op. 12 piano pieces; the Second Piano Concerto, fragments of which Prokofiev had played to Max and was completing at the time he received Max's suicide note; and, later, the Fourth Piano Sonata, composed in 1917 but based on themes dating from 1908 when he and Max had first become friends. These four works share an acid, biting edge, testimony to the caustic humour which bound the friends together.

To try to help her son overcome his grief, Maria persuaded him to join her on a trip to Paris, which was to be Prokofiev's first journey outside Russia. They left on 30 May, staying a week in a *pension* on the boulevard Malesherbes. Prokofiev was introduced to Diaghilev's Ballets Russes during their season held (for the first time) in the Théâtre des Champs-Élysées. Although he missed the scandalous première of Stravinsky's *Rite of Spring* by about a couple of weeks, while in Paris Prokofiev still managed to see *Petrushka*, Ravel's *Daphnis et Chloë*, Schumann-Folkine's *Carnaval* (orchestrated by Rimsky-Korsakov, Glazunov, Tcherepnin and Arensky), Rimsky-Korsakov's *Scheherazade* and Florent Schmitt's *La Tragédie de Salomé*. This last work was choreographed by Boris Romanov, a character dancer from Moscow who would later help Prokofiev in his own efforts to write ballet.

After a four-day visit to London, Prokofiev returned to Russia via Switzerland, staying three weeks with the wealthy Meshchersky family in Gurzuf, near Sevastopol. He had come to know the Meshcherskys several years previously in St Petersburg, and now flirted with one of the daughters, Nina. Sharp tongued, she was a highly intelligent young woman and a gifted writer. At first she found Prokofiev awkward, odd and affected: she was used to the uniformed young men from prestigious military and administrative institutions, and Prokofiev

Nina Meshcherskaya (left, with her sister Natalia in 1914) was Prokofiev's first great love, but the match was strongly opposed by her parents.

cut a precious figure in his striped grey trousers, handkerchief in pocket and smelling of Guerlain cologne. Nina and her girlfriends dubbed him 'The Martian', but in time she fell under the spell of his raw but real talent, his extraordinary mind and self-assurance.

Prokofiev practised his new concerto for an hour a day, made a few corrections to *Maddalena* and relaxed by swimming, hiking in the hills, racing in chariots pulled by fast Tartar horses and playing tennis and billiards. Meanwhile, Myaskovsky worked away in rainy Petersburg checking the concerto's orchestral parts and passing them on to the conductor Aslanov. At its performance on 23 August 1913 at Pavlovsk, its listeners were, according to Karatïgin, 'frozen with fright, hair standing on end'.

Prokofiev later lost the score and had to reconstruct the work from a piano short-score. Yet the published version's grotesque, even monstrous-sounding music in the third and fourth movements – possibly an expression of his turbulent emotions after Max's suicide – more than hints at what was inflicted on that first audience. The work's most powerfully conceived movement is the first, even if it sounds at times like a virtuoso show piece for piano, with the orchestra as an afterthought. There are many delights in the following movements – a dazzling second movement toccata, effectively shocking grotesquerie in the third, and a chilling pursuit in the final

movement that leads to soft but dissonant piano chords like light
refracted through shattered crystal, in turn heralding a Mussorgskian
lullaby. But after the impressively grandiose opening movement, these
movements seem too episodic, loosely assembled rather than
conceived as part of an entire coherent structure.

Prokofiev's time at the Conservatory was soon to finish and he was
determined to leave in most spectacular fashion. The gratifying
applause that had greeted his fiery pianism may have goaded him into
entering for the Rubinstein Prize. Each year, all the Conservatory's
best piano graduates entered into what was known as a 'battle of the
pianos': candidates had to play a classical concerto before the
examiners, the prize being a new Schroeder grand piano. Prokofiev
worked hard that winter, taking advantage of Esipova's illness by
selecting and studying his programme in his own idiosyncratic
manner: 'For example, in the Bach fugue from *Kunst der Fuge* I played
all the "subjects" *forte* and all the "answers" *piano*.' More audacious
was his decision, once he had qualified for the competition, to flout
the regulation requiring the performance of a classical concerto and
play his own First Piano Concerto instead. 'While I might not be able
to compete successfully in performance of a classical concerto there
was a chance that my own might impress the examiners by its novelty
of technique; they simply would not be able to judge whether I was
playing it well or not!'

Having made this decision, he persuaded Jürgenson to have the
score published in time for the examination, and on the day of his
exam he saw his concerto 'spread out on twenty laps – an
unforgettable sight for a composer who had just begun to appear in
print!' The deliberations of the examiners were heated, some of whom
were outraged at Prokofiev's audacity in playing his 'modernistic' work
instead of a classical concerto. But the decision was swung in his
favour by former students of Esipova and instructors like Tcherepnin.
Glazunov, with ill grace, announced the result almost inaudibly, much
to the jubilation of Prokofiev's supporters.

2

A young, svelte and typically
dapper Prokofiev, around
1915

*Red and flickering, like a flame, he rushed out
on to the stage, grasped our hands
enthusiastically, announced that he was a
devout Futurist and sat down at the piano …
It seemed that the café was on fire, and that the
rafters and door frames – in flame, like the
composer's hair – were crashing to the ground,
and we stood, ready to be burned alive in the
fire of this unprecedented music.*

The poet Vasily Kamensky on Prokofiev's
performance of *Suggestion diabolique* at the
Poets' Café, March 1918

Ballets Russes and Revolution 1914-18

Maria was delighted and proud at her son's graduation, and offered to finance a trip abroad for him. Prokofiev chose London, having heard from Walter Nuvel that the Ballets Russes were to be there in the coming season; furthermore, Nuvel could procure an introduction to the great impresario Sergey Diaghilev himself.

Armed with letters of introduction from Tcherepnin, Prokofiev set sail for England with Nuvel in June. It could scarcely have been a better time to visit: England's summer of 1914 was to be widely remembered as a warm idyll, with London enjoying one of her most extraordinary seasons. Prokofiev, when not revising his Sinfonietta (which the conductor Alexander Ziloti had agreed to perform the following season), attended several performances. At the Queen's Hall he saw Richard Strauss conduct three of his own tone-poems and Mozart's G minor Symphony No. 40. He also heard the great Russian bass Fyodor Shalyapin sing in one of the three operas Diaghilev produced that season: *Boris Godunov*, *Khovanshchina* and *Prince Igor*. On 3 July, Nuvel introduced Prokofiev to Diaghilev.

At that time Diaghilev was in the process of redefining the identity of the Ballets Russes. It was only the previous year that his leading star and one-time lover, the legendary dancer Nijinsky, had surprised everyone by marrying a Hungarian fan, Romola de Pulszky. Diaghilev was devastated, severing all connection in a fit of pique. This was a drastic move since Nijinsky was not only the *raison d'être* of the Ballets Russes' greatest success, *La Spectre de la rose*, but had choreographed their most notorious and possibly greatest ballet, Stravinsky's *The Rite of Spring*. The largest feather in Diaghilev's cap for this 1914 season was a highly expensive ballet-score by Strauss, *La Légende de Joseph*, originally commissioned as a vehicle for Nijinsky. The music was, according to an observer, 'vulgar beyond belief', saved only by the inspired interpretation of the Russians. In contrast, Diaghilev's production of Rimsky-Korsakov's *Coq d'or*, banned in Russia for its anti-royalist sentiments, was an unqualified hit. This, coupled with the extraordinary reaction to Stravinsky's *Rite of Spring*, convinced him that Russian composers were still a rich source to be mined. (Stravinsky's position as Diaghilev's favourite would soon be consolidated by his ballet *Les Noces*, which portrays a Russian peasant wedding.) So Diaghilev now received the 23-year-old Prokofiev, already hailed as Russia's bright young hope.

Prokofiev played to Diaghilev and his retinue parts of *Maddalena*, the Second Piano Sonata and the Second Piano Concerto. Diaghilev thought the opera hopelessly *passé*, and declined Prokofiev's proposal to write a new opera based on *The Gambler*, a novella by Dostoyevsky. He was most enthusiastic about the piano concerto: to Prokofiev's bemusement, Diaghilev toyed with the idea of turning it into a ballet, but then decided that Prokofiev should instead compose a new ballet. For the scenario Prokofiev was to seek out the writer Sergey Gorodetsky, famous for his book *Spring Corn*.

To familiarize himself with writing for ballet Prokofiev stayed on in London until late July attending many performances by the Ballets

The impresario Sergey Diaghilev (second from the right), with two of his legendary Ballets Russes colleagues, the stage designer Léon Bakst (adjusting his hat) and Diaghilev's greatest dancer, Vaclav Nijinsky, in 1913

Russes: he saw several of Stravinsky's works (*The Nightingale*, *The Firebird*, *Petrushka* and *Rite of Spring*) and also works by his teachers, *Coq d'or* by Rimsky-Korsakov and Tcherepnin's *Narcisse*.

Prokofiev returned to St Petersburg just before Germany declared war on Russia. Being an only son, he was spared from the army, but several of his friends, including Myaskovsky, now had to leave for the front. The European powers involved had expected a short war in line with Germany's previous wars – that of 1866 against Austria, and the 1870–71 war against France – but the war became a protracted affair of attrition. Russia's five million soldiers, commanded by officers with recent combat experience, had made her seem well prepared for a short war. But even at the outset, fewer than five million rifles were available, and men were expected to retrieve weapons from fallen comrades; it was even suggested that troops be provided with hatchets mounted on poles.

Prokofiev, blithely ignorant of the incompetence with which the Tsarist government was conducting the war, managed with Karatïgin's assistance to meet with Gorodetsky and work out an initial plan for his ballet for Diaghilev. *Ala and Lolli* was loosely based on ancient Scythian legends. (The Scythian Empire, centred on the steppes of what is now southern Russia, was at its most powerful around 400 BC.) The plot concerns Ala, daughter of the sun god Veles, and her mortal protector Lolli, a Scythian warrior. The villain, Chuzhbog, attempts to abduct Ala several times only to be vanquished by the all-powerful rays of Veles. Prokofiev, intrigued by the plot's central theme, the sun's atavistic power over mankind, began to keep an unusual autograph album entitled 'What do you think about the sun?' Over the years many great figures in the arts, as well as friends, contributed to it; one was the pianist Arthur Rubinstein who wrote, 'Le Roi-Soleil a dit: "L'état c'est moi." Vous, mon cher Prokofiev, pourriez dire: "Le Soleil c'est moi."'

That summer, by now fully enamoured with Nina, Prokofiev went to stay with the Meshcherskys in Kislovodsk. In the mornings he worked on his Sinfonietta, leaving the afternoons free for rambles with his lover, and the work's light, whimsical style seems to reflect the carefree spirit of this time. Unfortunately, Prokofiev's immediate plans for the Sinfonietta's performance were upset when the Hall of the Nobles, Ziloti's intended venue for his concerts, needed to be turned into a hospital to house the growing number of wounded soldiers from the front. But Prokofiev, who held the work in sentimental esteem, its creation being closely associated with his relationship with Nina, took considerable pains in his attempts to get it performed over the next couple of decades.

In the meantime Nina had made the suggestion of setting Hans Christian Andersen's *The Ugly Duckling* to music; perhaps she saw some parallel between the blossoming of the unprepossessing cygnet with the gawky youth who had won her love. Accordingly she wrote an adaption of the tale for Prokofiev, which he turned to in late September, in Petrograd, while waiting for Gorodetsky to complete his scenario for *Ala and Lolli*. This charming work, which lasts just under ten minutes, takes Mussorgsky's song cycle *The Nursery* as its stylistic starting point, with lively scene- and mood-painting by the declamatory vocal line and piano accompaniment. Prokofiev makes discreet use of recurring motifs to provide some musical coherence, but the overall effect is of a spontaneous and vivid setting of Andersen's fairy tale. The completed work was dedicated to Nina.

During 1914–15 Prokofiev met Boris Nikolayevich Bashkirov, a young amateur poet who published his work at his own expense under the name of Boris Verin. Through Prokofiev's connection with either the singer Anna Zherebtsova-Andreyeva, whom he met when travelling to London in 1913, or the harpist Eleonora Damskaya, a fellow Conservatory student, he had started attending Bashkirov's artistic-philosophical soirées. These included lectures on Kant, Aristotle and Socrates, recitals of new poetry and performances of musical compositions. Prokofiev did not restrict himself to providing music; he also wrote and recited his own, typically acidic poems. Other guests at these soirées included Karatïgen, and the philologist Boris Demchinsky, who was to become an important friend and advisor to Prokofiev, assisting him with the libretto for two of his operas, *The Gambler* and *The Fiery Angel*. Bashkirov was the son of a rich St Petersburg flour merchant, and had more charm than talent or application, but Prokofiev set one of his poems, 'Trust Me', in a song collection of 1915. The two became friendly, leading to several invitations to Bashkirov's parents' property in Finland.

Gorodetsky, rather tardily, delivered the scenario for *Ala and Lolli*, and by late autumn 1914 Prokofiev had produced the first sketches and played them to Nurok and Nuvel. They were taken aback by what they heard, and Nuvel reportedly wrote to Diaghilev, 'Prokofiev has written something absurd to an absurd plot.' Boris Romanov, another associate of Diaghilev's, joined Prokofiev and Gorodetsky to work on the ballet's choreography. Romanov was at that time associated with the Mariinsky Theatre, but his more daring choreography was to be seen at The Stray Dog, a basement club and regular haunt of many of St Petersburg's leading poets and writers. Karatïgin, another regular, would almost certainly have introduced Prokofiev to Romanov, and Prokofiev had already seen – if not recognized – Romanov's work for Diaghilev's production of Stravinsky's *The Nightingale*. In some ways Romanov's typically unrestrained approach would have been more congenial to Prokofiev than the rather conservative tastes of Gorodetsky, whom more than once Prokofiev chided for making the scenario 'much too pretty'.

With the late arrival of the ballet's scenario, Prokofiev had yet to complete the score when a telegram arrived from Diaghilev asking him to come to Rome, all expenses paid, to consult with him about the work. The war made travelling through Europe complicated. Russia had already suffered a considerable loss with the capture of her Second Army (over 70,000 had been killed or wounded and almost 100,000 taken prisoner by the Germans), forcing her to withdraw completely from East Prussia. In the face of this Prokofiev must have been far from certain that, even if he were to reach Italy, he would be able to return home.

For months he had been having discreet meetings with Nina Meshcherskaya; fearing an enforced parting, he made an impetuous proposal, demanding that she tell her parents about their relationship and come with him to Italy. Her parents were far from delighted at the idea of their daughter marrying a musician with uncertain prospects, and strongly opposed the match. There was a fraught scene between Prokofiev and Nina's father, to no avail. The lovers tried to elope, only to be discovered and stopped by a servant. Nina's mother then took her away to Ekaterinoslav. Many years later, in the 1920s, Prokofiev attempted to meet Nina when both were in Paris, but she, by then married, avoided what would have been an emotionally upsetting encounter. Prokofiev was never to talk of her again, and makes no mention of her in either of his autobiographies.

Igor Stravinsky, who initially inspired Prokofiev to compose his first successful ballet score *Chout*

No doubt shaken by losing Nina, Prokofiev travelled alone to Italy, carefully edging his way around the Black Sea via still non-belligerent countries – Romania, Bulgaria and Greece – to reach the Mediterranean. Diaghilev was extraordinarily accommodating and hospitable, despite Nuvel's recent discouraging communication about *Ala and Lolli*; he took Prokofiev on a sight-seeing tour of magnificent proportion around Rome, Milan, Naples, Palermo, Sorrento and Pompeii. He even arranged Prokofiev's first public performance outside Russia, and on 7 March Prokofiev appeared in the Augusteo in Rome, performing his Second Piano Concerto under the baton of Bernardino Molinari. The audience was small but vociferous, the reaction from the local press rather more mixed. A striking new line of criticism came from *Il Messaggero*: 'We had expected to find a new Stravinsky … but on the contrary we found an artist still lacking individuality and wandering between the old and the new.' Used to provoking shrieks of 'decadence' and 'modernist', criticism for being too attached to the old must have been quite a new, even humbling, experience for Prokofiev.

A second blow came from Diaghilev himself. He had now heard 'unfinished sketches' of *Ala and Lolli* and described its plot as 'trite'; yet it appears he was diplomatic enough not to indicate to Prokofiev how hopeless he thought the music, thus earning Prokofiev's trust and ready acquiescence over the major changes needed. In the event, *Ala and Lolli* was never staged. Diaghilev nevertheless believed in Prokofiev's potential and asked Stravinsky for his support in persuading Prokofiev to write a new ballet.

Prokofiev later salvaged material from *Ala and Lolli* and reworked it into a concert work, the *Scythian Suite*, but even this latter work reveals those precise elements to which Diaghilev had objected. Stravinsky's *Rite of Spring* was a very hard act to follow. Prokofiev, having been impressed by the 'barbaric' power of Stravinsky's masterpiece, was too self-consciously attempting to shock and dazzle with *Ala and Lolli*; the work, arguably, owes rather more to the grotesque, more truly barbaric music associated with the blackamoor in Stravinsky's *Petrushka*. Prokofiev seems to have mistaken the deliberately crude music for this boorish character as a microcosm for the *Rite*'s artful evocation of a primeval ceremony.

Diaghilev felt some trepidation in reintroducing the two composers: they had met two years earlier in St Petersburg when

Stravinsky played the introduction of his ballet *The Firebird* on the piano. Prokofiev had been bold enough to say the work had 'no music … and if there was any it was from [Rimsky-Korsakov's] *Sadko*.' Fortunately, when the two now met in Milan, in April 1915, Stravinsky made a point of praising the younger composer's Second Piano Concerto, and they joined forces in performing a four-hand arrangement of *Petrushka*. Stravinsky had brought with him a scholarly and comprehensive anthology of Russian folk tales collected by the ethnographer Alexander Afanasiev; it had been used as a source for Stravinsky's ballet-in-progress, *Les Noces*, and would be again for *The Soldier's Tale*. Both Stravinsky and Diaghilev urged Prokofiev to make a closer study of not only Russian folklore but also Russian folk music. Prokofiev's bemusement is evident from his letter to Myaskovsky: 'This is now the most *avant-garde* position, which both Stravinsky and Diaghilev advocate: down with sentimentalism, down with pathos, down with internationalism! They're turning me into the most Russian composer there is.'

On his departure, Stravinsky left the Afanasiev folk-tale collection with Diaghilev and Prokofiev, who worked together to find a suitable scenario for a new ballet. They chose a series of tales about a buffoon and his wife, focusing the action on a scam in which the couple sell a 'magic' whip, which supposedly brings the dead to life, to seven other buffoons. They soon mapped out a ballet plot in six scenes, 'and this time Diaghilev signed a proper contract with me for 3,000 rubles.' As Diaghilev was notorious for stringing his dancers and musicians along for little or no money, this princely sum was no mean achievement. Prokofiev would have been wary of venturing further into ballet without a contract, having had his first attempt axed, and he would also have been suitably advised by Tcherepnin, who had dealt with the impresario when composing and conducting for the Ballets Russes.

Back in Petrograd, Prokofiev spent most of the summer of 1915 working on the new ballet, *Chout* (or *The Tale of the Buffoon*). He had agreed to complete the piano score by August, and the full score by March 1916 ready for a Paris production two months thereafter. He intended to return to Italy later that summer for further consultation, but such a possibility became more remote as the war's tide turned against Russia. The papers were full of news of disastrous setbacks in Poland and Galacia, and Myaskovsky sent increasingly embittered letters from the front. Incompetence was rife among the Russian high command, and the losses were horrendous. By the autumn Russia's troops would be reduced to a third of their original number, and reserves of the Second Levy – those past their thirtieth birthday – had to be called into action. Facing possible conscription, the 24-year-old Prokofiev wrote to Stravinsky on 3 June 1915, expressing the hope that 'in a month I'll be in your affectionate embraces. Meanwhile, I'm enthusiastically caught up in writing the ballet, which goes easily, happily and persistently. Leafing through Russian folk songs opened up to me lots of interesting possibilities.'

The reference to Russian folk songs shows that Prokofiev had very much taken to heart Diaghilev and Stravinsky's recommendation that he should try to write 'real' Russian music. He avoided conscription by enrolling for the one remaining Conservatory course for which he was eligible, though organ-playing was scarcely suited to his temperament. Even so, he was still unable to return to Italy, as the Russian retreat had made travel through the Balkans impossible.

Prokofiev managed to finish the piano score of *Chout*, albeit several months after the agreed deadline, and sent it to Diaghilev, who was at that time in the United States. He then turned to create the four-movement *Scythian Suite* from the aborted *Ala and Lolli*, scoring it for huge forces of 140 players. Upon receipt of *Chout*'s piano score, Diaghilev sent Prokofiev half the advance. The childish delight with which the composer showed off his prestigious new link with Diaghilev was later recalled by pianist Heinrich Neuhaus:

I remember [Prokofiev] speaking highly of Stravinsky to K. Szymanowski [the Polish composer], after which the talk turned to Diaghilev. Prokofiev said he had signed a contract with Diaghilev for a ballet, and with a mischievous expression, he produced from his pocket a cheque signed by Diaghilev evidently to prove that he was telling the truth.

Diaghilev's contract gave increased lustre to Prokofiev's reputation, and engagements followed from previously wary or hostile concert organizers. Prokofiev gave various solo recitals and made several concert appearances, such as in performances of his two piano concertos, *Dreams* and his newly orchestrated Sinfonietta. Alexander Ziloti (who had said 'this music stinks' of the Second Piano Concerto)

Albert Coates, principal
conductor at the Mariinsky
Theatre from 1911; his
confidence in Prokofiev's
opera, The Gambler, ensured
that it went into production
despite opposition from more
conservative members of the
Theatre's advisory panel.

now agreed to schedule the first performance of Prokofiev's *Scythian Suite*. Given the score's complexity, Ziloti generously gave Prokofiev seven full rehearsals before the performance. More importantly, he introduced Prokofiev to the principal conductor of the Mariinsky Theatre, the Englishman Albert Coates. Coates was enthusiastic about Prokofiev's idea for an opera on Dostoyevsky's *The Gambler*, and promised to organize its performance. With this encouragement, Prokofiev began work on the opera in November, starting in the middle of what became Act I from the words 'good *Vater*'. This longish speech, or rather rant, by the young hero Alexis attacks the hypocritical values of the German upper-middle classes: setting this indictment in a characteristically impetuous, pointed and uncompromising manner, Prokofiev gave vent to his own feelings about the wealthy Mescherskys who had so recently taken Nina from him.

Even before the *Scythian Suite*'s first performance on 29 January 1916, the music provoked outraged reactions from the performers. Prokofiev joked that 'the price of rotten eggs has gone up in St Petersburg.' Yury Tyulin, a one-time fellow student, attended a rehearsal and saw the two harpists (on stage, as there was no room for them in the pit) hounding Prokofiev with ill-concealed hostility and, when not playing, using their wide collars to cover their ears. But Prokofiev 'continued his work with patience and concentration, as if nothing had happened, and came out after the rehearsal, serious but satisfied.'

Included in the strangely hotch-potch programme were Grieg's Piano Concerto, Glinka's *Kamarinskaya* and some Tchaikovsky arias. The audience, drawn as much by these works as by Prokofiev's growing notoriety, were shocked by the suite which, as Prokofiev reported, caused 'a tremendous hullabaloo'. *Birzheviye Vedomosti* ('Stock Exchange Newspaper') reported: 'The first movement was received in silence; the last called forth both applause and stormy protests. Despite this the composer, who had conducted his own "barbaric" work, took a number of bows.' Glazunov, whom Prokofiev had personally invited, 'lost his temper again and walked out, unable to endure the sunrise Finale, eight bars before the end.' But for many people the finale is the suite's most impressive moment, with bright, piercingly high brass creating the effect of staring straight into the sun.

Ziloti was delighted by the scandal and scheduled the work for a further performance at the beginning of the following season.

Prokofiev, who also relished the furore, knew that expectations were now running high over his projected *Gambler*. Having already completed the first act, he now gave free rein to his daring imagination. It proved too much for his usually supportive mother, who one day demanded, 'Do you really understand what you are pounding out of that piano of yours?' Deeply offended, Prokofiev did not speak to her for two days.

The Gambler, which continues the operatic style Prokofiev had been nurturing since seeing Mussorgsky's *Marriage*, sets a short story ill-suited to the requirements of conventional opera. Though the characters are strongly delineated, they lack the clear-cut, passionate emotions typical of late-nineteenth-century opera: the two central characters in particular, Alexis and Polina, are each subject to conflicting, even paradoxical, emotions which prevent them from taking any particularly decisive action. Ironically it is Alexis's one decisive act, his attempt to rescue Polina from debt by gambling at roulette, which tragically backfires on him. This scene represents the climax of the opera: Dostoyevsky's story, narrated by the excitable young Alexis, has minimal dialogue at this point and Prokofiev, who aimed to adhere closely to the original text, naturally found it hard to sustain the stage action on such material. Help came from Boris Demchinsky, whom Prokofiev knew through Bashkirov's soirées; together they evolved a *tour de force* in which speech fragments by various gamblers comment on and heighten the tension as Alexis wins and eventually breaks the casino's bank.

The entire piano score was completed by mid April. Albert Coates, true to his word, arranged – or rather engineered – *The Gambler*'s production at the Mariinsky. He delayed telling Vladimir Telyakovsky, director of imperial theatres, about the new opera until the regular panel (which included such stumbling blocks as César Cui, one of the *kuchka*, and Glazunov) had planned the season and departed. Coates then sprang news of *The Gambler*, and an impromptu panel, chaired by Telyakovsky, was held with the Mariinsky's young conductors. Telyakovsky disliked the opera, but was a minority of one. A contract was therefore signed with Prokofiev, securing him a 'substantial advance and the printing of the piano score in a hundred copies'.

Prokofiev was soon sought out by the press for his comments on his new opera. They are strikingly similar to Mussorgsky's comments

The Mariinsky Theatre, Petrograd, where *The Gambler* was originally to have been produced in 1917; later renamed the Kirov, the theatre was to witness triumphant productions of Prokofiev's opera *Love for Three Oranges* and his ballet *Romeo and Juliet.*

in letters written around the time he composed *The Marriage* and the first version of *Boris Godunov.* These letters were published in 1916 to mark the thirty-fifth anniversary of Mussorgsky's death, and Karatïgin, who edited and promoted Mussorgsky's music, may have drawn Prokofiev's attention to them. Like Mussorgsky, Prokofiev called for the abolition of set pieces in favour of naturally flowing dialogue. However, his dismissal of 'the custom of writing operas to rhymed texts' as 'an utterly ridiculous convention' – clearly echoing Mussorgsky – sounds very odd from one who admired, and would continue to admire, the verse dramas of Pushkin, but is consistent with his decision to set Dostoyevsky's prose text unchanged. Finally Prokofiev stated his faith in opera, defying the avant-garde trend as exemplified by Diaghilev in particular: 'I believe that Wagnerian grandeur had a disastrous effect upon the development of opera, as a result of which even the most advanced musicians came to consider opera a dying form. However, given an understanding of the stage, flexibility, freedom, and expressive declamation, opera should be one of the most vibrant and compelling of the scenic arts.'

Prokofiev spent most of the summer of 1916 in the countryside outside Petrograd on the Gulf of Finland. With just a break in July to cruise down the Volga to the Caucasus, he completed scoring *The Gambler* by October. On delivering his opera to the Mariinsky, he then composed 'in one breath' (13–16 November) five songs to poems by Anna Akhmatova. These remarkably sensitive and beautiful settings – tender, poignantly lyrical with transparent piano accompaniment – perfectly reflect Akhmatova's precise, spare yet intimate style, and present a striking contrast to the near-expressionism of *The Gambler*.

Late in 1916, Prokofiev left Jürgenson – having become increasingly frustrated with the firm's cautious publishing policy and reluctance to pay large advances – to join the list of Gutheil, a firm now owned by the double bass player and self-taught conductor Serge Koussevitzky who would do much to champion Prokofiev's works. Flamboyant and egocentric, Koussevitzky had a sound instinct for talent. He had championed Skryabin and would later nurture such musicians as Leonard Bernstein and Benjamin Britten. He had bought Gutheil to enable him to publish the contemporary composers he supported and the Akhmatova songs were among the first of Prokofiev's works to be published by him. The première was given by Zinaida Artemyeva, accompanied by Prokofiev at a Concert of Modern Music in Moscow on 5 February 1917. Most of the critics were surprised at the songs' lyricism, deemed unusual for Prokofiev. Yet, as Karatïgin, perceptive as ever, had earlier pointed out, 'the Andante of the Second Sonata, the Andante of the Sinfonietta, surely this is the purest lyricism – stern and harsh, to be sure, but genuine, sincere, and moving.' Before the year was out, Prokofiev was to give fuller voice to this lyricism in one of his most beautiful scores, his First Violin Concerto.

The winter of 1916–17 was exceptionally cold. Blizzards and freezing weather immobilized thousands of railroad cars loaded with food and fuel intended for the cities, and conditions were so harsh that peasant women refused to cart food to the towns. The lack of basic supplies in the cities meant that people, increasingly, had to brave the freezing weather and stand in queues overnight in the hope of obtaining some bread. Factories had to close through lack of fuel, leaving tens of thousands of laid-off workers milling the streets.

It was against this background that rehearsals for *The Gambler* started in January. Singers were soon complaining that the roles were unsingable, and before long the stage manager resigned from the production. The breach was filled by the innovative and highly controversial director Vsevolod Meyerhold, who was to become famous for creating an anti-realist theatrical style which anticipated

A scene from *The Gambler*, in which the forthright *Babulenka* (grandmother, seated right) upsets the plans of her avaricious relatives by gambling her fortune away

such artists as Berthold Brecht and, later, Dario Fo. It may seem extraordinary that Prokofiev's supposedly ultra-realist drama appealed to him, but it did. Meyerhold's experience in producing opera for the Mariinsky included *Boris Godunov*, Richard Strauss's *Elektra*, and Wagner's *Tristan und Isolde*. He took an intelligent interest in how the rhythmic ebb and flow of music gave emotional power to drama and applied his observations even to plays without music, choreographing his actors according to the rhythm inherent in the text and the dramatic action. Such principles were to be inherited by one his most famous pupils, the film director Sergey Eisenstein.

Meyerhold had a particular interest in *commedia dell' arte*, and while directing *The Gambler* introduced Prokofiev to Carlo Gozzi's theatrical tale, *The Love for Three Oranges*. This theatrical extravaganza was originally written in the 1760s in reaction against the then new style of 'realistic' comedies, Gozzi's intention being to revive the old style of theatre where actors, wearing colourful masks and costumes, played types as opposed to characters capable of development. The trade-off was a more spontaneous, improvisatory style of performance

Vsevolod Meyerhold (1874-1940), the revolutionary theatre director who took over the production of *The Gambler*; his pupil, the Soviet film director Sergey Eisenstein, would become one of Prokofiev's principal collaborators.

that could be as topical as any of the actors wished it to be. Though naturally such an improvisational approach would have been impractical even for Prokofiev's operatic style, Meyerhold's anti-realist ideas and the irreverent style of Gozzi's comedy greatly appealed to him. Gozzi's style may also have reminded Prokofiev of the semi-improvised plays he and his childhood friends used to put on in Sontsovka. He was to return to *The Love for Three Oranges* only two years later to create what was in his lifetime his most successful opera.

Nadezhda Dobychina, a Petrograd art dealer for whom Prokofiev had performed the previous year, invited him to take part in a concert held during an exhibition she was organizing in February, and offered to dedicate the entire second half of the programme to his music. Prokofiev, who rather naïvely regarded this shrewd and influential woman as 'a kind, warm and simple person', readily accepted. He proved to be in most distinguished company: in the first half of the concert, Maxim Gorky read from his autobiography *My Childhood*, and before the interval the pre-eminent violinist Jascha Heifetz gave his final performance before leaving Russia for America.

Prokofiev's half of the concert consisted of the *Scherzo* – arranged for four bassoons – from his Op. 12 pieces, his Études, *The Ugly Duckling* and *Sarcasms*. As Prokofiev remembered, 'Gorky showed much interest in the *Sarcasms* and *The Ugly Duckling*.' Gorky is reputed to have said of the latter work, 'but this he has written about himself!' Boris Asafyev, the critic and one-time fellow student of Prokofiev, had in fact already made this observation at the work's first performance; Gorky, who by then was employing Asafyev on his journal *Novaya Zhizn* ('New Life'), had presumably borrowed this insight. Gorky nevertheless spent some time with Prokofiev asking him about his work and from then on took a friendly interest in the young composer. *The Ugly Duckling* was heard again in Petrograd nine days later in a chamber concert sponsored by the Russian Musical Society. That very day Tsar Nicholas II left the capital on the assurance of Protopopov, Minister of the Interior, that no serious disturbances were anticipated in the capital. But in just two weeks the Tsar was to lose power in what became known as the February Revolution.

On 23 February 1917, International Women's Day, a large procession of women marched down Nevsky Prospekt demanding equality, interspersed with cries for bread. After almost two months of subfreezing temperature the weather had suddenly improved and people were out in the streets enjoying the sun. A journalist from the British *Daily Chronicle*, reporting on the strikes and demonstrations, remarked on the good temper of the crowds, the broken windows aside, and said that far from presenting a popular uprising, they were simply making 'an unusually insistent demand for a vigorous solution of the food problem'. But the calm did not last. The military controller of Petrograd received a telegram from Nicholas II demanding that the disorders be suppressed by military force: without warning, the police fired into the crowds on Nevsky Prospekt. The crowd's mood became particularly ugly and even the troops baulked at firing at unarmed citizens as they shared many of their grievances. By 27 February the tsarist forces had lost control of the capital. Soldiers guarding key buildings such as the Small Arms Factory and Arsenal turned against their officers and the police when ordered to open fire at the crowd. Mobs of armed men and boys, including criminals liberated from Krestovsky Prison, set about to hunt down and kill any policemen they could find. The headquarters of the Okhrana (the secret police), several police stations and the District Court were sacked and ignited to destroy all incriminating records. By midday, all of Petrograd and the surrounding districts were in the hands of the people, with several buildings aflame.

In his autobiography, written decades later in Stalin's Russia, Prokofiev claimed that he had been in the streets of Petrograd while the fighting was going on: 'No. 19 of the *Visions fugitives* written at this time partly reflected my impressions – the feeling of the crowd rather than the inner essence of the Revolution.' Referring to the 'inner essence of the Revolution' was misleading if not consciously ironic, for the collapse of tsarist authority had taken everybody, even professional revolutionaries, by surprise. This was a truly popular uprising, but one that was in effect leaderless and, at its height, anarchic. It was dangerous to be seen out without a red flag or armband to signify sympathy with the people, who continued pounding the streets throughout the night, waving red flags and singing revolutionary songs, the sky aglow from burning buildings. Even the Duma hesitated to seize absolute power, awaiting orders from the Tsar. It was only when the Tsar abdicated on 2 March and

The first revolutionary stirrings
of 1917 were demonstrations
demanding bread; here in
Petrograd people process
before the monument to Tsar
Alexander III.

his brother, Mikhail, refused the throne, that the Duma proclaimed itself a Provisional Government.

Apart from his own safety, only one issue, how *The Gambler* had 'fared under all these overthrows', remained paramount for Prokofiev. The opera's production, originally scheduled to start in late February, had been postponed due to the Revolution, and for a while it seemed that it could only be staged in a production without scenery. In mid April street demonstrations flared up again, provoked by news that the Duma intended to pursue a punitive rather than defensive war against Austria-Hungary and Germany. The demonstrations, though originally spontaneous, were stirred further by Lenin, and Petrograd's more timid citizens were forced to stay behind their boarded-up front doors.

The fate of Prokofiev's opera was fully announced on 27 April by the paper *Vercherniye Birzheviye Vedomosti* ('Evening Stock Exchange Newspaper'):

> *The prevailing sentiment among the artists is that Prokofiev's opera* The Gambler *should be dropped from the repertory, for while this cacophony of sounds, with its incredible intervals and enharmonic tones, may be very interesting to those who love powerful musical sensations, it is completely uninteresting to the singers, who in the course of a whole season have scarcely managed to learn their parts.*

Even Ziloti, who had succeeded Telyakovsky as director of the former imperial theatres, was unable to persuade the Mariinsky artists to relent. The possibility of a concert performance in May came to nothing, and shortly afterwards *The Gambler* was removed from the repertory. Throughout the summer Prokofiev carried on negotiations for the opera's production at Moscow's Bolshoi Theatre, but even with the help of friends he was unable to secure this.

By way of consolation, Ziloti agreed to programme a number of Prokofiev's works in his forthcoming concert season in November: these included a projected Violin Concerto, the Third and Fourth Piano Sonatas, and *Visions fugitives*, all works yet to be completed. Prokofiev took himself off to a quiet town outside Petrograd to try to meet this commitment, but he was clearly upset by the blow the revolution had dealt to *The Gambler*, and disturbed by the volatile scenes he had witnessed. In a letter to Myaskovsky he confessed that he had 'fallen into a depression' and spent much time losing himself in contemplating distant stars with a telescope.

Visions fugitives were nevertheless completed that spring after two years of sporadic work. This set of twenty short piano pieces includes some of Prokofiev's most haunting music – sometimes mournful, often charming – and passages of great melodic invention. There is considerable skill and subtlety not only in the harmonic transitions between one piece and the next, but in creating a coherent emotional journey overall. Prokofiev scrupulously dated each piece with its year of composition: those of 1915 – numbers 5, 6, 10, 16 and 17 – tend to be light, playful and even mischievous; those of 1916 – numbers 2, 3, 7, 12, 13 and 20 – are predominantly mournful, slow and somehow haunted. In many of these one can hear harmonies typical of Maurice Ravel's *Valses nobles et sentimentales*, published in 1911, such as the bittersweet triads towards the end of Prokofiev's seventh piece, 'Arpa'; and his second piece, with its *fin-de-siècle* feel and ripely chromatic harmonies, ends with high, chiming grace notes strikingly similar to those which end Ravel's waltz suite. Prokofiev revealed that number 19, frantic and volatile, was inspired by scenes during the February Revolution. The biting scherzo that opens number 4, and the urgent, almost desperate character of numbers 14 and 15 – all written around the time of the Revolution – also seem to offer his impressions of that unsettling period.

On completing *Visions fugitives*, Prokofiev retreated into a musical idyll by returning to his long projected Violin Concerto. He had composed its first, dreamily melodious theme early in 1915, when romantically involved with Nina Mescherskaya. The piece had been envisaged originally as a concertino for violin and orchestra, and its glorious fruition as a full-length concerto was probably due to his encounter with the Polish composer Karol Szymanowski. (They had met in 1916 through a mutual friend and one of Prokofiev's leading champions, the publisher Pierre Suvchinsky.) Szymanowski had just completed his own first Violin Concerto with the help of the Odessa-born violinist Paul Kochanski, a recent recruit to the staff of the Petrograd Conservatory as violin professor, and undoubtedly recommended Kochanski to Prokofiev for assistance in matters of violin technique.

Kochanski's playing, noted for its sweet-toned lyricism, matched Prokofiev's original inspiration perfectly, and in a matter of weeks the concerto was fully sketched. Prokofiev, needing a break from the turmoil of Petrograd, took a steamboat trip along the Volga and Kama rivers, orchestrating the concerto en route. The work's fresh, clear textures seem to reflect the 'virginally pure' landscape through which the boat sailed up the Kama river into the Ural Mountains.

The light and lucid orchestration of this work is a perfect framework for an open-hearted lyricism quite exceptional from Prokofiev; hitherto he had punctuated, even punctured, his lyrical moments – whether in the First Piano Concerto or *Visions fugitives* – with a touch of irony or whimsical humour. In the Violin Concerto, despite some quirky playfulness in the first movement's second theme, and in the central movement, where the violin line tumbles like an acrobat with mischievous humour, these parts of the concerto are subsumed in the final movement by the sheer charm and warmth from the violin's lower D-string register floated above sumptuous harmonies, and especially by the rapt recollection of the opening theme to lush orchestration at the work's close. Although it would be five years before the concerto was first performed, it subsequently became one of Prokofiev's best-loved works, its lyricism and unorthodox structure (two slow outer movements with a scherzo central movement) admired and emulated by several composers, most notably William Walton in his Viola Concerto.

Having completed the concerto, Prokofiev – still on his Volga trip – prolonged this retreat into a calm, harmonically 'purer' musical language by planning the completion of a 'Classical' symphony, a project he had worked on intermittently over the past few years. The inspiration for this had come five years earlier from Tcherepnin, whose own great enthusiasm for the symphonies of such late eighteenth-century Classical composers as Mozart and Haydn came at a time when Haydn in particular was scarcely performed. Prokofiev, who had despised Mozart in preference to Skryabin's richly orchestrated and over-heated harmonic style, now found the Classical composers' clean-cut, orderly style and economical yet piquant orchestration a revelation. First to be finished for the symphony was a Gavotte, possibly after he conducted a Haydn symphony in 1913. Here he clearly demonstrates his lesson gained from Reger's *Serenade* of how to juxtapose distant tonalities as if they were tonic and dominant; the phrases appear to balance each other perfectly but for the fact that each cadence takes the music into increasingly alien keys before abruptly returning to the correct, 'home' tonality through an unlikely modulation. Similar tricks appear throughout the symphony, which he began in earnest in 1916, composing without the piano in order to achieve 'more transparent orchestral colours'. (Curiously, although it was another four years before the 'neo-classical' movement was fully launched with the première of Stravinsky's *Pulcinella*, Reger, also in 1916, completed orchestrating his *Suite im alten Stil*, a similarly affectionate tribute to a past master, in this case Bach.)

Prokofiev returned from his boat trip in time to perform his First Piano Concerto in Pavlovsk on 20 May. Between this and a repeat performance on 10 July at the Petrograd Theatre of Musical Drama, he stayed in the same small town outside Petrograd, where he 'crossed out' the original version of the Symphony's finale and, walking in the surrounding fields, recomposed the movement trying to avoid all minor chords.

The resulting bright, mock-elegant and joyous work has become one of his best-known and loved compositions. Prokofiev himself chose the name 'Classical' to 'tease the geese, secretly hoping that he would be proved right 'if the symphony really did turn out to be a "classic" piece of music' and enter the repertoire. (In the event, its première the following year ruffled no feathers but simply charmed its audience.)

Life in Petrograd, meanwhile, became ever more unsettled. Early in July, street demonstrations – provoked by Lenin's Bolsheviks in an attempted *putsch* – converged on the Tauride Palace where the government was in session, demanding, 'All power to the soviets!' Just when it seemed the government was about to fall, news – leaked by the Minister of Justice – spread of Lenin's financial dealings with the German General Staff. Several military units, determined that their government was not to fall at the hands of an 'enemy collaborator', descended on the Tauride, scattering the mob and dispersing the Kronshtadt sailors mobilized by the Bolsheviks.

With this disturbance over, Maria and Sergey Prokofiev travelled south to the Caucasus, where Sergey gave a performance of his First Piano Concerto at the Kislovodsk Kursaal, and finished orchestrating the 'Classical' Symphony. Pleased with the result, he conceived the possibility of writing a 'Russian' Symphony, dedicating it to Diaghilev in recognition of his concern for Prokofiev's 'Russian style'. But by the time he returned to Petrograd in late August another, more explosive idea was clamouring for his attention and subsequent expression. He turned to a ferocious 'Chaldean evocation', 'engraved in cuneiform characters on the walls of an ancient Akkadian temple', which had been deciphered by the German archeologist Hugo Winkler, and paraphrased by Balmont in his poem, *Seven, They Are Seven*. Balmont was in Kislovodsk himself, and may well have suggested the text to Prokofiev, who planned a setting for choir and full orchestra. According to the unusually detailed account he later gave in his Soviet autobiography of the work's genesis, Prokofiev sketched its general outline during one week in September, working 'at fever pitch … visualizing some passages with such startling clarity that I would find myself breathless with excitement and would have to leave my desk and go for a walk in the woods'. The significance, perhaps even the necessity, of completing the work's outline in September – a whole month before the Bolshevik revolution – becomes clear from the text, which could be construed, embarrassingly, as being hostile to the events of October:

Charity they know not,
Shame they have none,
Prayers they heed not, to entreaties they are deaf.
Earth and heaven shrink before them,
They clamp down whole countries as behind prison gates,
They grind nations, as nations grind grain.
They are Seven! They are Seven! They are Seven!

The final four lines, penned by Prokofiev himself, may well have been in response to the menace that had approached Petrograd in mid August. That month Russia's Commander-in-Chief, General Kornilov, announced to an aghast audience at the Moscow Conference that the army was no longer fit to resist the invading Germans. Privately he accused the Provisional Government, now led by the fiery socialist orator Kerensky, of becoming a mere instrument of the Petrograd Soviet, in turn increasingly dominated by Lenin's Bolsheviks. It was well known that Lenin, ever since his arrival in Russia, had called for Russia to cease her fight in the 'imperialist war'. Kornilov's worst fears, shared by many of the bourgeoisie, were realized when on 20 August Russian troops, with scarcely a struggle, withdrew from Riga – about three hundred miles from Petrograd – letting it fall to the Germans.

Conditions at Petrograd had been steadily deteriorating. The wooden sidewalks were in a severe state of disrepair and queues for bread and kerosene had become a common sight. A new type of queue, made up of respectable people who would normally shun such a practice, now appeared: they were queuing for trunks and cases.

Konstantin Balmont (1867–1942), the Symbolist poet who wrote the words Prokofiev set in his most overt response to the events of 1917 – the savage 'Chaldean evocation', *Seven, They Are Seven*

Prokofiev was one of those many people now making preparations to leave Petrograd. He sent a case of his manuscripts to Moscow for safekeeping in the vaults of the Gutheil publishing house, then travelled south to Essentuki. It was a perilous journey; Prokofiev had to disguise himself in a peasant's blouse to avoid being recognized as a bourgeois should the train be stopped by deserting troops or looting bands of mercenary cossacks.

But he joined his mother safely at Kislovodsk, and continued to work on *Seven, They Are Seven*; he also revised an early piano sonata from his student days to create his fourth published sonata. Prokofiev wrote to Myaskovsky, on 27 October, that he was planning to leave Kislovodsk shortly (for piano recitals in Moscow and Petrograd), unaware that only two days previously the Bolsheviks had launched their *coup d'état* in Petrograd. The Provisional Government, taken by surprise, was toppled with so little resistance that there was hardly any bloodshed; at first the citizens of Petrograd did not notice any change. Within a week, however, pro-Kerensky forces were fighting back, and street battles broke out in both Petrograd and Moscow. Those in Moscow were particularly bloody, as the Bolsheviks there had been poorly prepared for the take-over: it took them five days to overcome their opponents. Prokofiev had received only confused accounts of these events from local papers, and so attempted to travel to Moscow. A train with its windows smashed pulled in at the local station, disgorging 'a panic-stricken bourgeois crowd' who told Prokofiev, 'There's shooting in the streets of Moscow and Petrograd. You'll never get there.' Now persuaded that it was futile, even dangerous, to travel, Prokofiev remained in Kislovodsk. There he was trapped after General Kaledin led his cossacks against the Bolshevik forces who then seized the town of Rostov on the River Don. Although the fighting was several hundred miles away from Kislovodsk, posing no direct threat to the Prokofievs, travel to Moscow became impossible.

Prokofiev therefore concentrated on completing the score of *Seven, They Are Seven*. The result is one of his most startling works, its impact quite disproportionate to its mere seven minutes' duration. An initial orchestral maelstrom – reaching bursting point with loud, dissonant brass reinforced by bass drum and repeated cries from the chorus – heralds the tenor's incantation against the terrible Seven. This is punctuated with some of Prokofiev's most ferocious choral writing and

dazzingly aggressive orchestral writing. A percussion-heavy procession
with blood-chilling howls from the womens' voices leads to a final,
churning climax for chorus and orchestra which gradually winds
down to men's voices in a monotone above a low, dark-toned chord,
with soft tam-tam strokes like billows of smoke over a smouldering
wreckage. Prokofiev was never to write a work quite like this again:
more than his *Scythian Suite*, this was his atavisitic outburst to mirror
Stravinsky's *Rite of Spring*. When Prokofiev showed Balmont his
completed work, in March 1918, the poet was ecstatic, describing it as
being 'like a whirlwind of fire, such a score has not yet existed on this
earth.' But Prokofiev, after the great productivity of 1917, had come to
a creative impasse, having failed to start any new work since moving
to Kislovodsk. Although he made some attempt to continue work on
a Third Piano Concerto, using some material rejected from the First
Concerto, he was undoubtedly distracted and distressed by his
uncertain future. It was by no means clear that any artistic activity was
going to be possible under the Bolsheviks; city refugees would have
told him that many theatres and halls had closed in protest against the
Bolsheviks' illegal seizure of power. Many of the upper and middle
classes did not believe that the Bolsheviks, whom they considered
unable to handle the complexities of Russia's economy let alone
manage her international relations, could last more than a month.

He now considered the possibility of going to the United States.
The previous summer he had met Cyrus McCormick, an American
magnate who had come to Petrograd as part of a delegation led by
Senator Reid 'to welcome the advent of our Republic'. Because of
McCormick's interest in music Prokofiev drew up a list of 'the best of
our new music' for him, and had a copy made of the *Scythian Suite*.
As a result, McCormick invited Prokofiev to get in touch should he
ever come to America. Another option, which Prokofiev took more
seriously, was to tour South America. As the Ballets Russes had toured
there in the summer of 1917, Prokofiev wrote to Diaghilev early in
January of his plan to go to South America in the spring, asking for
advice and recommendations. Prokofiev recieved no reply, but was
determined to leave: he had nothing to do, as he recalled in his
autobiography, and 'time hung heavily on my hands.'

His first Bolshevik encounter was with local Soviet forces who
came to hunt down White officers ('Whites' being any forces who

opposed the Red Army) based in the hotel in which the Prokofievs were staying. Prokofiev must have sustained sufficiently friendly relations with the local soviet, for when the 'Kaledin front' collapsed he set off for Moscow on 16 March armed with a safe-conduct pass. He had missed a number of major developments during his five months in Kislovodsk. He is likely to have read the appeal by Lunacharsky (Commissioner of Public Enlightenment) in *Pravda* on 1 December 1917, calling on 'all comrades – painters, musicians, and artists – who wish to work towards the rapprochement of the broad popular masses with art in all its aspects, as well as the comrade-members of the Union of Proletarian Artists and Writers, to report to the office of the Commissar of Public Enlightenment in the Winter Palace.' This may have prompted Prokofiev to write to Derzhanovsky with what otherwise seems a naïve request to 'drop me a few lines about Moscow musical life.' In the event only a few responded to Lunacharsky's appeal, although those who did included such distinguished cultural figures as the poets Blok and Mayakovsky, the artist Altman, and the theatre director Meyerhold, who had introduced Prokofiev to *The Love for Three Oranges*.

Prokofiev may not have known of the fate of the Constituent Assembly, Russia's first truly democratic parliament. One of the Provisional Government's final acts before the coup was to fix an election date; the Bolsheviks, on seizing power, did not dare cancel this. But within days of the elections – won by the Social Revolutionaries in an overwhelming majority – the Bolsheviks brazenly claimed that events had moved so rapidly that the Assembly was no longer truly representative of the people. Several key opponents who had been elected were arrested, particularly members of the Kadets, a non-socialist party supported by the liberal intelligentsia. The Assembly met on 5 January 1918 regardless, but the Bolsheviks brought in the Red Guard to close the meeting and disperse the representatives once and for all.

Prokofiev's journey from Mineralnye Vody to Moscow took eight days. Although 'once or twice the train was fired at', as he later recalled, he reached what was shortly to become the capital (Lenin had decided to transfer government from Petrograd to Moscow, which was further behind the frontier and thus easier to defend). There Prokofiev gained some income from a deal with Koussevitzky, now head of the

Votes are cast for Russia's first, short-lived democratic parliament – the Constituent Assembly; the Bolsheviks achieved a poor result and Lenin ordered that the Assembly be closed by the Red Army.

first State Symphony Orchestra. Koussevitzky readily agreed to buy publication rights to a number of large-scale works (including *Scythian Suite*, *Chout* and *The Gambler*), paying 6,000 rubles – a sum that reflected more the inflation-ravaged state of the Russian currency than the value of Prokofiev's music.

Prokofiev also reacquainted himself with Mayakovsky, whom he had met the previous year in Petrograd. Mayakovsky was then working for Gorky's journal *Novaya Zhizn*, and it may have been through Gorky that the meeting was effected. According to Asafyev, who worked on the same journal, the poet became a great fan of Prokofiev's music, once turning on Asafyev (whom he regarded as a desiccated academic) to say, boorishly, 'What do your Beethovens mean to us? I'd give up all the old music for one Prokofiev!' Mayakovsky was one of the few artists to have responded to Lunacharsky's appeal. Now he not only wrote poems glorifying the Bolshevik revolution, but also conceived and designed posters intended to generate support for the new government. In Moscow he was often to be seen at the Poets' Café in Nastasyinsky Pereulok, where with a group of other 'Futurist' poets

Portrait of Prokofiev by
Alexander Benois, 1918;
an important instigator of
St Petersburg's cultural
renaissance – the so-called
'Silver Age' – Benois was
instrumental in helping
Prokofiev gain permission
to leave the newly formed
Soviet Union.

The truculent Russian poet,
Vladimir Mayakovsky
(1893–1930), embraced the
new Bolshevik government,
and was one of Prokofiev's
greatest admirers.

such as Kamensky he recited his aggressive, hyperbolic poetry to
enthusiastic and rowdy audiences. Prokofiev attended one of those
sessions and played some of his piano pieces, including *Suggestion
diabolique*. Mayakovsky, as a token of his esteem, presented Prokofiev
with a copy of his poem *War and the World* with the inscription: 'To
the World President for Music from the World President for Poetry. To
Prokofiev [signed] Mayakovsky.'

Prokofiev left Moscow for Petrograd, where he gave four premières:
in the hall of the former Tenishev School on 15 and 17 April he gave the
first performance of his two new piano sonatas and *Visions fugitives*.
Then on 21 April he conducted the former Court Orchestra in the
première of the 'Classical' Symphony in the hall of the former Court
Chapel. Lunacharsky was present, and this was almost certainly the
first occasion on which the two men met. According to Prokofiev's

autobiography, he was introduced to the Commissar by both Gorky, who acted as go-between between the new government and various artists, and Alexander Benois, who was busily helping to restore the Winter Palace (Lunacharsky's base), which had been shelled during the Bolshevik seizure of power. It was at the Winter Palace that Lunacharsky and Prokofiev met together, a meeting which was to prove a turning-point in Prokofiev's career. Unlike many of his colleagues, Lunacharsky was a highly cultivated man of some conscience. On at least two occasions, appalled by the increasingly dictatorial behaviour of the Bolsheviks, he had tried to tender his resignation. But Lenin, who recognized Lunacharsky's usefulness in gaining party support from intellectuals and artists, managed to persuade him to stay. Lunacharsky in turn, having heard great things of Prokofiev from both Gorky and Mayakovsky, now felt it his duty to try to persuade Prokofiev to stay in Russia, telling him, 'You are a revolutionary in music, we are revolutionaries in life. We ought to work together.' But coercion was not his style; when Prokofiev told him quite firmly that he needed a rest and 'would like the physical air of seas and oceans', Lunacharsky finally agreed to let Prokofiev go and arranged for his passport 'and an accompanying document to the effect that I was going abroad on an art mission and to improve my health.'

And so on 7 May 1918, Prokofiev took a train on the Trans-Siberian line to Vladivostok on the Pacific coast with the aim of sailing to South America, in search of fame and fortune.

3

A publicity shot of Prokofiev
posing improbably with a
pipe in a Chicago hotel
room, 1918

M. Prokofiev is a very young musician – slender,
svelte – who carries himself like a student.
As soon as the musicians are seated,
M. Prokofiev sweeps on, like some elemental
force. He moulds them, he explains his ideas
and his aesthetic, and they work with joy, for
the musicians recognize that he is a real master.

Le Gaulois, 14 May 1921

A Tale of Three Cities 1918–22

Prokofiev's journey to America was long and arduous. At the best of
times the Trans-Siberian rail journey to Vladivostok would have taken
thirteen days. But the Bolshevik signing of the ruinous Brest–Litovsk
peace treaty with Germany – by which Russia lost one quarter of her
arable land – plunged the nation into civil war. About a week into
Prokofiev's journey, the Czech Legion (essentially an anti-German
force armed by the Provisional Government) rebelled, seizing the
Siberian town of Cheliabinsk, about one third of the way along the
Trans-Siberian line. Fortunately for Prokofiev, he had set out just
weeks before Trotsky, Commissar for War, could form a properly
disciplined and uniformed Red Army. At this point there was hardly
any serious resistance to the Czechs, and the Legion – who after all
only wanted to get out of Russia – allowed Prokofiev's train to pass. A
potentially more dangerous delay was caused at Chita by roving
mercenaries, but local forces eventually drove them back, and the train
could proceed.

Prokofiev appears to have been almost oblivious to all that was
going on; he calmly spent most of his time reading about Babylonian
culture, an interest sparked by his setting of the Chaldean inscription
in *Seven, They Are Seven*. Balmont, who encouraged this interest, may
well have lent Prokofiev the book. Certainly it would have told of
Babylonian priest-magicians healing the sick and combating malign
spirits through the use of necromancy – a foretaste of the kind of
subject-matter Prokofiev was to deal with just a year later in one of his
most ambitious operas, *The Fiery Angel*. Prokofiev also had pleasant
distraction from his fellow passengers. One was a wealthy Japanese art
collector called Motu Otaguro, who also owned a journal entitled
Music and Literature. Otaguro took an interest in Prokofiev and his
music and invited him to stay over at his summer home in Japan
before travelling on to America. When Prokofiev duly arrived in
Yokohama, he discovered that he had just missed the boat to the
Chilean port of Valparaiso; the next boat to South America was in a
month's time and by then the concert season would be over. At this

point Prokofiev was persuaded that he would be better received in New York than in South America.

So while Prokofiev awaited his American visa, he stayed on with Otaguro, whose journal published a laudatory article on 'the brilliant young Russian composer who is seeking a new world for his music'. This opened sufficient doors for Prokofiev to give a recital at Tokyo's Imperial Theatre. 'The Japanese did not understand much about European music,' he later recalled, 'but listened attentively, sat incredibly quietly and applauded technique.'

Prokofiev caught his steamer for America. After a 'delightful stop-over in Honolulu' he reached San Francisco, where he was detained by American immigration; as he later explained, he had come from Russia 'where the "Maximalists" (as the Bolsheviks were called in America at that time) were in power – a strange and evidently dangerous lot'. More to the point, he had arrived with less than the statutory $50 in his pocket. America was wary of taking in impecunious immigrants, and Prokofiev was held for questioning on Angel Island. Fortunately he was able to contact another fellow-traveller, Anglon, who had convinced Prokofiev in favour of New York and who now organized a collection from Chicago's large Russian community to bail him out. Once released, Prokofiev made his way to New York, where he stayed initially with Adolf Bolm, one of Diaghilev's leading dancers. Through Bolm Prokofiev met some of the leading figures of New York society; it was also through Bolm that Prokofiev was able to arrange his first American appearance. This was at a 'Russian concert', held on 29 October 1918 in the Auditorium of the Brooklyn Museum to open an exhibition of works by the painter Boris Anisfeld (once associated with the Mariinsky Theatre).

But more important to Prokofiev's American career was his début at the Aeolian Hall on 20 November. Adolf Bolm evidently did his part to spread Prokofiev's fame, as the concert was fully booked and attended by many leading musicians, including émigré Russians such as Rachmaninov. Prokofiev performed his own Études and the Second Piano Sonata, leavening his programme with two Skryabin Études and three Rachmaninov Preludes. It was a sensation: so thrilled were the Americans by the 'novelty' of Prokofiev's hard-edged virtuosity that they would not let him go until he had given them several encores.

Much to Prokofiev's satisfaction, his concert was widely reported in the press: 'Even its unfavourable comment was served up in a somewhat sensational manner.' Notoriously, the *New York Times* critic said that the finale of Prokofiev's sonata 'evoked visions of a charge of mammoths on some vast immemorial Asiatic plateau'. Other journalists reported that Prokofiev himself cut an impressive figure, a 'blond Russian giant' with the 'size and build and strength of a football guard'. What impressed his Aeolian Hall audience, and all those who subsequently heard Prokofiev, was his no-nonsense, almost relentless style of playing, with little variation of tempo, and evident yet understated musical expression. Béla Bartók, the Hungarian composer-pianist to whom Prokofiev's playing-style is perhaps closest, was not yet known internationally, and such piano playing was a startling contrast to that of the late-Romantic pianists such as Ignacy Friedman, or even near-contemporaries such as Samuel Feinberg ('he doesn't play, he suffers', Prokofiev scornfully commented on the latter's playing some years later). None the less, Prokofiev's unpretentious, straightforward character made a favourable impression, and he was described as an unusual and charming young man whose demeanour contrasted with the 'volcanic eruptions' he produced on the piano.

Offers followed in the wake of his Aeolian Hall recital. The first American contract secured was to make Duo-Art piano roll recordings; then a New York publishing house offered to publish any new piano pieces he chose to compose: Prokofiev responded with two sets of miniatures – *Old Grandmother's Tales*, and Four Pieces Op. 32. In the end, however, Prokofiev found the publisher's terms so unfavourable that he did not enter into a contract with them (the two suites were eventually published by Koussevitzky). Prokofiev contacted Cyrus McCormick in Chicago who, as good as his word, arranged introductions for him. Chicago was to prove even more receptive to Prokofiev than New York, and offered, particularly through the Chicago Symphony Orchestra and their conductor, Frederick Stock, higher quality performances of his work. Early in December, Stock and Prokofiev gave two performances of the *Scythian Suite* and the First Piano Concerto. The directors of the Chicago Opera were present and, impressed by what they heard, discussed with Prokofiev the possibility of producing *The Gambler*. Unfortunately Prokofiev had brought with him only the vocal score (the full score was in the Mariinsky Theatre Library), but, remembering Meyerhold's suggestion for a possible opera, mentioned to them Gozzi's *The Love for Three Oranges.* At this the expatriate Italian conductor, Cleofonte Campanini, was delighted: 'Our dear Gozzi! But that is wonderful!' By January 1919 a contract had been signed, and Prokofiev was to deliver the opera by the following autumn.

Prokofiev went straight back to New York for his début at Carnegie Hall, where he was to perform his First Piano Concerto with the Russian-born conductor Modest Altschuler, who had founded a Russian symphony orchestra in New York under the auspices of the Tsarist Embassy in Washington. As Prokofiev wryly recalled, 'New Yorkers could not see why anyone needed a "Russian orchestra" in which most of the musicians were Americans, and with a mediocre conductor besides.' Yet it was through this concert that Prokofiev first became known to the woman who was to become his wife.

Carolina Codina – Lina to her friends – was then twenty-one, dark-haired, slender and strikingly attractive. Spanish on her father's side, part Polish and part French-Huguenot on her mother's, Lina's maternal grandfather had held an important government post in Poland, and had spoken both Russian and Polish fluently (Poland then being part of the Russian Empire). Lina's parents were both singers, and she was being trained by her mother to pursue the same career. Her mother was especially knowledgeable about Russian music and musicians, and was already acquainted with Rachmaninov. Lina had come to Prokofiev's symphony concert with some girlfriends, who found Prokofiev's music and his on-stage mannerisms – especially his

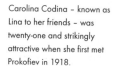

Carolina Codina – known as Lina to her friends – was twenty-one and strikingly attractive when she first met Prokofiev in 1918.

stage bow, 'as though he would break in half' – deeply eccentric. Lina, on the other hand, was excited by what she had heard. Her friends teased her, daring her to go backstage to see her 'hero', but shyness almost prevented her from meeting him. Even at a later concert, which she attended with some other friends, the Staals, she had initially stayed outside the Green Room while her friends went to meet Prokofiev. After waiting what seemed an inordinate length of time (testimony, perhaps, to how charismatic Prokofiev could be), she peered in to see if the Staals were ready to leave. Prokofiev saw her and was smitten. They were introduced and the Staals, noticing Prokofiev's interest in her, rather mischievously invited the two to lunch together at their Staten Island home the following weekend.

So started what became a gentle but persistent courtship by Prokofiev of his future wife. Lina's mother, though a devotee of Russian music, was at first wary of allowing her daughter to be seen in public with Prokofiev, fearing she might be taken to be his mistress – a considerable stigma at that time for a young woman hoping to make a good marriage. When she herself met Prokofiev over lunch, however, she was utterly charmed by him and from then on did all she could to encourage the relationship.

Prokofiev and Lina, very early in their relationship, strike a quirky pose for the camera while spending a weekend on Staten Island.

Now that he had signed the Chicago Opera contract, Prokofiev was able to cut down on performing engagements and concentrate on *The Love for Three Oranges*. But in March he fell seriously ill with scarlet fever, and needed to be hospitalized after developing 'an abscess in my throat that very nearly choked me'. It was possibly at this time that he was introduced to Christian Science, a sect founded in the late nineteenth century by Mary Baker Eddy (a former Calvinist from New England), which preaches a philosophy based on the premise of 'mind over matter' and spiritual healing. It may well have encouraged Prokofiev's rapid recovery. He was to turn to Christian Science years later when suffering a crisis of self-confidence; as a pragmatic man, his faith at that time must have been based on an earlier compelling experience of its apparent effectiveness.

Once discharged from hospital, Prokofiev set to work on his opera with renewed vigour. Perhaps remembering the fraught rehearsals of *The Gambler*, he deliberately considered the prevailing American taste and chose 'a more simple musical language'. Unlike *The Gambler*, promoted as a revolutionary new work, *The Love for Three Oranges* was intended to be no more than a colourful, entertaining extravaganza. But although *The Love for Three Oranges* has often been paraded as a 'comic opera', its style is utterly different from the kind of Italian or German fare that suited conservative American taste: there are no recognizable 'flesh and blood' characters such as one might find in Mozart, or even Rossini. The closest equivalent was not the American musical – then in its infancy – but pantomime, with its colourful stage-effects and fairy-tale plot involving archetypal, pasteboard characters. Meyerhold, when discussing with Prokofiev the possibility of turning Gozzi's play into an opera, may have told him of his ideas for a new kind of anti-realist theatre which – even as *The Love for Three Oranges* was being produced – was reaching the stages of the Soviet Union: circus techniques of slapstick and acrobatics (including juggling and tight-rope walking) were being used by Meyerhold and his disciples to interpret even classical Russian dramas by Gogol and Ostrovsky. Prokofiev almost certainly had something of this kind of staging in mind when writing the opera. Significantly, its most successful production in his lifetime was to take place in Leningrad in the late 1920s, when Meyerhold's theatre was at its most influential.

Much is made of Prokofiev's love of the fantastical and grotesque, but the work also shows considerable charm: the court jester, Truffaldino, is made believably more lithe through his music than through anything else, and the lyricism associated with the princesses in Act 3 – particularly the love music between the prince and Ninette – is genuinely touching despite the satirical text and the underlining of its parody by the appearance of an approving chorus of Romantics. (One personal touch Prokofiev made was to change the first of the princesses' names from Violetta to Linetta, reflecting his new relation-ship with Lina.) The well-known march parodies a triumphant symphonic march with a cheekily insouciant tune and a final series of chords which teasingly delay its final cadence.

Prokofiev completed the short score by June and spent the summer working on its orchestration, which was completed, as the contract stipulated, by 1 October. Boris Anisfeld had been commissioned to design the sets, and all seemed set for Prokofiev to see one of his operas staged at last. But in December Campanini died, suddenly and unexpectedly, and Chicago Opera's season was thrown into disarray as the management, losing their nerve, postponed the production of *The Love for Three Oranges*. Prokofiev, who had put all his energies into the opera, found himself 'left high and dry without the opera and with no concerts to speak of'.

At a loose end, Prokofiev – perversely yet typically – decided to throw himself into writing another opera immediately. Perhaps pro-voked by the fact that even his attempt at lightweight entertainment had been jinxed, he was determined to write something 'meaty', more

Isaak Rabinovich's costume designs for the Kirov Theatre's production of *The Love for Three Oranges*, the most successful production of the opera in Prokofiev's lifetime

worthy of the genre for which he most cared. Casting around for a suitable subject, he came across a novel by Valery Bryusov entitled *The Fiery Angel*, originally serialized in 1907–8 in a Russian Symbolist magazine. Its plot – set in medieval Germany beset by both black magic and the inquisition, with a hysterical heroine and a would-be knightly lover – was just the kind to appeal to Prokofiev, as indicated by the fatal heroines of his earlier operas *Maddalena* and *The Gambler*, and the kind of lugubriously supernatural subject-matter he had immersed himself in after writing *Seven, They Are Seven.*

Prokofiev started planning an opera on *The Fiery Angel* in January 1920, but was quite aware that there was no hope of getting it produced in America:

> *I had come here too soon; the child (America) was not old enough to appreciate new music. Should I go home? But how was I to get there? Russia was blocked on all sides by White Guard fronts, and besides who wants to return home a failure!*

Perhaps more of a decisive factor was the news that his mother – in the tumult of the Russian civil war – had managed to retreat south to Constantinople and was hoping to sail from there to Italy or France. Prokofiev decided to go on to Paris where he knew Diaghilev was running a season, and in the hope of meeting his mother. By then low in funds, he would have been given money for this European trip by a number of his New York émigré friends – including possibly Vladimir Bashkirov, brother of the poet Boris in whose house Prokofiev had enjoyed cultural evenings at Petrograd.

Prokofiev found Paris and London swarming with émigré Russians. Russia's civil war had driven out not only many dispossessed aristocrats (only a few had managed to salvage some jewels for capital) but writers, artists and musicians no longer able to make a living in their homeland. Hospitality that had once been forthcoming to such refugees had now, inevitably, dried up. Most were now thrown back upon their own resources and talent. Prokofiev was fortunate in already knowing Diaghilev, who had soon become weary of the many émigré Russian composers hoping for his help, but was pleased to hear from Prokofiev again. He was much preoccupied, however. The Ballets Russes, having regrouped after the upheavals of the war, were undertaking a heavy schedule of seasons at Monte Carlo and Paris, including the première of Stravinsky's new ballet, *Pulcinella*. Diaghilev suggested, therefore, that Prokofiev meet him later in London during their Covent Garden season; he would then have more time to discuss sensibly the possibility of producing *Chout* (the advance for which had been paid as far back as 1916).

Prokofiev went to London ahead of Diaghilev, hoping to make further contacts before the Ballets Russes season began. He visited exhibitions of work by Russian artists, including Nicolas Roerich, who had designed the sets and costumes for the original production of *The Rite of Spring*. Émigré Russians gave Prokofiev bleak news. The Bolshevik government had not been toppled, as so many had predicted, and in the ensuing social and economic chaos, Russia was on the brink of famine. People had to queue for several hours for bread or anything they could get. Many had become 'numb, hungry stomachs on two legs' before fleeing Petrograd. Musicians were lucky if they could get work in cinemas – instrumentalists by accompanying silent films, singers by performing popular arias. The stories only confirmed what had been implied by Maria Prokofieva's flight from Russia. For the time being, at least, Prokofiev would have to abandon any idea of a return and instead find some means of living in Europe and the States. His best hope, it seemed, was to reaffirm his links with Diaghilev and his circle.

The Ballets Russes had undergone a dramatic change of style since Prokofiev had last seen them before the war. The former opulence represented by Bakst's décor and Russian nationalist-style music had been replaced respectively by the clean-cut, post-Impressionist style of Picasso and Matisse, and a clean, spare Italianate neo-Baroque musical style epitomized in Stravinksy's *Pulcinella*. (This was quite different to the stylistic 'homage' of Prokofiev's 'Classical' Symphony. It consisted of various short arias and chamber pieces attributed to the eighteenth-century composer Pergolesi, vividly orchestrated with occassional, piquant dislocations of the original harmonies. Stravinsky went on from this to create his own so-called 'neo-classical' style, exemplified by his opera-oratorio *Oedipus Rex* composed in 1927.) Given these circumstances, it was extraordinary that Diaghilev should have even considered using Prokofiev's music. Yet Diaghilev, quite apart from his appreciation of Prokofiev's obvious talent, must have felt some

Prokofiev in a London street,
1921; Ernest Ansermet, who
was then conducting for
Diaghilev's Ballets Russes,
stands behind him.

responsibility towards his 'second son': the plot of *Chout* had, after all,
been chosen by the impresario himself, and having trashed Prokofiev's
first ballet, written at his own behest, Diaghilev did not have the heart
to turn him down again.

Probably in response to Prokofiev's communication of intent to
come and see him, Diaghilev had the original score of *Chout*
handsomely bound. Prokofiev was flattered and touched by this
gesture, and therefore prepared to accept Diaghilev's recommendations
for improving the ballet: he agreed to rewrite a number of parts, to
compose five symphonic entr'actes to allow the six scenes to be
performed without interruption, to revise the finale completely and
to reorchestrate the entire work. But the ballet's very beginning, 'with
all its whistling and rattling sounds, as if someone were "dusting the
orchestra" before the beginning of the spectacle' was to be left intact.

Before the season started, however, Prokofiev had to get back to
Paris to greet his mother, who had finally arrived from Constantinople.
Suffering now from rheumatism and rapidly failing eyesight, the
deprivations Maria Prokofieva had suffered over the past few years had
taken their toll on her health. Acting on medical advice, her son
immediately placed her in a hospital where doctors would decide

whether or not to operate on her eyes. In the meantime, Lina had travelled to Europe to further her singing studies, and Prokofiev, who was about to return to London, asked her to visit his mother in hospital on a regular basis and to keep her amused. Lina soon proved to be most sympathetic company for Maria, talking with her about the arts, the latest news, and chiefly – as this was what Maria wanted to hear about above all – everything she knew about Prokofiev's life after he had left Russia.

When Prokofiev returned, he was told that the operation on Maria's eyes had succeeded only in preventing complete blindness. She was now only able to see figures in silhouette and had to occupy herself, when not talking with Lina, with learning Braille and mastering the art of knitting. Maria was totally dependent on her son's support.

In order to find some peace and quiet to revise *Chout*, Prokofiev rented a small house near Mantes-la-Jolie, a village on the Seine an hour away from Paris. He also spent time at the piano 'grinding out' pieces he needed to get 'in his fingers' for his next American tour. Lina often visited the Prokofievs and, concerned that Sergey might be overworking, insisted that he take her for walks in the neighbouring woods. During these walks Prokofiev would bring her up to date with his work in progress, and it seems to have been then that Lina's love for Sergey truly flourished: she admired his creativity and was deeply touched by the trust he showed her in talking of his work. Indeed, she was so enamoured with this side of Sergey that when three years later he proposed to her in Munich, and asked her whether she was worried about marrying 'a poor, unknown composer', she was genuinely astonished. She did not know, of course, how or why Prokofiev had been rebuffed over Nina Mescherskaya, and how much hurt pride lay behind this apparently humble question. Maria became jealous of the intimacy that was growing between them, and begged her son to share with her all that he had been telling Lina. This irritated Sergey, and he lost his temper on at least one occasion. It says much about Lina's generosity but also, perhaps, about how much Maria had charmed her that she usually backed her future mother-in-law against his fury.

In late October Prokofiev returned to America, and had a 'battle royal' with the director of the Chicago Opera. Although the company was prepared to produce *The Love for Three Oranges* during the 1920–21 season, Prokofiev demanded compensation for the year's postponement, arguing that he had turned down all possible

Sergey and Lina with friends in the 1920s: (left to right) the Russian-born musicologist Pierre Suvchinsky, the mezzo-soprano Nina Koshetz, Prokofiev, Zosia Kochanski, the violinist Paul Kochanski, Lina

engagements as a performer in order to produce the score in time for the original deadline. The director was unsympathetic and claimed a right to stage the opera whenever he wanted without the composer's permission. With Prokofiev's threat of legal action, the opera, once again, failed to reach the stage.

Prokofiev travelled on to California where he had some concert engagements in December and January. There he was able to forget his tribulations in Chicago, enjoying the state's spectacular landscape and the warm climate, and he was also well received in Los Angeles and San Francisco. It was then that he composed *Five Songs without Words* for the mezzo-soprano Nina Koshetz, who had emigrated from Russia in 1920. His mellow mood is reflected in the haunting, wistful yet suavely urbane melodies, with hints of passion in the first and last songs. Unlike the vocalises of Rachmaninov and Villa-Lobos, Prokofiev's highly mobile melodies are less brilliant and more intimate in character, and were to be more successful in their later arrangement for violin, made at the suggestion of Paul Kochanski. (Kochanski had now left Russia, and was eventually to take a teaching post at the Juilliard School in New York.)

Back in New York by late January, Prokofiev met Karol Szymanowski, this time in the company of Arthur Rubinstein, Paul Kochanski and his wife Zosia over breakfast at the Ritz Grill. Prokofiev made a very good impression on Szymanowski, who had been brought to America by the Kochanskis and Rubinstein in an attempt to raise interest in his music. Indeed, Prokofiev was in

particularly good humour after his Californian trip, and also because
he had recently met Mary Garden, the legendary soprano who had
taken over as director of Chicago Opera. She had made her reputation
creating the role of Mélisande for Debussy's revolutionary opera,
Pelléas et Mélisande, and had sung the demanding title-role in Strauss's
Salome, so was well acquainted with the demands of contemporary
opera. She declared herself interested in producing *Love for Three
Oranges* and shortly afterwards signed a contract with Prokofiev to
present the opera in the 1921–2 season.

By April 1921 Prokofiev had returned to Paris, and Diaghilev sent
him on to Monte Carlo where rehearsals of *Chout* were in progress.
Chout reached production, unfortunately, just as Diaghilev had – yet
again – lost his choreographer. Léonide Massine, who had filled the
position vacated by Nijinsky, found working with Diaghilev,
professionally and emotionally, an increasing strain. His abrupt
departure meant that the choreography of *Chout* passed into the hands
of a totally inexperienced dancer, Taddeus Slavinsky, supervised by the
designer Mikhail Larionov. Diaghilev nevertheless rushed *Chout* into
production, having heard that Koussevitzky intended to be the first to
introduce Prokofiev's work to Paris that month with the *Scythian Suite*.
Determined not to have his thunder stolen, Diaghilev sent
Koussevitzky a series of brusque telegrams to try to persuade him to
postpone the performance. Not surprisingly Koussevitzky refused to
comply, and Prokofiev must have soured his relations with Diaghilev
by agreeing to conduct Koussevitzky's concert. The performance, on 29

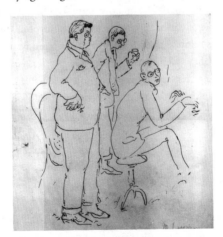

This caricature by Mikhail
Larionov shows Prokofiev, at
the piano, playing the score
of *Chout* for the benefit of
(left to right) Diaghilev and
Stravinsky

Portrait of Prokofiev by Henri Matisse, April 1921; Prokofiev was amused by how Matisse lengthened his face, and on asking why, was told by the artist that it helped to convey his considerable height.

April at the Salle Gareau, went well, yet it convinced Prokofiev of the need to revise the *Scythian Suite* further, and by the following year the third movement had been cut substantially.

The première of *Chout* eventually took place on 17 May, lavishly produced with Larionov's colourful sets, and a glossy programme including a portrait of Prokofiev by Matisse. Diaghilev, as always, had found a way of cutting costs; for this season he held his Ballets Russes at the Gaieté-Lyrique, a venue for operetta situated on the working-class boulevard de Sebastopol. The Ballets Russes' usual audience, arriving for the first night in their top-hats and tails, finery and jewellery, were greeted with whistles and boos by the locals. Diaghilev's gamble paid off, however, as the new location brought him a new audience. *Chout*, conducted by Prokofiev, was a tremendous success. The brightly coloured music and garish sets made their impact despite the loosely structured and unmemorable choreography: Roland Manuel of *Éclair* hailed the ballet as 'the most important work that the Russians have shown us since the War'.

By now Prokofiev was being perceived, and presented, as a potential successor to Stravinsky. A journalist who had attended rehearsals for *Chout* had predicted that the première would be 'a date to remember in the history of Russian music just as not so long ago was the appearance of *The Firebird*, which signalled the dawn of the young glory of M. Stravinsky'. But this was misleading, since Stravinsky was already well advanced in mapping out a style of musical discourse quite different from Prokofiev's. The elder composer's works from *The Rite of Spring* onwards – instead of following the conventional musical syntax he (and Prokofiev) had inherited from Rimsky-Korsakov, in which musical ideas balance or 'answer' each other in a continuous musical narrative or argument – tended to be built on monolithic musical ideas which were then fragmented and juxtaposed with contrasting yet equally monolithic musical ideas. And though Prokofiev's colourful orchestration, repetitive melodic patterns and 'audacious' and 'modern' harmonies were indebted to Stravinsky's pre-war works, Prokofiev was to think always in terms of late-nineteenth-century narrative discourse (such as might be found in Tchaikovsky's operas and symphonies) throughout his entire composing career.

Chout is nevertheless one of Prokofiev's most colourful and attractive scores, a considerable achievement for a composer still in his

A scene from the original production of Chout: (left to right) M. Jazwinsky, Lydia Sokolova and Taddeus Slavinsky, who was responsible for the choreography; Larionov's costumes and décor were strikingly garish, and well complemented Prokofiev's colourful score.

twenties, and it compares favourably against Stravinsky's more derivative *Firebird* (written when the same age). Though *Petrushka* influenced particularly the sparkling orchestration of *Chout*, Prokofiev was clearly forging his own distinctive approach to the Russian folk material he arranged. There is a certain tartness, combined with a wistful edge – for example, in the opening cor anglais theme set against gusting woodwind chromatics – which is more romantic in feel than the astringent style Stravinsky had adopted in such recent works as *The Soldier's Tale*. Prokofiev's sweet-sour harmonies and his use of a large but purposeful orchestral palette seems to anticipate the sound of Kodály's later folk-inspired works such as the *Peacock Variations* and *Háry János*. Prokofiev also succeeded in developing the style he had used in the more atmospheric moments of *Ala and Lolli*, creating highly effective spooky music (such as the twining clarinets playing while the buffoon brandishes his magic whip) in a style that owes nothing to Stravinsky.

That summer Prokofiev took refuge in Etretât, on the coast of Brittany. There he worked on completing his Third Piano Concerto on what Lina described as 'a horrible old upright piano'. Most of its themes had been composed over the past ten years, some of them for a two-movement string quartet he had started after challenging himself to write a diatonic work that could be played solely on the white keys of a piano. Prokofiev ultimately found the task too difficult, and divided the quartet's themes between *The Fiery Angel* and the new concerto.

The Third Piano Concerto is easily the best-known of his cycle of five; despite its long gestation and the different origin of some of its themes, the impression is of a spontaneous, continually inspired,

Konstantin Balmont on a beach near St Brevin-les-Pins, summer 1921; Prokofiev was also on holiday there, and Balmont was inspired by the composer's nearly completed Third Piano Concerto to write a sonnet – 'Prokofiev! Music and youth in bloom/In you, the orchestra yearns for forgotten summer sounds ...'

effortlessly colourful and enchanting work. Most impressive are the second movement's theme (written as far back as 1913) and variations, each distinctly characterized, and showing Prokofiev's skilled use of the piano's timbre supported by felicitous orchestration. Those inclined to think Prokofiev incapable of vivid scene-painting without labouring his forces should try the fourth variation, where quietly sonorous piano writing combines with silky-dark orchestration, highlighted by fleeting high strings and flecks of woodwind: it is a nocturnal landscape, vividly drawn with an astonishing economy of instrumentation.

Balmont was a close neighbour at Etretât. Prokofiev visited the poet frequently, and could see that he had fallen on hard times. Partly in response to this, but also in recognition of the inspiration Balmont's work had been to him, Prokofiev set five of his newly written poems as a song cycle, which he dedicated to Lina. Each performance he and Lina gave of the cycle would, of course, earn author's royalties for Balmont; furthermore, on his next trip to America, Prokofiev made efforts to persuade wealthy benefactors to sponsor Balmont. The poet expressed his admiration of Prokofiev's art with a sonnet on his almost completed Third Piano Concerto; Prokofiev in turn dedicated his Concerto to him.

After finishing the concerto in September, Prokofiev took Lina on a tour along the French Atlantic coast. The following month he set off for America, accompanied by Bashkirov, to supervise the forthcoming production of *The Love for Three Oranges*. It would be designed by Boris Anisfeld, whose New York exhibition Prokofiev had helped open with his first American recital, and Prokofiev had hoped that their mutual friend, Adolf Bolm, would be in charge of the production. The task was, however, given to Jack Coini, 'a colourless personality'. Prokofiev became increasingly frustrated by Coini and eventually took it upon himself to explain the roles to the singers and – quite openly on stage – to the chorus. Coini, outraged at having his authority so brazenly affronted, finally lost his temper demanding, 'Who is in charge here, you or I?' Prokofiev replied, 'You – so as to carry out my wishes.'

Before his opera's première, Prokofiev gave the first performance of his new concerto on 16 December 1921 with the Chicago Symphony Orchestra under Frederick Stock. The reception was moderately enthusiastic, the concerto's success only being confirmed with the tremendous welcome it would receive the following year in Europe. As for *The Love for Three Oranges*, though lavishly produced, the Chicago audience was apparently 'both proud and embarassed to be presenting a "modernist première" which, according to the newspapers, had already cost some 250,000 dollars.'

In mid January Prokofiev took part in what he later described as 'a grand concert arranged by the Chicago branch of the Friends of Soviet Russia'. It seems the 'Soviet' part of the concert was something of an invention, given that his mother and many of his friends, such as Balmont and the Bashkirovs, had fled Soviet Russia; the concert was essentially for the benefit of Chicago's Russian community, who had bailed Prokofiev out when he had first arrived. Significantly, when writing his biography in the intolerant environment of Stalinist Russia, Prokofiev omitted to mention to his Soviet readers that also taking part in the concert was the singer, Nina Koshetz, who had left the Soviet Union in 1920, and never shared his later interest in returning to Russia. Despite her evident importance to Prokofiev – she gave the first performance of his *Five Songs without Words*, appeared many times with him in concert, was a regular correspondent, and as late as 1928 sang the lead role of Renata in the first performance of part of *The Fiery Angel* – she does not feature once in his autobiography.

Shortly afterwards Prokofiev left Chicago for New York where, on 14 February, *The Love for Three Oranges* received a single performance which, Prokofiev wrote to a friend afterwards, was 'splendidly accepted by the audience. But the critics did not like it and wrote columns and columns of nonsense.' Typical was the *New York Times*'s review: 'The audience was large, and after the first shock of surprise, evinced considerable amusement in the proceedings onstage ... There are a few, but only a very few, passages that bear recognizable kinship with what has hitherto been recognized as music ...'

Prokofiev performed his Third Piano Concerto again, this time conducted by his friend Albert Coates. He then stayed in New York just long enough to sort out visas and passports for himself and Boris Bashkirov to travel to Germany, the refuge he intended would enable him to work on his opera *The Fiery Angel*.

4

Sergey, Lina and Maria
Prokofieva holding her
grandson Sviatoslav in the
garden in Bellevue, Paris
1924

*My concert engagements at this period took me
all over France, England, Belgium, Italy and
Spain. Strange to say, though I lived for a year
and a half in Germany within two hours' ride
of a city like Munich, I did not establish any
contacts whatever with the German musical
world. The March and Scherzo from the Three
Oranges and the Overture on Hebrew Themes
had been performed in Berlin, and one or two
piano pieces were played by professional pianists,
but they did not make much impression and
Paris remained my musical centre.*

Sergey Prokofiev, *Autobiography*

Lina and The Fiery Angel 1922-7

Looking for a quiet haven, and with only limited funds at his disposal, Prokofiev needed somewhere modest to rent. Germany was now the cheapest European country in which to live thanks to the weakness of the Deutschmark, and by late March 1922, Prokofiev had found a Bavarian-style chalet for himself, his mother and Bashkirov, initially available for one year's rent. Situated in the southern German hamlet of Ettal, Haus Christophorus was an ideal base, and for almost two years it was Prokofiev's home. He was exhausted by his itinerant existence over the past four years, and now relished the rural peace of the Bavarian Alps. Ettal – within striking distance of the Passion-Play village of Oberammergau and of the Harz mountains (traditionally associated with Witches' Sabbaths) – seemed the ideal setting to inspire his new opera.

The Fiery Angel was the most problematic opera Prokofiev had composed to date, in at least its staging and interpretation. Part of the complications lay in the libretto, which juggles characters of psychological depth with deliberately 'stagey' and anti-realistic happenings. The story, set in medieval Germany, is reasonably straightforward: Ruprecht, a knight freshly returned from his travels in the New World, meets an attractive but hysterical young woman, Renata, who believes herself tormented by evil spirits. She tells Ruprecht of a fiery angel called Madiel, her playmate from childhood who encouraged her to lead a holy life then abandoned her when she tried to consummate their relationship. She subsequently convinces herself that she has found the angel in mortal form, in the person of one Count Heinrich, who forsakes her after a brief relationship. Taking pity on Renata, Ruprecht agrees to assist in her (clearly insane) quest for Heinrich with the use of black magic (courtesy of the philosopher-magician Agrippa). Ruprecht is led into a near-fatal duel with the Count, after which Renata declares undying love for her apparently mortally wounded suitor. But when Ruprecht later recovers and attempts to persuade her to sleep with him, Renata draws a knife

Haus Christophorus, Ettal –
the Bavarian chalet which
was Prokofiev's home from
March 1922, and where he
composed his gothic opera,
The Fiery Angel

on him and flees. In the final act she appears as a novice in a
monastery, where all is peaceful but for mysterious knockings and
disquiet among her fellow nuns. The Grand Inquisitor arrives to
question Renata, but as she denies all association with the forces of
darkness, her fellow sisters succumb to possession – or mass hysteria –
one by one. The opera ends as the Grand Inquisitor accuses Renata of
having carnal knowledge of the devil, thus condemning her to be
tortured and burnt as a witch.

Here again is Prokofiev's favourite theme of a man locked in a
destructive relationship with an attractive but unbalanced woman.
But in the time since he had treated such a subject in *The Gambler*,
Prokofiev had been radically affected by Meyerhold's anti-realist theories
of drama. An obvious manifestation of this different approach to opera
occurs at the end of Act Two when, as Agrippa denies that he has any
dealings in necromancy, two skeletons wave their arms and shriek, 'You
lie!' And just as there had been a chorus of spectators commenting on
the action in *The Love for Three Oranges*, a chorus of demons (which
arguably include the skeletons) make the odd appearance.

Theatrical style aside, *The Fiery Angel* is Prokofiev's most overtly
nihilistic work, a near-masterpiece of its kind. Renata's obsession with
her fiery angel, related as it is to her moral degeneration and
schizophrenic behaviour, can be seen as an uncanny premonition of
the destructive hero-worship that was to grip both Soviet Russia and

Nazi Germany. Ultimately, most (if not all) of the mortal characters appear foolish or deluded, which is what makes the music so compelling and horrifying. Except for the 'comic relief' provided in Act Four by Mephistopheles, the music itself betrays little or no sense of irony. Rather, from Renata's first appearance there is an intense sense of foreboding and increasing menace. The music builds to a powerful near-climax in Act Two as Renata attempts to summon Heinrich through black magic, culminating in ferocious malevolence when in the following scene Ruprecht tries to enlist Agrippa's help. This latter scene seems particularly to bring what Prokofiev had learnt from Schopenhauer (which he had been re-reading) to its logical conclusion:

> The composer reveals the innermost nature of the world, and expresses the profoundest wisdom in a language that his reasoning faculty does not understand. [Music] gives the most profound, ultimate, and secret information on the feeling expressed in the words, or the action presented in the opera. It expresses their real and true nature, and makes us acquainted with the innermost soul of the events and occurrences, the mere cloak and body of which are presented on the stage.

As the characters on stage are seen foolishly pursuing 'the explanation of all mysteries' (Agrippa's portentous claim for 'true magic') or twittering superstitiously over patterns made by egg white, the real force of the drama, through the music, is potently present throughout. It is no accident that Prokofiev makes Mephistopheles seem rather ridiculous and tiresome. The malign presence expressed – or rather, given expression – by the music is, by implication, infinitely greater than anything that could be conceived by the mumbo-jumbo of the necromancers, and certainly greater than opera's favourite pantomime devil.

Yet if all human endeavour – as shown by the characters – appears morally futile, why should one care about any of them? By not allowing his characters any degree of self-awareness regarding their predicament, Prokofiev prevents his audience from feeling much sympathy for them and so any sense of tragedy is lost. Significantly, Prokofiev was not to attempt 'flesh-and-blood' characters again for many years. If one discounts his ballet *The Prodigal Son* (the central character of which is arguably something of a self-portrait), it was more than ten years before Prokofiev successfully portrayed living characters in his music, and this was in the form of his ballet *Romeo and Juliet*.

While working on *The Fiery Angel*, Prokofiev supported himself, his mother and Bashkirov by making several tours as a pianist. In April 1922 he performed his Third Piano Concerto in Paris under Koussevitzky, with a follow-up performance in London. Prokofiev wrote to his friend in Chicago, Ephraim Gottlieb, that the reception of the concerto in both cities was 'quite remarkable, much bigger than in Chicago, and the critics called me "genius"(!)'

Altogether Prokofiev was beginning to feel that Europe was far more congenial to his work and its reception, not to mention his well-being, than America had ever been. Increasingly he was to turn down requests from America to make concert tours there: although the States could offer higher concert fees, he was in greater demand in Europe and the fees he commanded were more than adequate to cover Ettal's modest living costs.

Indeed such was Prokofiev's success in Europe that when Diaghilev gave a revival of *Chout* in Paris in June, the initial run of three performances had to be extended to five. The contrast between the reception of this and the rather cooler one given to Stravinsky's latest offering – the half-hour opera *Mavra* – was striking enough to make the older composer, according to their mutual friend Pierre Suvchinsky, 'terribly worried'. The help and support he had given Prokofiev seemed to be leading to his own undoing. No doubt Stravinsky had also been disturbed by Diaghilev's increasing references to Prokofiev as 'my second son'.

When Diaghilev invited Prokofiev to play through *The Love for Three Oranges* for a possible production by himself, Stravinsky was present. According to Prokofiev, after hearing Act One, Stravinsky was sharply critical and refused to listen to any more. He appears to have accused Prokofiev of using a musical language 'unsympathetic' (i.e., too personal and original) to the original *commedia dell'arte* drama; he may even have referred to his own arrangements of Pergolesi for *Pulcinella* as a more sympathetic accompaniment for such theatre. As Prokofiev recalled, 'I hotly defended my opera and the result was a quarrel. For my part I did not approve of Stravinsky's … 'pseudo-Bachism' – or rather I did not approve of adopting someone else's

argument with Stravinsky

idiom and calling it one's own. True, I had written a 'Classical' Symphony myself, but that was only a passing phase.'

Hardly surprisingly, relations became strained between the two composers, and were only shakily patched-up several years later once Stravinsky had re-established his pre-eminence. Until then, it seems that Stravinsky did much to poison Prokofiev's reputation with many of Paris's leading arbiters of taste in the arts, including Diaghilev himself. As a result Diaghilev, despite the success of *Chout*, not only failed to issue Prokofiev with an immediate commission for a new ballet, but abruptly dropped *Chout* from the repertory of the Ballets Russes.

The loss of Diaghilev's support was a blow for Prokofiev, who must have been counting on gaining a further advance for either a production of *The Love for Three Oranges* or a new ballet commission. His fall from Diaghilev's favour was so marked that when Vladimir Dukelsky (later known by his Broadway name Vernon Duke) was first introduced to Diaghilev two years later, he was positively discouraged from making any contact with Prokofiev: 'Prokofiev is an utter imbecile,' Diaghilev said haughtily. 'He can always be counted on to do the wrong thing. Fancy calling a symphony Classical! It's almost as ridiculous as Skryabin labelling his orchestral poem Divine.'

Prokofiev now had to rely more than ever on income generated from tours as a pianist. He also depended increasingly on the support of Koussevitzky, in many ways Diaghilev's rival for championing all that was new in music. Koussevitzky agreed to publish a number of works through his firm, Gutheil, including *Old Grandmother's Tales*, the Op. 32 piano suite, the *Overture on Hebrew Themes*, the *Songs without Words*, a suite from *Chout* and the vocal score and an orchestral suite of *The Love for Three Oranges*. With two new orchestral suites and a piano reduction to prepare, as well as all the proofing necessary prior to publication, Prokofiev now had plenty to do on top of his continuing work on *Fiery Angel*. Balmont found Prokofiev to be 'completely wilted' with a 'sad and harried' face when they met that autumn.

That he had reached something of a spiritual crisis is clear from a list of Christian Science precepts he wrote for himself at this time, from which he obviously tried to draw strength. At the top of the list is a single sentence which provides the key both to his state of mind, and to what motivated his subsequent behaviour: 'Depression is a lie of the mortal mind, consequently it cannot have power over me, for I am the expression of Life, i.e., of divine activity.'

Although Prokofiev never became a full member of the Christian Science church (he took too much hedonistic pleasure in clothes, scent and haute cuisine to be fully sympathetic to its anti-materialistic stance), he embraced a number of its precepts, particularly those which seemed in harmony with what he had learnt from Schopenhauer – above all, Schopenhauer's idea that music, by not exhibiting 'the *Ideas* of grades of the will's objectification, but directly the *will itself*, transcended more material laws. A number of precepts in Prokofiev's list, which he wrote in English, also appear to have shored up certain of his traits, such as industriousness and self-belief, to the point, in some cases, of cock-sure arrogance that was not only unattractive but even potentially hazardous to himself:

I am the expression of spirit, which gives me power to resist all what [sic] is unlike spirit.

My fidelity grants my uninterrupted adherence to all what [sic] is untrue.

As I am the expression of spirit, I am capable of vigorous creative thinking.

As I am the effect [or result?] of the one great Cause, I ignore everything which does not proceed from this Cause.

I am honest to myself and therefore will do the work which is the best.

As activity is my inherent quality, the desire to work is natural.

I am eager to work, as action is the expression of Life.

I rejoice in tribulations, for the contact with them gives me the opportunity to prove their unreality.

With much of his time in Ettal taken up with his own composition, Prokofiev had little energy to follow musical developments in Germany. Yet despite his punishing timetable, Prokofiev found time in November to make a trip to Berlin with Diaghilev to see Mayakovsky, one of Prokofiev's most devoted fans. Mayakovsky, obtaining a visa through Diaghilev, then came to Paris to discuss possible projects, in the course of which the poet tried to persuade Diaghilev to return to Russia. Although there is no record to confirm this, one assumes that Mayakovsky also talked to Prokofiev about a possible return. If so, this would have been the first of what were to be many such propositions.

By February 1923 Prokofiev had finished the piano score of *The Fiery Angel*, writing jubilantly to his Parisian friend Fatima Samoilenko, 'I am indescribably happy, and have even forgotten that this whole mass of music still has to be orchestrated.' Prokofiev was much delayed in this task, however, not least due to his developing relationship with Lina, now pursuing her singing studies in Milan. It was a relatively easy rail journey from Milan to Ettal, and Lina became a regular visitor. As in France, the two often took walks together, visiting Richard Strauss's house in Garmische-Partenkirchen, and made plans for a walking tour through Switzerland. Prokofiev, a keen chess-player, also tried to teach Lina the game: 'At first I showed some talent ... he gave me the nickname of an outstanding young professional player. But the chess problems he gave me became more and more difficult, and I would end up in tears trying to solve them. Then he would say: 'Stop, Ptashka, let's go to bed,' and we would later sing his songs, play Debussy, discuss the Flaming Angel ...' The only other chess partner available, Boris Bashkirov, had left Ettal; in order to get a decent game Prokofiev had to visit him at the house of Dr Anton Lang in Oberammergau. Boris and Lina had not got on; aware of Prokofiev's struggle to make ends meet and possibly jealous of the friendship between him and Bashkirov, Lina resented the poet's indolence and also – it seems – his over-free manner with what she regarded as their property (she later accused him of having used a car without their permission while they were abroad).

In May 1923, Lina made her singing début in Milan as Gilda in *Rigoletto*. Prokofiev gave a piano recital in the city, and the couple followed this with a joint concert in which they gave a successful première of Prokofiev's song cycle to poems by Balmont. They returned to Ettal, and their romance intensified. That summer Prokofiev wrote a new piano sonata – his fifth and his last for sixteen years. Dedicated to Suvchinsky, its deceptively calm, 'classical' opening theme has led a number of writers to describe the sonata in terms of 'serenity' and 'pastoral elegance', even to suggest that it may somehow reflect the love between Sergey and Lina. There is an

Prokofiev in his first car, a French convertible Ballot; his friend, the poet Boris Bashkirov, is at the wheel, with Lina in the back, c. 1923.

unmistakeable chill, however, in the second subject, and even a hint of *The Fiery Angel*'s eerie atmosphere in the pervasive chromaticism and in some of the ethereal, at times almost Bartókian effects. The second movement is quirky, once described by a British pianist as a 'tango for tortoises', full of mildly clashing major second intervals which give a futuristic sound typical of the 1920s; the balletic final movement follows, very much in Prokofiev's acidic scherzo style.

That summer Lina became pregnant. To have a child out of wedlock – certainly as far as both Lina and Maria were concerned – was out of the question, and so, on 14 September 1923, Sergey and Lina applied for a marriage licence at the Municipal Office at Ettal; they were married quietly on 29 September with Boris Bashkirov and Maria as witnesses. Lina's pregnancy had not begun at the most propitious of times, as the owner of Haus Christophorus announced that he planned to sell the property. Faced with having to find somewhere else to live, the newly-weds opted for Paris; not only was Prokofiev's most constant champion, Koussevitzky, based there, but it seemed sensible for Lina to have her child within easy reach of medical assistance.

Just days after their marriage, therefore, Sergey and Lina travelled up to Paris, arriving in time for the long-delayed première of his Violin Concerto. This was held in the Paris Opera on 18 October, with Koussevitzky conducting and the orchestra's leader, Marcel Darrieux, as soloist. Many of Prokofiev's friends – including Szymanowski, Arthur Rubinstein, Szigeti and Kochanski – were

Lina in a dressing-room, possibly in Milan, where her singing career began in earnest in 1923 with her début as Gilda in *Rigoletto*

present, as were Picasso, Anna Pavlova and Benois. The reception given to the concerto was inevitably coloured by its sharing the programme with Stravinsky's latest work, the Octet for wind instruments. Stravinsky's supporters turned out in force, among them members of Les Six (the group of French composers so-named by the journalist Henri Collet, who, referring to Russia's *kuchka*, had drawn parallels with 'Les Cinq Russes') and the pedagogue Nadia Boulanger. After the performance they made a point of praising Stravinsky's witty and sophisticated work at the expense of Prokofiev's more straightforwardly melodious, 'Mendelssohnian' Concerto. Ironically, Stravinsky himself, as he demonstrated more and more openly over the decades, had a particularly soft spot for Prokofiev's most magical score.

Prokofiev was wounded by the dismissive reception in Paris, but was encouraged by news of its highly successful Moscow première only days later, performed by Nathan Milstein with Vladimir Horowitz playing the orchestra's part on the piano. Myaskovsky, who was present, wrote to Prokofiev about the performance in detail, concluding that as a result of the Moscow première Prokofiev's popularity was 'almost indecent. You've eclipsed even the Moscow idols, Rachmaninov and Medtner!'

Lina's mother arrived in Paris for the birth of her grandchild. Prokofiev's finances were at a low ebb, but Lina's family friends gave financial support which enabled her to stay at 'a magnificent clinic in Muette' where their son, Sviatoslav, was born on 27 February 1924. Used to Lina's undivided attention, Prokofiev was at first jealous of the demands of his new son, nicknaming him 'the oyster'. It was only later, when Sviatoslav became a toddler, that the future composer of *Peter and the Wolf* was to show a delighted interest in him. When their child was two months old, the Prokofievs moved into rented accommodation – a small top-floor apartment in rue Charles Dickens, situated in the well-to-do suburb of Passy across the Seine from the Eiffel Tower. With no commissions forthcoming from Diaghilev, Prokofiev continued to rely on what performances he could get, particularly those brought about by Koussevitzky. Fortunately, as Prokofiev had expended most of his compositional resources on *The Fiery Angel* over the past two years, there was a backlog of compositions awaiting premières; apart from the Violin Concerto there was *Seven, They Are Seven* and a revised version of the Second Piano Concerto. Asafyev had written from Leningrad that the piano concerto's original manuscript had been used as fuel 'to cook an omelette', so necessitating a rewrite of the score. In his new version Prokofiev increased the complexity of the independent melodic lines, simultaneously improving the flow and detail in the piano and orchestral parts.

Much to Lina's consternation, Prokofiev practised the revised concerto continually, in particular the ferocious first movement cadenza, in their cramped apartment (the baby had to sleep in the same room as the piano). Sergey's practice prior to the première also displeased the neighbours, who called every day to complain about the noise. Finally the apartment manager came to demand that Prokofiev cease playing his piano. Lina recalled Prokofiev's response:

> 'All right, you don't want to hear my music, but I have the right to do whatever I like in my own apartment. Instead of playing music I'll start hammering boxes together.' Placing a box on the floor, he started banging on it with a hammer. That's how it ended – apparently the neighbours threw up their hands and gave in.

On this occasion, maybe. But according to one friend, Serge Moreux, Prokofiev (and with him his family) was often 'turned out of various lodgings for making too much noise'. This would explain his complete failure to hold down a single Parisian address from one year to the next.

After the altercation over the practising of the revised concerto, its première on 8 May (according to Harlow Robinson) was positively tame. Much more exciting for the sophisticated Parisian audience was the first performance of *Seven, They Are Seven*, conducted by Koussevitzky on 29 May in the final concert of his 1924 spring series. To ensure the work made its impact, Koussevitzky insisted on playing

it twice in the same concert. As he had already been appointed the
new conductor of the Boston Symphony Orchestra from the
following autumn, Koussevitzky's activities in Paris were of particular
interest to American readers. Olin Downes of the *New York Times* was
there to report, and wrote of *Seven*, 'How it would have sounded
under a conductor less sympathetic to its nature than Koussevitsky it
is hard to say. But on the evening in question and under the
circumstances the work made a powerful impression.' It was certainly
applauded enthusiastically by the Parisian audience. Koussevitzky,
after the success of *Seven*, gave Prokofiev an advance for a new
symphony, encouraging him to try to compose a 'hit'. He also
promised to programme a number of Prokofiev's works during his first
Boston season, including the *Scythian Suite*, the Third Piano Concerto
with Cortot as soloist, and the Violin Concerto.

The Prokofievs took their summer retreat in the village of St-Gilles-
sur-Vie on the Atlantic coast in Brittany. There Prokofiev worked at

Sergey and Lina with Serge
Koussevitzky and his wife
Natalia, c. 1925; after
Prokofiev quarrelled with
Stravinsky and Diaghilev in
1922, he increasingly relied
on Koussevitzky's support
both as a conductor and as
a publisher.

his Second Symphony, determined to repeat the success of *Seven*. He had begun to establish a daily routine: each day started with a short stroll to 'air himself out' before settling down to compose solidly, only stopping for another little walk just before lunch. In the early afternoon he would either rest – 'nestling down' as he called it – or attend to any business matters, before turning to the more mundane aspects of composing, either orchestrating or correcting proofs. Prokofiev regarded the latter task almost as a recreation, enthusiastically and conscientiously correcting scores even when travelling. He took almost malicious pleasure in the fact that Stravinsky's scores, for all the neatness of their writing, were always peppered with basic errors whilst his own were immaculate.

In mid October, the family moved to the Paris suburb of Bellevue, a much more pleasant location than the crowded apartment in rue Charles Dickens. But life in Bellevue was increasingly clouded by Maria, who, enfeebled and now almost blind, had become petty-minded and suspicious. Lina could not buy a new piece of clothing without Maria demanding to know its cost, insisting that Lina had to be 'careful with Sergey's earnings'. Maria also mistrusted the elderly Russian couple who kept house for them, and even tried to make Lina count the sugar cubes. Maria finally died on 13 December 1924. Sergey, according to Lina, 'found this loss very hard to bear and was totally submerged in his grief for a long time'; but, as with the death of his father, he said almost nothing about his mother's death to even his closest friends.

Sergey wheels his son Sviatoslav in his pushchair, c. 1926; the future composer of *Peter and the Wolf* took particular delight in watching the antics of his toddler son.

Prokofiev completed his Second Symphony by the end of May, after nine months of 'feverish work'. He had been clearly encouraged by the stir caused by the première of *Seven, They Are Seven* which had led to Koussevitzky's commission, and perhaps also by Honegger's recent *Pacific 231* (an orchestral evocation of the power and sound of a American-style locomotive). Prokofiev declared that this was going to be a work of 'iron and steel'. He raised the stakes further by attempting the intellectual rigour of basing the work's structure on that of Beethoven's last piano sonata – a sonata-form first movement followed by an extensive set of variations on a theme. Prokofiev's immense relief on completing the work is all too obvious in his letter to Myaskovsky: 'Anyway – Schluss – now, they won't get anything complicated from me for a long time.'

The symphony opens with an exhileratingly noisy sonata movement, a direct answer to Honegger's locomotive. The second movement initially appears more restrained, a charming modal theme being played against an undulating accompaniment, but the variations which follow cover an extraordinary range of moods from dark foreboding through boisterous playfulness to pastoral reflection. In the final two violent and vigorous variations, themes from the first movement emerge and blend with the varied theme of the second movement, building to a horrifying juggernaut of a climax before the almost comforting return of the original theme. And yet its close is sinister – a hair-raising whistle of string harmonics above lugubrious low clarinets. To the Parisian audience at its première on 6 June 1925, the symphony seemed a gratuitously hideous work, all too self-consciously trying to sound tough and relentless. Most of the critics hated it. André George of *Nouvelles Littéraires* noted in some frustration: 'A strange artist, splendidly gifted, Prokofiev is in urgent need of something that is not denied to much less important musicians: he has buckets of gold, but not two sous' worth of reflection.' Prokofiev was severely disappointed, but not, apparently, because he felt the audience and critics had failed his work. He wrote afterwards to Derzhanovsky, 'Neither I nor the audience understood anything in it,' and years later confessed, 'This was perhaps the first time it occurred to me that I might perhaps be destined to be a second-rate composer.' In fairness, the work's failure seems to have been partially due to shortcomings in Koussevitzky's performance, for when it was given its second performance in February 1928, conducted by Walter Straram after eight rehearsals, Prokofiev's verdict was that it sounded better. Even so, he expressed the wish one day to revise the symphony and 'express the same ideas more lucidly'. Given the sheer effort that went into writing the work, these statements strikingly display Prokofiev's lack of faith in its intrinsic worth.

It was much to his surprise, therefore, that in the wake of its première he was approached with a new commission from an entirely unexpected quarter. Diaghilev deemed the symphony's style, with its hard-edged, aggressive sound and churning ostinatos (repeating rhythmic and melodic patterns), ideal for a new ballet he had in mind. Back in 1923 in Paris he had attended peformances of Alexander Tairov's Moscow Chamber Theatre. Tairov had been a colleague of

Meyerhold's, and his bio-mechanical productions with their highly-choreographed and acrobatic players intrigued Diaghilev, who conceived the idea of staging a ballet about life in the new Soviet Russia. That Diaghilev took so long to approach Prokofiev about it suggests that he initially attempted to find a Soviet composer to do the work. But, as Prokofiev noted, most Soviet artists were wary of Diaghilev, regarding him 'as a bird of prey, constantly on the look-out for new and good things to peck at and pin down'. Diaghilev therefore resorted to his former 'second son'.

Not immediately understanding what Diaghilev wanted and still piqued by receiving the cold shoulder, Prokofiev pointedly told him he was incapable of writing in the style he approved of. Diaghilev reassured him, 'You must write in your own style,' and explained that he wanted Prokofiev to write a ballet on the theme of Soviet constructivism. Diaghilev hoped that the Soviet artist Georgy Yakulov, who had recently exhibited in Paris with great success, would design the ballet, with possible collaboration from Prokofiev's friend Meyerhold.

In the event Meyerhold was unable to be involved, but Prokofiev seized the opportunity to work on the ballet, partly because he felt much more at home with the stage than with symphonic abstractions, and partly because he wanted to find out (from Yakulov) what had been going on in Russia under the Bolsheviks. To mirror the reportedly hard-edged and matter-of-fact new life in the Soviet Union, Prokofiev clarified his textures and returned to his earlier experiment of gravitating his music towards the white keys on the piano. This is presuambly what Prokofiev meant by his description of his turning away 'from the chromatic to the diatonic', for the music is still full of grating dissonances, including uncannily realistic imitations of the mechanized grindings and bangings of a contemporary factory.

In the midst of composing *Le Pas d'acier* (the almost untranslatable title literally means 'The Steel Step' – though the French word, *pas*, is used in the sense of a ballet step, as in *pas de deux*), Prokofiev set sail with Lina on 23 December for a long joint concert tour in the States. This was Prokofiev's first visit there for almost four years, and he still found American audiences very conservative, complaining to one journalist, 'You all ride in automobiles, and yet you lag behind in music. I would prefer your rode in horse-drawn carriages but were more up-to-date in music.' Between engagements, Prokofiev hurriedly orchestrated *Le Pas d'acier*, but found it almost impossible to work in the swaying carriages of trains. He devised, through necessity, a method of writing his music in piano score that enabled him to include detailed instructions about instrumentation, dynamics and even articulation and bowing. A side effect of this was that the arduous task of writing out the full score could now be passed to an assistant (the young composer, Georgy Gorchakov, was his first). This development later led to erroneous accusations, from Shostakovich in particular, that Prokofiev no longer did his own orchestration.

Much to Prokofiev's disappointment, Diaghilev postponed production of the new ballet by a year and a half until 1927. In the meantime, however, *The Love for Three Oranges* finally reached the stage in the Soviet Union: a production mounted in Leningrad on 18 February 1926 was very well received, with much attention from the press. Prokofiev was bemused by some of the notices he received: 'some reviewers were very sensible; others wanted to know whom I was laughing at: the audience, Gozzi, the operatic form or those who had no sense of humour. They found in the *Oranges* mockery, defiance, the grotesque and what not; all I had been trying to do was to write an amusing opera.' Nevertheless, the opera's success, and hearing that the Persimfans (a conductorless Soviet orchestra formed with the communist ideal of having perfect equality among the players) were giving several performances of his music in Moscow, must have given the composer a tremendous boost of self-confidence.

In the spring of 1926 Prokofiev's old friend and collaborator, Vsevolod Meyerhold, came to Paris on a visit. Prokofiev went to meet him and took him to a rehearsal of the Ballets Russes. The two men discussed the possibilty of producing *The Gambler* in the Soviet Union, with Meyerhold encouraging Prokofiev to come and see what the Bolsheviks had done for Russia. This, and above all news of the great success his works were enjoying in the Soviet Union, had their effect; by late May Prokofiev was communicating to both Asafyev and Myaskovsky his eagerness to come and visit.

That autumn he corresponded with the Persimfans and the Leningrad Philharmonic Orchestra, negotiating a concert tour in the Soviet Union, and in January 1927, he set off with Lina to visit his homeland for the first time since he had left almost a decade before.

5

Serge Lifar and Felia
Dubrovska in *The Prodigal
Son*, 1929; the ballet,
Prokofiev's last commission
from Diaghilev, appears a
curious augury of Prokofiev's
own disillusionment with the
decadent West.

*During the interval I ask that no one be
allowed into the Green Room. Only Tsukker is
there, very pleased with the [Grandmother's]
Tales and their success, and is saying, 'This is
the kind of music that the public should
be getting!' Whereupon I round on him, saying
that the public must be educated by being made
to accept more profound and complex works ...*

Sergey Prokofiev, *Soviet Diary 1927*
(4 February)

The Prodigal Son 1927–9

Prokofiev was conscious as always about keeping up appearances, so chose to travel to the Soviet Union in the luxurious North-Express train to avoid other people's condescension ('Poor wretches, what they must be in for, going back to the Bolsheviks!'). His assistant Gorchakov was left in charge of the Prokofievs' Parisian apartment, with Sviatoslav taken care of by a Christian Science nurse. Prokofiev and Lina travelled via Germany and Lithuania, stopping over in Riga to give a concert. An advance telegram ensured their passage through customs with only a superficial inspection of their baggage, which included several musicological books for Asafyev and a bag full of woodwind reeds for the Persimfans orchestra. They crossed the border on 19 January.

Prokofiev had the disconcerting experience of finding that his home had become a foreign country. The Soviet Union in turn

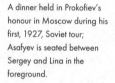

A dinner held in Prokofiev's honour in Moscow during his first, 1927, Soviet tour; Asafyev is seated between Sergey and Lina in the foreground.

Lina with two of Prokofiev's
Conservatory colleagues,
Asafyev and Myaskovsky,
photographed by Prokofiev,
1927

regarded Prokofiev, at least officially, as a 'foreigner' – as designated in the official papers drawn up for his concert tour. A committee had been organized to meet him, with Asafyev included as the Leningrad representative. Although nervous of officialdom, Prokofiev was glad to know that Asafyev would be there: 'he at least will tell me how to behave.' His anxiety was relieved on being met by his old friend Derzhanovsky, accompanied by the chairman of the Persimfans, Lev Tseitlin, and a government official called Tsukker. That evening the group was joined by Asafyev, who looked fatter and more healthy, and Myaskovsky, who was reassuringly little changed, although, as Prokofiev noted: 'he looked intently at me for a long time, smiling all the while, probably wondering how I could have put on so much weight and become so bald.'

Russia had already enjoyed six years of what was known as the New Economic Policy (NEP), implemented by Lenin in 1921 in response to popular uprisings against the Bolsheviks. Lenin recognized the need for a popular safety-valve, and officially allowed limited capitalist enterprise, instantly relieving the desperate food and fuel shortages. Stores, cafés, restaurants, theatres and cabarets proliferated for the first time under Bolshevik rule. On their first day in Moscow the Prokofievs were taken to one of the NEP restaurants where they feasted on 'hazel-grouse, whipped cream, cranberry juice ... and many exquisite long-forgotten dishes'. The next day they attended a rehearsal by the Persimfans at the Great Hall of the Moscow Conservatory; their arrival was greeted with a rendition of the March from *The Love for Three Oranges*. It was an auspicious start to what proved to be a triumphal home-coming for Prokofiev. He gave eight concerts in Moscow, all sell-outs, including two programmes with the Persimfans – one with his Third Piano Concerto, and one with his Second – and two piano recital programmes, with each pair of programmes repeated.

But in spite of the tremendous reception given him, and being 'completely stunned by Moscow', Prokofiev was nonetheless aware that all was not rosy. Only days after their arrival, Sergey and Lina visited Nadya Rayevskaya, wife of Prokofiev's cousin Shurik (who as a boy had taken part in the first performance of *The Giant*). Shurik had been imprisoned as a 'political suspect' – a charge grounded solely on the fact that he had studied at the St Petersburg Lyceum, a college for the nobility. The Prokofievs, fearing they too might be under surveillance, stopped the cab some distance from the house and tried to slip through the gate without drawing attention to themselves. But, as Prokofiev said, 'Ptashka's leopard-skin coat made her so obvious that no one would be likely to forget seeing us.' They saw Shurik's children: 'puny creatures, sweet but plain and much smaller than they should be.' Sergey told Nadya he would get some of the family to come and help look after them, and would try, if he could, to obtain Shurik's release. Throughout his visit to the Soviet Union, Prokofiev repeatedly tried to make good his promise, even asking the help of Tsukker, who was effectively his political minder during the tour; sadly, Prokofiev's efforts came to nothing.

He travelled on to Leningrad, where, to even greater acclaim, he performed the same four programmes he had given in Moscow. In the intervals between concerts he enjoyed walking the streets and embankments of the city, delighting in the memories they brought back of his student days, though he noted with some regret that the Mariinsky Theatre, once a glorious yellow, had now been painted red to match the Winter Palace.

The highlight of his Leningrad visit was attending the first Russian production of *The Love for Three Oranges* directed by a friend from his youth, Sergey Radlov, who was a disciple of Meyerhold. Prokofiev was most enthusiastic about the production, which showed several trademarks of Meyerhold's theatre: various groups of the chorus were seated in the auditorium – the 'Tragicals', presented as critics, seated in the box near the stage; the 'Blockheads' seated in the dress circle! Prokofiev, unsurprisingly, was rather more struck by the resulting 'curious counterpoint: the right ear gets one lot of voices, the left another.' But he was, overall, astonished and delighted by the ingenuity and liveliness of Radlov's production, and embraced his old chess partner after the performance. There was optimistic talk about the possibility of touring the production in Paris, though in the end nothing was to come of this. But the renewed friendship between Prokofiev and Radlov was to lead to further collaborations including one of the most famous stage works of Prokofiev's career: *Romeo and Juliet*.

Prokofiev was introduced to a number of young Leningrad composers, who played their compositions for him on the piano.

Prokofiev with the cast of the revived Leningrad production of *The Love for Three Oranges*, 1927; the conductor Vladimir Dranishnikov had been a fellow student of Prokofiev's at the Conservatory.

Of these, Prokofiev was most struck by the 21-year-old Dmitry Shostakovich, playing his First Piano Sonata, and Gavriil Popov, who performed his Septet. Prokofiev took a score of Popov's Septet which he later helped to promote in the West (he was directly responsible for its performance in America at a concert organized by Dukelsky in 1938). Prokofiev also saw Meyerhold to discuss changes he felt were needed to *The Gambler* before its production at the Mariinsky; he particularly wanted to revise the ending 'where the love-making of Polina and Alexey seemed to me visually unpleasing'. On the other hand, when he played through the score which he had not seen since leaving Russia in 1918, Prokofiev was especially pleased with the Grandmother's music which he felt needed very little change. He was most touched when Meyerhold, as soon as he heard about Shurik, promised to have a word with 'friends in the GPU' – something Prokofiev did not hesitate to compare favourably in his diary to Tsukker's 'negative attitude'. Unfortunately, esteemed as the 'Red Army' director was, Meyerhold's efforts were to prove just as fruitless.

After touring Kharkov, Kiev and Odessa, Prokofiev gave a final concert in Moscow with the Persimfans on 20 March before leaving for France with Lina. He spent a few days in Paris to check on his son Sviatoslav – who had celebrated his third birthday while his parents were away in Russia – then travelled down to Monte Carlo to attend rehearsals of *Le Pas d'acier*. On the eve of the first performance,

rumours were circulating that émigré White Russians were going to
turn up in force to demonstrate against this work of 'Bolshevik
propaganda'. Prokofiev, whose attitude to the ballet had been
opportunistic and even apolitical, could only have been amused by
such heated reactions. The programme distributed to the audience
had just two, cryptic lines on the ballet: 'The two tableaux of this
ballet present a series of scenes giving two aspects of Russian life:
village legends and the factory's mechanism.'

Each of the first tableau's scenes were given mystifying titles: 'Battle
of Baba-Yaga with the Crocodile'; 'The Sailor and the Three Devils';
and most bewilderingly, 'Le Chat, la chatte et les souris'. The action
on stage bore only the most tenuous relationship to these titles; there
were scenes involving soldiers, country-women in voluminous skirts,
rubber-suited workers, and a sailor, evidently the main character,
danced by Diaghilev's new male star Serge Lifar. But most of the time
it was far from clear to the audience what was going on: as Prokofiev
noted afterwards, the libretto had clearly been written not by a
playwright but 'a painter guided by his visual impressions'. One scene,
'Street Pedlars and Countesses', deeply shocked Diaghilev's émigré
friends: the street pedlars were shown fondling old women, then
snatching their possessions in exchange for a bag of flour. The political
significance of this scene, though, seems to have been lost on most of
the Parisian audience, who watched the ballet with bemusement (at
least until the final scene). What they heard, initially, could not have
stirred them much either. Although *Le Pas d'acier* bears some stylistic
resemblance to *Chout* in such passages as the quirky, somewhat acid
scherzo in the fourth scene, or the astringent charm of the woodwind
music accompanying the courtship between the sailor and a female
worker, the work is several degrees cooler emotionally than *Chout*,
which has a readier warmth and charm.

The audience's attention, though, was seized by the climax. The
dancers seemed transformed into the very machinery of a factory,
vividly evoked by Prokofiev's whirring, stamping and grinding music:
lights flashed, wheels spun and – much to Stravinsky's distaste – huge
hammers crashed on to the stage. For visceral excitement, the final
scene almost matches *The Rite of Spring* – its brutal power updated to
a contemporary setting – though it lacks the *Rite*'s unbridled savagery
and sheer wealth of invention. But *Le Pas d'acier* was topical and

Lina with Serge Lifar,
Diaghilev's new star dancer,
who triumphed both in *Le
Pas d'acier*, and later in the
lead role of Prokofiev's final
ballet for Diaghilev, *The
Prodigal Son*

Georgy Yakulov's constructivist set for the final factory scene of *Le Pas d'acier*, in which the dancers seem to be transformed into parts of the machinery

thrilling. As the critic Pierre Lalo noted, despite its 'next to unintelligible' plot and 'extremely severe production conceding little to grace', the final scene, 'made alive by the power of the music, excited and uplifted everyone' who rose with thunderous applause at its end. It was Prokofiev's greatest hit since *Chout*, and became a runaway success in both Paris and London.

That summer, satisfied with what had been a highly successful 'home tour' in the Soviet Union and with his latest Parisian hit, Prokofiev rented a seaside villa, 'Les Phares', in St. Palais-sur-Mer, on the Atlantic Ocean near Royan. He spent some time scoring *The Fiery Angel* for a Berlin Staatsoper production scheduled for the 1927–8 season, but his short-scoring method meant that much of this task could be passed to his assistant. This enabled Sergey and his family to take breaks, motoring around the local countryside and entertaining visitors – including Sergey's old Conservatory friend Boris Zakharov.

By September the score of *Fiery Angel* was completed, but Bruno Walter, who claimed that the orchestral parts had arrived too late for sufficient rehearsal, cancelled the production. A piano score of the opera with German text had already been specially printed, and it is likely that Walter, on seeing this, was not only taken aback by the extreme demands made on the singer of the leading role of Renata, but had been shocked by the opera's amoral and nihilistic plot. Prokofiev certainly suspected Walter of using the parts' late arrival as a pretext; he was particularly irked that Walter did not consider producing the opera the following spring, calling his behaviour 'despicable' in a letter to Myaskovsky. Bitterly disappointed, he begged Koussevitzky to perform at least part of the opera in his Paris season and, when Koussevitzky agreed, proposed a concert performance of extracts from Act Two.

Then came the news that the Mariinsky première of *The Gambler*, scheduled for the spring, had to be postponed until the autumn. Prokofiev cancelled his planned trip to the Soviet Union, and now with time on his hands, took a leisurely drive in April, accompanied by his friend Vladimir Dukelsky, down to Monte Carlo where Diaghilev's Ballets Russes were in rehearsal. Neither Prokofiev nor Dukelsky had ballets being performed that season, but Diaghilev was to be reminded of their existence. En route they made a gastronomic tour of the area, stopping at high-class hotels and restaurants to sample specialities. On arrival at Monte Carlo Dukelsky was feeling ill from an over-indulgence in *pâté de foie gras*.

Prokofiev found the impresario still keen to commission a new ballet from him, and Boris Kochno was asked by Diaghilev to think of a subject – 'something simple which would not need to have a long scenario printed on the programme … something which would be familiar to everyone.' Kochno remembered a scene from a Pushkin tale, *Le Maître de poste*, in which a traveller sees on the wall of an inn a series of pictures representing the biblical story of the prodigal son: the final picture in particular, of the son dragging himself home on his knees, struck Kochno as a potentially powerful scene to realize on stage. Diaghilev was taken with the idea and, together with Kochno, presented it to the composer.

The Prodigal Son was to become one of Prokofiev's greatest works for the Ballets Russes, although he was initially reluctant to commit himself. Diaghilev had only produced *Le Pas d'acier* after some delay, and Prokofiev moreover had more immediate prospects elsewhere: Meyerhold's production of *The Gambler* was scheduled to be produced at the Mariinsky that autumn, and Prokofiev hoped to couple this with a second, triumphant tour of the Soviet Union that winter rather than start work on a new ballet.

Back in Paris by May, Dukelsky took Prokofiev and Diaghilev to the Opéra to hear a new American talent, George Gershwin, whose Piano Concerto was being performed on 29 May by Dmitry Tiomkin. Diaghilev shook his head – 'good jazz and bad Liszt' was his opinion – but Prokofiev, as Dukelsky recalled, was more enthusiastic, and invited Gershwin to his apartment. Gershwin came the next day and 'played his head off'. The Russian admired Gershwin's melodic invention but criticized his concerto as consisting of 'thirty-two-bar choruses ineptly bridged together'. Overall, he thought highly of Gershwin's unusual gifts as composer and pianist, and predicted a great future for him if he left 'dollars and dinners' alone.

In June Koussevitzky conducted a programme that included excerpts from Prokofiev's *Fiery Angel*. Nina Koschetz sang the demanding role of Renata. In the audience were Diaghilev and Suvchinsky, and neither of them liked what they heard. Prokofiev complained to Myaskovsky that 'apparently they are obsessed with deciding what can be called modern, the latest thing and the very latest thing, while *Angel* was conceived in 1920.'

Myaskovsky this time was unable to send back encouraging news: excerpts from *Le Pas d'acier* performed in Moscow at the end of May had met with only 'moderate success' with both the Soviet critics and the audience. Prokofiev confessed himself 'unnerved and angered' by this, but was determined to get the complete ballet staged in Moscow, convinced that it would win over the Russians in the form that had convinced the Parisians.

The Prokofievs left Paris in mid July to stay in the Château de Vetraz, in the Haute Savoie near the Swiss border. There Prokofiev endeavoured to salvage a concert work from *The Fiery Angel*, initially considering a suite, as with *The Love for Three Oranges*. While working on this, however, he became convinced that the opera's almost symphonic development of its themes (particularly in the entr'acte portraying the duel between Ruprecht and Count Heinrich) made its material suitable for a symphony.

The result, Prokofiev's Third Symphony, is the most genuinely 'symphonic' of the symphonies he composed in France. The explosive duel entr'acte, which became the central crux of the first movement, is in fact the closest the symphony gets to symphonic-style development, and is taken wholesale from the opera without alteration. The main addition was a highly effective recapitulation, which takes music associated with the trance-like singing of the 'possessed' nuns in the final act as its starting-point. For the next three movements, Prokofiev cobbled together themes not so much to symphonic purpose but for the sake of dramatically effective contrast: after the hectic drama of the first movement, the second launches into the deceptively calm, beautiful music associated with the convent. One can, however, feel the clouds gathering through the proliferation of insinuatingly chromatic lines. The storm bursts instantly with the third movement scherzo: here Prokofiev made use of the extraordinary multiple string-part writing, with its shrieking glissandos, originally heard in Act Two when Renata attempts to summon Heinrich through black magic. This leads, almost inevitably, to the baleful roar of the finale, with music taken from the scene between Ruprecht and Agrippa.

While at Château de Vetraz Prokofiev received a letter from Diaghilev asking if he was still interested in writing *The Prodigal Son*, and also wanting information about Soviet composers. Prokofiev provided a detailed survey of the young Soviet composers he had

At Koussevitzky's summer retreat at Plombières in the Vosges Mountains – Lina with Sviatoslav on her lap, and Prokofiev with a boxer dog

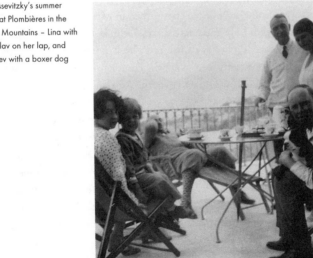

Dmitry Shostakovich, the brilliant 21-year-old composer Prokofiev met when visiting the Soviet Union in 1927; Prokofiev described him to his friend Nicolas Nabokov as a 'shy and self-centred youth with a great love for sports'.

earlier mentioned to Diaghilev, recommending Mosolov, Shostakovich and above all Popov – even though Shostakovich was the more prominent. He added that 'Shostakovich's difficult character forces one to be careful when doing business with him …' Prokofiev also told Diaghilev that he intended to spend six weeks in the Soviet Union in the autumn, and another two months in the winter, and so was reluctant to commit himself to writing a major new ballet score. He urged Diaghilev to revive *Chout* – shelved since 1922 – or to stage a ballet based on a pair of piano pieces he had written, *Choses en soi*.

But soon after his return to Paris in early October, Prokofiev heard that the Mariinsky production of *Gambler* had been cancelled yet again. As Lina was now seven months pregnant, and Prokofiev faced the prospect of having two children to support, he decided to accept Diaghilev's commission after all. The Prokofievs found it difficult to find accommodation in Paris; initially staying in a hotel for some weeks, they eventually moved into a furnished apartment on rue Obligado. Prokofiev worked furiously at the ballet, finishing a rough piano score – according to his autobiography – in November. Diaghilev was astounded by the rapidity of his work, but was delighted with the result, writing to Serge Lifar: 'Much of it is very good. The last scene, the prodigal's return, is beautiful. Your variation, the awakening after the orgy, is, … [a] sort of profound and majestic nocturne. Good, too, is the tender theme of the sisters, and very good, … the pilfering scene: three clarinets performing miracles of agility.' Since the 'failure' of his Second Symphony, Prokofiev had had time to reassess his style and approach to music, and *The Prodigal Son* was something of a breakthrough. Contrary to the still fashionable trend of providing light, brittle entertainment (such as the children's ballet *L'Éventail de Jeanne*, collectively composed by members of Les Six, Ravel, Jacques Ibert and others in 1927), Prokofiev wrote expressive, lyrical music, avoiding the equally modish practice of reusing the styles – and even the music of – dead composers (as Stravinsky continued to do after *Pulcinella*, using Tchaikovsky for his ballet *The Fairy's Kiss* in 1928).

Once again Lina's relations provided the necessary financial support for the Prokofievs' second son, Oleg, to be born in the Muette clinic on 14 December. The following spring saw *The Gambler* produced at last; it took place on 29 April, in French, at Théâtre Royal de la

Monnaie in Brussels. Prokofiev had revised the work extensively, smoothing many of the rough edges of the original and improving the congested scoring. He took particular pains over the final two scenes between Alexis and Polina, the latter newly abandoned by the scheming Marquis; Polina is no cold-hearted man destroyer, as had so often been the case with women portrayed by Prokofiev up until the early 1920s. The music reveals her to be a young woman who is psychologically deeply wounded: her emotive words, 'He's not the same man ...', are sung to a powerfully haunting theme. This same theme wells up again from the orchestra when Alexis returns with his winnings, and Polina reveals her feelings: 'Buy me then, if you want me. Buy me for fifty thousand francs ...' All her longing, memory of a hope betrayed and utter despair are invested in that poignant musical phrase. It is a fleeting moment, but when revealed by a fine singer-actress the effect is potentially even more powerful than any of Renata's pathos in *The Fiery Angel.* The Belgian production, compared to the lavish one planned for the Mariinsky, was quite modest, but Prokofiev was delighted with the care with which the music had been prepared. But in his laudatory letter to the producer, Prokofiev did not hesitate to make a few practical suggestions, such as that Alexis, when leaving the roulette table, should drop a few gold coins 'which would be more effective than bank notes'.

Within a month of *The Gambler*'s first night he attended two further major premières, 'like a bee between three hives' as he wrote to Myaskovsky. On 17 May Pierre Monteux conducted the première of the Third Symphony. 'Conscientious, but earthbound' was Prokofiev's verdict, though both Diaghilev and Stravinsky liked the result. *The Prodigal Son* opened on 21 May at the Théâtre Sarah Bernhardt, with choreography by Balanchine, sets and costumes by Georges Rouault, and Serge Lifar in the title role. Because of his involvement in the première of *The Gambler*, Prokofiev had only been able to attend rehearsals for *The Prodigal Son* after many details of the production had already been agreed. He approved of Rouault's sets, but hated Balanchine's stylized choreography, having imagined something much more realistic – 'like *Rigoletto*,' Balanchine scornfully remarked years later. 'He complained so insistently that Diaghilev finally told him, "Look, this is how we're doing it. If you don't like it, you can just get out of here."'

Near-disaster shook the ballet's première when Lifar had an attack of nerves and took to his bed, saying that he felt 'out of sympathy' with the part of the Prodigal. He only pulled himself together by recalling all that Diaghilev had done for him. He then rushed to the theatre, got into costume and, having kept the rest of the company waiting an extra fifteen minutes, went on stage. The result, conducted by Prokofiev, was a triumph: the naked emotion of the final scene where Lifar dragged himself across the stage on his knees to be welcomed by his father and enfolded in his cloak brought many of the audience to tears. The critics were equally enthusiastic, Émile Vuillermoz of *Excelsior* noting that 'Together with the explosiveness and vibrant energy we have come to expect, [Prokofiev] shows us gifts of feeling and simplicity that our public did not suspect in him.'

Only days later, Prokofiev received bad news from the Théâtre Royal de la Monnaie: their production of *The Gambler* had had to be suspended due to the illness of the singer playing Polina. He was naturally astonished that there was no understudy, but he made the best of things and took the opportunity to revise certain parts of the opera which had struck him as unsatisfactory, particularly in Act One. Prokofiev was further angered when on 29 May Roger Désormière took over the conducting of *The Prodigal Son*. Prokofiev had invited a number of American musicians to attend what he had hoped to be an impressive execution of one of his most profoundly emotional works. The result, in the pit at least, was an embarrassing mess. Ensemble fell apart several times and the virtuoso passage for three clarinets became a horrible scramble. Prokofiev wrote to Désormière the next day:

During the interval [...] I had to field a number of ironical questions: was the orchestra composed of Conservatory debutants? Or perhaps people who had never seen the music before? Naturally, the Americans told me that in New York you could hear better playing at a café.

I tried to defend our musicians as best I could, but they looked at me with pity: poor devil, he's tone deaf!

Prokofiev was altogether in a foul mood when Balanchine approached him, requesting a cut from the composer's royalties on *The Prodigal Son*. This was before choreographers officially received any percentage

for ballet productions on which they had worked; often they had to
resort to gentlemen's agreements with the composer, who got by far the
largest share. Balanchine had reached such an agreement with Stravinsky
over *Apollon* the previous season and hoped that the same could be
achieved with Prokofiev. But, frustrated by the latest developments on
The Prodigal Son and *The Gambler*, and having in any case thoroughly
disliked Balanchine's work, Prokofiev roared at him: 'Why should you
get money? Who are you? You're nothing but a lousy ballet master. Get
out!' (His friend Nicolas Nabokov asserted that Prokofiev never let
himself be exploited, describing Prokofiev as being usually a friendly
and jovial man, but with an inflammable temper. Outbursts were of
short duration, but would often lead to childish sulking.)

Lina, as was increasingly noted by their friends, was often at the
receiving end of Prokofiev's foul moods. She did everything she could to
smooth his relationship with professional colleagues and to make their
home life conducive to his work, but her husband was capable of being
outrageously boorish, even cruel, to her. In Balanchine's case, however,
Prokofiev's temper-tantrum proved to be self-defeating. He was not to
know that before the year was out Diaghilev would be dead – destroyed
by diabetes, at that time non-treatable – and that Balanchine would
become a major ballet-master in his own right. In one stroke, Prokofiev
had lost a potentially useful, indeed influential, collaborator.

That summer, needing a thorough break from Parisian life,
Prokofiev took his family on retreat to 'a beautiful medieval castle on
the top of a hill, with excellent views all round'. This was the Château
de la Flechère, the grandest house that the Prokofievs were ever to
inhabit. It was near Lake Burze in central France and was so large that
its two pianos, placed at opposite ends of the château, could be played
simultaneously without either pianist hearing the other. Stravinsky
came to stay that summer. According to Lina, her husband had
become well disposed towards him, possibly because both of them had
had problems with Diaghilev during the previous season. Stravinsky
played them his new *Capriccio*, which Prokofiev claimed to like very
much, though when writing to Asafyev he more guardedly described it
as 'less derivative' than some of Stravinsky's other music. Pierre
Suvchinsky and Ernest Ansermet were among other visitors to the
château. Mikhail Astrov was another. A musician, formerly employed
at Koussevitsky's publishing house, he had been hired to act as

By the summer of 1929, Stravinsky and Prokofiev were again on speaking terms; here they are photographed with Lina and their respective sons, Soulima and Sviatoslav, in the garden of Château de la Flechère.

Prokofiev's secretary; by then there was a very large amount of correspondence to deal with. Astrov took over from Lina in assisting Prokofiev with foreign languages, and corrected him on points of grammar and phrasing. He also acted as Prokofiev's copyist.

After the frantic pace at which *The Prodigal Son* had been composed, together with the three premières that year, Prokofiev had little energy to devote to new work. He revised the Sinfonietta yet again, and created one new opus; a Divertimento for orchestra. This consisted of arrangements of two movements from the *Trapeze* ballet composed five years earlier, and a movement originally conceived for *The Prodigal Son* but rejected from that ballet. To these, Prokofiev added one slow, lyrical movement he had composed the previous year. Prokofiev did admit Stravinsky's influence in the 'ascetic' style of the orchestration.

When Stravinsky returned to his holiday home at Echarvines, he immediately gave Prokofiev the news he received there: Diaghilev had died in Venice on 19 August. Prokofiev had become increasingly distant from Diaghilev, and their relationship had ended with a lawsuit in which Prokofiev and Édition Russe de Musique had to pay a fine for not crediting Kochno as co-author of *The Prodigal Son* in the published score. But he nonetheless recognized the vital influence Diaghilev had been on artists and composers, including himself, and was to remain faithful to his memory even in the politically

beleaguered milieu of 1930s Stalinist Russia. If the eulogy Prokofiev
wrote at the time appears forced and otiose, it should be borne in
mind that Prokofiev was rebutting Soviet accusations that Diaghilev
was an anti-patriotic, cynical capitalist who exploited musicians,
artists and dancers for his own financial gain: 'his services in
popularizing Russian art cannot be overestimated. He left no money
after his death, only a very interesting collection of books and sketches
made by the artists he worked with. He had been in constant touch
with our [Soviet] representatives in London and Paris and, had he
lived, would no doubt be working with us now.'

Apart from Prokofiev's loss of a valuable mentor, the ballets he had
written for Diaghilev abruptly dropped out of the repertory – hence
the frantic attempts to get as much mileage as possible out of *The
Prodigal Son*, which had enjoyed just one season before Diaghilev's
death: Prokofiev not only drew from it a symphonic suite, but it
formed the basis of his Fourth Symphony and a substantial part of his
Six Pieces, Op. 52. Now with two children to support, this need to
spread his work thinly was symptomatic of the struggle Prokofiev felt
he had to cope with in order to keep his family in Paris. Increasingly
disillusioned, and with one less patron to support him, a return to the
Soviet Union seemed more and more attractive.

6

Prokofiev conducts a rehearsal
for a broadcast by Radio
Moscow, 1934

*Foreign air does not suit my inspiration, because
I'm Russian, and that is to say the least suited of
men to be an exile, to remain myself in a
psychological climate that isn't of my race.
My compatriots and I carry our country about
with us. Not all of it, to be sure, but a little bit,
just enough for it to be faintly painful at first,
then increasingly so, until at last it breaks us
down altogether.*

Sergey Prokofiev speaking to Serge Moreux,
June 1933

Return to the USSR 1929-36

Early in October 1929, Prokofiev was driving his family back to Paris
when, at full speed, a rear wheel flew off. The car overturned and
crashed. The family, miraculously, escaped without serious injury, but
Prokofiev lost a tooth, was quite seriously bruised, and had pulled a
muscle in his left hand which prevented him initially from playing an
octave spread on the piano. With a major tour in America coming up
at the end of the year, he was indeed lucky to have escaped so lightly.
Just as fortunately, his three-week visit to Russia prior to the tour
involved no piano recitals, enabling him to rest his sprained hand and
attend to new and forthcoming productions in the Soviet Union. As it
turned out, this alone was to prove testing enough.

The political climate in the Soviet Union had changed significantly
since his visit of more than two years earlier. Under Lunacharsky's
benevolent patronage, the arts had enjoyed a relatively liberal
atmosphere that encouraged new and innovative means of expression,
Eisenstein's early great films (*Strike* and *Battleship Potemkin*) and
Meyerhold's constructivist theatre productions being two such
examples. Prokofiev's friend Asafyev, one of the most perceptive
connoisseurs of avant-garde music, had been in his element working
for the Association of Contemporary Music (ACM), importing
between 1925 and 1927 such works as Schoenberg's *Gurrelieder*, Berg's
opera *Wozzeck*, and Stravinksy's *Pulcinella* and *Renard*. The ACM also
encouraged such composing talents in the Soviet Union as Mosolov,
Shebalin, and above all the young Shostakovich, whose First
Symphony, written when he was only eighteen, had been acclaimed
internationally just one year before Prokofiev's visit of 1927.

But an alternative group – the Russian Association of Proletarian
Musicians (RAPM) – had formed almost simultaneously with ACM
to promote 'music by workers for the workers'. Virulently against
anything 'bourgeois' or modern, it placed itself in direct opposition to
everything the ACM stood for. Unfortunately, the population at large
was indifferent, even hostile to avant-garde music, and the ACM
steadily lost ground to the RAPM, the tastes and policies of which

Joseph Stalin (1879–1953),
General Secretary of the
Communist Party from April
1922

superficially chimed in with those of the Bolshevik government's increasingly powerful chairman, Joseph Stalin.

Stalin's self-effacing manner had deceived nearly all his colleagues, who took him for a moderating influence between the 'Right' and 'Left' blocs of the Communist party. His reserve and extraordinary patience concealed an ambition greater and more ruthless than that of any other Bolshevik: almost from the start, his ultimate aim was total control of an all-powerful communist state. In political manoeuvrings from 1923 to 1929, Stalin made and broke alliances as he saw fit, steadily ousting all his political rivals starting with Trotsky. In 1928 he introduced the first Five Year Plan, a radical programme for the collectivization of agriculture and the development of heavy industry. It was an uncompromising attempt not only to catch up with the West but to surpass the economic achievements of the United States. All energies, both ideological and cultural, were subordinated to this aim; dissent became treason. 'Show trials' served to wipe out Stalin's political opponents and provide scapegoats for the woes of the Soviet people who were struggling to meet unrealistic production targets. 'Saboteurs', who allegedly were damaging overworked and poorly serviced machinery, were continuously 'unmasked'; citizens were encouraged to betray their neighbours – and even their own family – to Stalin's secret police, the GPU (renamed the NKVD in 1934).

This all-embracing policy had an inevitable knock-on effect on Soviet culture. Imports of foreign films and translations of foreign authors were drastically reduced. Both 'leftist' (avant-garde) and 'rightist' (bourgeois intellectual) cultural tendencies were mercilessly denounced by the young party cadres and Komsomols (young Communist League members) who made up most of the membership of the proletarian arts organizations. By March 1929, the ACM's magazine – *Contemporary Music* – had been closed down. In coming to Russia, Prokofiev himself was unwittingly to become the catalyst to the RAPM's final act of routing the 'decadent' modernists.

He arrived on 30 October 1929. Most of his time was spent in meetings with Meyerhold and Asafyev in Moscow and Leningrad, who undoubtedly did their best to fill him in on political developments, and discussed with him the production of some of his major stage works. On 13 November he attended the Bolshoi revival of *The Love for Three Oranges*, a production with décor so lavish and complicated to set up that the intervals seemed to be longer than the

acts. '"Love for three intervals," joked the weary spectators,' was
Prokofiev's wry comment. The following day he attended the Bolshoi's
'audition' of *Le Pas d'acier*. Members of the RAPM were present, as
were Bolshoi officials and Meyerhold (who would direct the
production). Meyerhold had tried to smooth the way for the ballet in
his report of 9 October by answering the charge that Prokofiev was a
bourgeois émigré. 'Because of certain personal circumstances,
Prokofiev lives in Paris and not in Moscow. But we should not say that
he is not one of us ... [He] can still agree with us because, in himself,
he is with us. A street address does not mean anything. The language
and the subject of his writing are far more important.'

At the Bolshoi's listening session Meyerhold added further to his
defence of Prokofiev and *Le Pas d'acier*. The ballet should be staged,
he argued, as it could illustrate 'the construction of the Soviet Union
under the conditions of class warfare'. This did not stop the ensuing
cross-examination. The RAPM asked whether the factory scene
portrayed 'a capitalist factory, where the worker is a slave, or a Soviet
factory, where the worker is the master? If it is a Soviet factory, when
and where did Prokofiev examine it, since from 1918 to the present he
has been living abroad and came here for the first time in 1927 for two
weeks [sic]?' Prokofiev, enraged by what he considered presumptuous
and arrogant questioning, retorted, 'That concerns politics, not music,
and therefore I won't answer.' Answers he did give were delivered,
according to an article published in the RAPM's *Proletarian Musician*,
'with the same irritability and rudeness found in his music'. A second
article in the same paper delivered the RAPM's verdict – a
condemnation of the ballet as a 'flat and vulgar anti-Soviet anecdote, a
counter-revolutionary composition bordering on Fascism'. The
Bolshoi directors had no choice but to turn the ballet down.

Prokofiev must have been profoundly shaken by this decision. But
he stayed in Moscow a little longer to conduct a broadcast
performance of his newly revised Sinfonietta, prefaced by a laudatory
talk by Meyerhold. He then returned to Paris, whence he wrote to
Koussevitzky: '... life in Russia has become more difficult ... but there
are still a lot of interesting things going on there. The attitude toward
me was extremely cautious, so in the spring I'm planning to go again,
and with Ptashka.' The restraint of his language indicates how
reluctant he was, even then, to admit the extent to which his standing
in the Soviet Union had deteriorated. Evidently he still hoped that the

Soviets would warm to him with increased exposure. In the same letter
Prokofiev discussed terms for a symphony that Koussevitzky wished to
commission for the fiftieth anniversary of the Boston Symphony
Orchestra. Stravinsky, who had also been commissioned, responded
with one of his greatest works: the *Symphony of Psalms*. Prokofiev, for
his part, objected to what he considered to be far too low a fee, and
allowed the Boston Symphony Orchestra only to purchase the
manuscript for the offered fee, but not to commission it.

At the end of December, the Prokofievs sailed first class to America.
Sergey went directly to Cleveland to conduct a concert of his music,
then to New York, where his train was met by Dukelsky. Over supper
that evening, Prokofiev confessed that the state of the Soviet Union
was 'very bad indeed'. How upset he had been by his Soviet reception
can be gauged by the almost desperate arrogance with which he tried
to push his American fortunes. He wrote to Koussevitzky, berating his
long-term champion for setting up a festival of Glazunov's music, and
insisting that he do the same for him: 'It's especially important pour
me poser bien à New York, where fighting for a spot is so hard. If you
devote so much energy to Glazunov, couldn't you reserve a tiny bit for
me, damn it all!' Koussevitzky replied by return of post:

> *I must tell you that in spite of all my propaganda during these past five
> years, your name is not so popular as that of Bach, Beethoven and Brahms,
> nor so popular that I can transport my orchestra to New York to give a
> Prokofiev festival. This doesn't mean that festivals should be given only to
> honour the dead – I hope that I will live to the time when a festival will be
> given in your honour – but we must be patient and not allow any silly
> little things, any pleasant nonentities, like your Sinfonietta, to be performed.*

Now effectively slapped in the face by both the Soviet Union and his
main champion in the West, Prokofiev turned towards his own
certainties. Early in 1930, the *New York Times* published a revealing
interview he gave to the critic Olin Downes:

> *We want a simpler and more melodic style for music, a simple, less
> complicated emotional state, and dissonance again relegated to its proper
> place as one element of music... I think we have gone as far as we are
> likely to go in the direction of size, or dissonance, or complexity in music.
> Music, in other words, has definitely reached and passed the greatest degree*

of discord and complexity that can be attained in practice. I want nothing better, more flexible or more complete than the sonata form, which contains everything necessary for my structural purposes.

Six years earlier Schoenberg had invented the dodecaphonic – or twelve-note – method of composition (to gain structural cohesion within his highly chromatic musical language), which was to have far-reaching effects on Western classical music over the next fifty years. In the light of this, Prokofiev's categorical statement – 'Music has definitely reached and passed the greatest degree of discord and complexity that can be attained in practice' – may seem more a justification of his own new-found lyrical style than a fair reflection of Western musical trends of the time. But both he and Schoenberg were responding, in their different ways, to a crisis in which avant-garde composers found themselves during the 1920s. Just as Prokofiev had indulged in harmonic experimentation, culminating with his crisis over the Second Symphony in 1925, leading composers such as Bartók and Hindemith had made extensive use of dissonant harmonies in their radical works of the 1920s before realizing that, by so doing, the basic principle of building large-scale musical structures through tension (dissonance) and its resolution (consonance) had been severely undermined. The choice facing composers in the late 1920s was simple: they had to find a new way of structuring their music or somehow renovate past practices.

In a roundabout way, Prokofiev chose the latter by returning to Schopenhauer, whom he read a great deal in the 1920s. Schopenhauer's discussion of musical theory is – given his expected readership – fairly rudimentary, but his insistence on the primacy of the harmonic series (the series of tones that may be heard when a low string is plucked and left resonating) as the basis of diatonic harmony must have impressed Prokofiev, as did his insistence on music being built on 'constantly renewed discord and reconciliation' – hence Prokofiev's stated desire to have 'dissonance again relegated to its proper place as one element of music'. Another dictum of Schopenhauer's – which Prokofiev virtually made his own maxim – appears in the third book of *The World as Will and Representation*: 'The invention of melody, the disclosure in it of all the deepest secrets of human willing and feeling, is the work of genius.'

On 16 February, in the middle of a hectic three-month tour of America, Prokofiev wrote to Mrs Elizabeth Coolidge, patron of the

Library of Congress in Washington, accepting their commission for a string quartet for the relatively modest fee of $1,000. This composition was to be a decisive turning-point in Prokofiev's output, further developing the expressive lyricism that he had first brought to fruition in *The Prodigal Son*. His decision to make a preliminary study of Beethoven's quartets, rather than approaching the works of Haydn as he had for the 'Classical' Symphony, may have been influenced by Schopenhauer's enthusiasm for the Romantic composer. Prokofiev spent many hours on trains during the tour, working on the string quartet concurrently with his Fourth Symphony which reworked themes from *The Prodigal Son*.

He and Lina sailed back to Europe at the end of March. The concertizing did not end, though. Over half-a-dozen concerts awaited Prokofiev, and in April he wrote to Derzhanovsky: 'I thought that I would rest after America, but nothing of the sort. Yesterday I waved and played through the sixth concert (Brussels, Turin, Monte Carlo, Milan), and in all there will be thirty-three concerts this season. If this continues, goodbye Moscow until the fall.' Perhaps most significant was his postscript, 'I am deeply grieved about Mayakovsky.'

Prokofiev had just received news of the poet's death. Over the past year Mayakovsky had been increasingly hounded by the RAPP (Russian Association of Proletarian Writers), who branded him a 'class enemy', his work 'unintelligible to the masses'. No doubt this charge had been provoked by his satirical play, *The Bath House*, produced by Meyerhold who was increasingly under attack himself. Mayakovsky had responded by exhibiting his works, including propaganda posters and poems written in support of the Bolshevik government, and appreciative notes and letters he had received from workers. On 14 April, alienated and embittered, Mayakovsky shot himself while playing Russian roulette. He was only thirty-six.

The mood of despair was endemic amongst the Soviet Union's intellectuals: the day after Mayakovsky's death, Asafyev wrote to Myaskovsky: 'I cannot work. Nothing succeeds. My job was to infect myself with music and to write in such a way as to infect others … I have no other concept of musicology or criticism. Now, alas, one cannot write this way. So I've turned sour.' Prokofiev did not know under what terrible pressures Asafyev was working, and was bewildered by his apparent reluctance to arrange concerts in Leningrad.

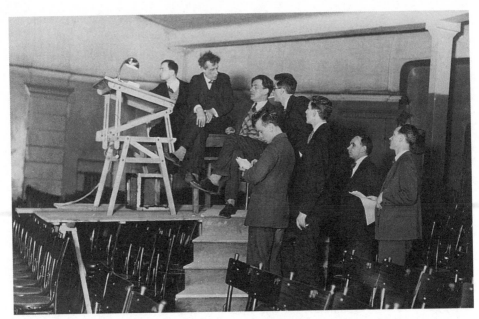

Meyerhold (second from the left) in conversation with the poet Mayakovsky during rehearsals of his drama *The Bath House* 1930; the RAPP attacked the play so viciously that Mayakovsky was driven to commit suicide only months later.

Things became more clear with a letter from Myaskovsky. It contained depressing news of the fall-out from Prokofiev's visit in the previous year:

> *The Association of Proletarian Musicians does not want to forgive you for your careless treatment of them during the listening sessions for* Le Pas d'acier, *and, even more, considers* Le Pas d'acier *a mockery of our revolution. In good conscience, I have to agree with them that the titles of many of the ballet's numbers now appear tactless. It seems to me that Yakulov did you a dirty trick.*

Even Lunacharsky, a leading champion of Prokofiev's who had battled for so long with the proletarian organizations to maintain standards of artistic excellence, suddenly lost power; just two months after the Bolshoi débâcle over Prokofiev's *Le Pas d'acier,* the Commissariat for Enlightenment was abolished. Lunacharsky was shunted off to Geneva to represent the Soviet Union at the League of Nations, well out of the way while the proletarian organizations continued to savage the intelligentsia.

Facing such bleak prospects in the Soviet Union, Prokofiev cancelled his proposed May tour. That spring, he and Lina rented their first unfurnished flat in Paris – a clear sign that he had resigned himself to settling in France. This was 5 rue Valentin-Haüy, in the fifteenth arrondissement near the place de Breteuil. Most of that summer was spent bargain-hunting for furniture before leaving Paris in mid August for a summer holiday at La Naze, par Valmondois, on the Seine – about twenty miles from Paris. Here Prokofiev continued to work painstakingly on his string quartet, and also started a new ballet – *On the Dnieper* – commissioned by Serge Lifar, now appointed artistic director of the Paris Opéra's *corps de ballet*. In the wake of *Le Pas d'acier*'s rough reception in Moscow, Prokofiev and Lifar deliberately kept the details of the plot quite vague, leaving room for the story-line to be altered to suit the ideological requirements of Soviet theatres.

Towards the end of their holiday, the Prokofievs were visited by Meyerhold, whose theatre troupe had come to Paris. Possibly learning from him further depressing details of what was going on in Russia, Prokofiev cancelled a planned tour there in late October. He did, however, keep in regular correspondence with both Asafyev and Myaskovsky, deeply worried by how his music had fallen out of favour thanks to the actions of the RAPM.

The winter of 1930–31 was spent in Paris, and Prokofiev finished his string quartet just after the New Year. He also made sketches for a Concerto for the left hand, written for the pianist Paul Wittgenstein (who had lost his right arm in World War I). Furnishing the new apartment, providing for his family and now arranging schooling for Sviatoslav created heavy financial demands, and by mid April Prokofiev had spent the advance Wittgenstein had paid for the new concerto (half the total fee). Fortunately, royalties had started coming in from America. In April Stokowski conducted the Philadelphia Orchestra in the American première of *Le Pas d'acier* at the Metropolitan Opera House, New York. Prokofiev described it as 'an excellent production', and the audience, unaware of the scandal *Le Pas d'acier* had stirred in Moscow, enjoyed the frisson of seeing a 'genuine' piece of Bolshevik art. In that same month, two days after Prokofiev's fortieth birthday, the Brosa Quartet played the première of his First String Quartet in Washington.

The quartet begins with what appears to be a typically scherzo-like first subject, and yet the severe, almost 'classical' second subject reveals a seriousness quite new for Prokofiev's music – most clearly

showing Beethoven's influence. After an enigmatic second movement
– a slow introduction followed by a frenetic yet guarded scherzo –
comes the final slow movement, which Prokofiev recognized as 'the
most significant in the whole piece'. Mournfully lyrical at first, the
movement builds to an impassioned climax on a distinctly Slavic
theme. Then, suddenly and shockingly, the music seems to fall apart
emotionally: against a wailing ostinato, an abrupt melodic figure
tumbles downwards from first violin to viola; then, after a return of
the opening lyric theme, the music winds tortuously down to a
desolate coda. Intentionally or not, this is Prokofiev's most eloquent
expression of his despair at being disowned by his own homeland.

To mark his fortieth birthday, Prokofiev took his family to the
highly fashionable resort of Biarritz at the end of July. Renting a villa,
they mingled with such celebrities as the great Russian bass Fyodor
Shalyapin (who had emigrated to the West in 1922), the violinist
Mischa Elman and Charlie Chaplin. Evenings were spent watching
Shalyapin and Chaplin improvising comic scenes. In the midst of
these pleasant diversions, Prokofiev found time to compose, and by
mid September he was able to tell Myaskovsky: 'I have learned to
swim and I am done with the one-handed concerto.' Unlike Ravel and
Korngold – two other composers who wrote concertos for
Wittgenstein – Prokofiev did nothing to create the illusion of two
hands playing; he concentrated on developing the new style of
understated lyricism created in *The Prodigal Son* rather than creating a
brilliant virtuoso display. On receiving the concerto in the autumn,
Wittgenstein sent a terse note: 'Thank you for the concerto, but I do
not understand a single note in it and I will not play it.'

This, for Prokofiev, was just another, if more blatant, rejection of
one of his works. Though most of his older works were being
performed, few of his recent ones were accepted into the repertoire,
and he had not had a single 'hit' since Diaghilev's death. Part of the
problem may have been that his favoured forms (stage and symphonic
works) were those least likely to be performed in the parlous economic
climate of 1930s America and Europe. After the Wall Street Crash,
financial backing for large-scale projects was at a premium: a proposed
production of *The Fiery Angel* at New York's Metropolitan Opera had
been cancelled, and a ballet staged in Paris to the 'Classical'
Symphony in May 1931 had to close shortly after opening.

To improve the lot of composers, a number of performance societies were set up in Paris around this time. One of Prokofiev's émigré friends, Nicolas Nabokov, was involved in La Sérénade which organized chamber concerts in the Salle Gaveau. Prokofiev had some association with La Sérénade, although, according to Nabokov, he did not like the concerts' atmosphere, complaining that the music was insubstantial and the audiences were made up of snobbish 'society ladies who really don't know what to say'.

In his book *Old Friends, New Music*, Nabokov gives a vivid description of Prokofiev at this time. Delivering some of his own songs to Lina at No. 5 rue Valentin Haüy, Nicolas was ambushed by Sergey:

> *'What are you doing here on my beat?' said a jovial Russian voice behind my back. 'Don't you know that this is my own private terrain?' I turned round and saw Sergey Sergeyevitch Prokofiev ... I explained [my business] and [that] now I was going home. 'Oh, no,' he said in the same jovial baritone, 'you aren't going home, you're going with me. We're going to circumscribe a circle around that thing there ...' He put his cream-coloured gloves on my shoulders, turned me around and said: 'Forward, march!'*

Nabokov found himself accompanying Prokofiev on his regular pre-lunch circuit around Napoleon's Tomb, and got an earful of Sergey's denigration of the Parisian audiences and their superficial tastes. He went on to attack all the major French composers of the century – 'There hasn't been a first-rate French composer since the time of ... Chabrier and Bizet' – and evidently enjoyed Nicolas's scandalized response. Several biographers have since taken Prokofiev's claim on that occasion that Ravel was 'the only one in France who knows what he's doing' rather too seriously; significantly, Ravel was one major figure who had fallen foul, as had Prokofiev, of such arbiters of fashion as Jean Cocteau, who, along with 'that old crank Satie', denounced Ravel as 'ring-leader of the sub-Debussyists'. Cocteau had appointed Satie as godfather of the chic new group of composers, Les Six, whose considerable success Prokofiev resented, referring to their 'over-inflated' reputation. Perhaps it was their heavy involvement in La Sérénade that lay behind Prokofiev's disaffection with the organization.

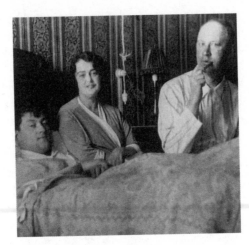

Prokofiev and Lina with Nicolas Nabokov, ill with flu in 1931; Nabokov was one of the few Paris-based musicians with whom Prokofiev remained on friendly terms.

More to his liking was Le Triton, a rival group founded by the highly talented composer Pierre-Octave Ferroud. Its *comité d'honneur* included such composers as Bartók, Falla, Schoenberg and Stravinsky. New works by these and other European composers, such as Dallapiccola and Hindemith, were performed, alongside those by French composers including – it is true – three of Les Six (Milhaud, Poulenc and Honegger), as well as the young Olivier Messiaen. Le Triton was altogether a much more serious enterprise, and Prokofiev wrote for them one of his finest pieces, his Sonata for two violins (1932). Its resourceful handling of the two instruments and the sometimes astringent harmonies are akin to Ravel's masterly Sonata for violin and cello, composed some ten years earlier. But Prokofiev's work is more frankly lyrical and less radically 'modernistic' in sound. Moreover it gives voice to the poignant and very Russian lyricism heard in the finale of his string quartet, particularly in its anguished first movement and sweetly nostalgic third movement. By contrast, the second movement is alternately brusque and balletic, while the ostensibly bright C major of the finale, with its disconcerting chromatic inflections and suddenly sprung dissonances, brings to mind the equally fragile emotion of the finale from Schubert's great C major Quintet.

In 1932 the countenance of the Soviet music scene suddenly changed. By an important Central Committee Resolution of 23 April, all existing 'creative associations' (including the RAPM) were formally dissolved, their leaders arrested and removed from the positions they had usurped in the conservatories, universities and other artistic centres. Unions, previously banned by Lenin as hotbeds of independent thought, were resurrected, the much hated RAPM being replaced by the Union of Soviet Composers. The abolition of the proletarian arts organizations was greeted in the Soviet Union with such widespread relief by creative artists that few questioned the reasons behind the government's measure. One reason was that many members of the RAPP, to the embarrassment of Stalin and his henchmen, had taken a *Pravda* editorial asking for 'a vital, gripping description of our socialist construction, of all its gigantic achievements, and of all its failings' all too literally. They had started to criticize not only the shortfalls of the Five Year Plan but also the very system Stalin was creating, emphasizing the loss of socialist ideals and, in particular, the growing bureaucracy. Stalin's abolition of the RAPP and its sister organizations was in fact a prelude to taking direct state control of the arts as social-engineering and propaganda. The Resolution's stipulation – that musical works should have a socialist content, and should be expressed in a readily understood language addressed to the people at large – was essentially little different from the policy Stalin had hoped the RAPM *et al* were to have implemented.

According to Nicolas Nabokov, 'Prokofiev welcomed the official edict as a realization of some of his own ideas about the function of music. "I always wanted to invent melodies ... which could be understood by large masses of people – simple, singable melodies." This he considered to be the most important and difficult task of the modern composer.' Soon Prokofiev was considering establishing a permanent residence in Moscow, and investigated the possibility of taking up a part-time teaching post at the Moscow Conservatory.

The signs continued to be encouraging. An article in *Pravda* attacked the recent rule of the Proletkult for 'cliqueism, left vulgarization, and time-serving'. Former RAPM members, true to their 'time-serving' nature, now adopted a more positive attitude toward Prokofiev and his music and, as Myaskovsky triumphantly reported later that year, were even anticipating beneficial results from his forthcoming visit in late November. Prokofiev magnanimously wrote back that former RAPM members had 'a right to exert influence, provided they straighten out their policy line somewhat'.

At the end of July 1932, the Prokofievs set off for their holiday in the south of France. They had rented a remodelled farmhouse, Les Pins-Parasols, on the Mediterranean coast in Saint-Maxim. The house, which was situated on a hill overlooking the light blue sea, belonged to the old, well-known French Communist, Jacques Sadoul, then a correspondent for the Soviet paper *Izvestiya*. Prokofiev appropriated the largest room, where he finished his Fifth Piano Concerto. He gave its première in Berlin on 31 October – with no less than Wilhelm Furtwängler directing the Berlin Philharmonic – and it was a great success, the audience delighted to see the composer-pianist back in glittering action. Prokofiev's technique was, if anything, more polished than ever. Francis Poulenc, who rehearsed a two-piano arrangement of the new concerto with Prokofiev, noted that 'on a level with the keys he was capable of producing sonority of fantastic strength and intensity,' and that his 'long spatulate fingers held the keyboard as a racing car holds the track.'

The piano concerto was equally acclaimed in Paris and America, although, significantly, Prokofiev failed to record how its subsequent performances in Moscow and Leningrad were received. Despite its beautiful, limpid slow movement, Prokofiev later dismissed the work as one of his unsuccessful attempts to create a new simplicity in style. That Myaskovsky was instrumental in this rejection can be judged by a letter he wrote to Prokofiev, criticizing the desiccated Op. 54 Sonatinas along with his Fifth Piano Concerto. Rather than offering a 'new simplicity', observed Myaskovsky, Prokofiev was in fact creating 'a more intellectual style. You no longer follow the creative stream, but try to direct it consciously into a foreordained and … more narrow river bed … if formerly you tried to stun, then now you try to impress and intrigue, which does not possess the same spontaneity.' Prokofiev wrote back to Myaskovsky: 'One may invent, but one must not lose touch with life … The more you get carried away in your quest for new melodies and new simplicity, the less you notice how far away from shore you have swum. If in doing so you really do discover a new idiom, it's all right; but if your efforts lead you to dryness and the merely bizarre, then you're finished. In this respect your letter was like a good shout that pulled me back …'

That winter, after a short but highly successful tour of the Soviet Union, Prokofiev gave an interview to *Evening Moscow* in which he made clear his intention to return by April, claiming that he found the Soviet Union – or perhaps, rather, Russia – far more conducive to his creative work: 'The dead end to which the search for subject matter has led in the West only intensifies my desire to find Soviet material. There, one has no feeling of necessity. One subject is as unnecessary as the next.' Prokofiev revealed that he had been conferring with a Soviet film studio on a project that would give him his first opportunity to work with 'Soviet' material. This was *Lieutenant Kizhe*, based on a story by Yury Tynianov, then head of the screenwriting department at Lenfilm. Tynianov had himself suggested that Prokofiev write the music, sensing in the 'Classical' Symphony the composer's empathy with the late-eighteenth-century Classical style.

Prokofiev had at first been wary about composing for film, not knowing 'what kind of sauce to put on it', but was won over by Tynianov's story. It is based on a true incident from the days of Emperor Paul I (who reigned from 1796 to 1801), and hinges on a clerical error which added a non-existent lieutenant to a list of soldiers presented to the Tsar. Paul I, intrigued by the unusual name of Kizhe, demands that the lieutenant be promoted to his élite guard – which his subordinates, too terrified to contradict him, proceed to do, thus bringing into existence an entirely fictitious soldier. Tynianov was one of the first Russian authors to write historical fiction as a means of writing anti-Bolshevik parables. Although Prokofiev may not have grasped this entirely, he was canny enough to recognize that Tynianov's tale of bureaucracy run riot was essentially tragic in character, and affirmed his agreement to write the music.

Back in Paris, Prokofiev was almost immediately involved in a number of performances. Most important was the long-delayed première of his first post-Diaghilev ballet, *On the Dnieper*, on 16 December at the Paris Opera. Immediately preceding this was another Paris première, this time of the Sonata for two violins performed at the inaugural concert of Le Triton by Samuel Dushkin and Robert Soetens. 'Fortunately the ballet came on half an hour later,' recalled Prokofiev, 'and so immediately after the sonata we dashed over to the Grand Opéra – musicians, critics, composer all together.'

On the Dnieper had received much advance publicity, and there was tremendous hope that it would revive the panache and style of the Ballets Russes. Prokofiev left for America the next day, and so was

Oil painting of Prokofiev by the Soviet artist, Peter Konchalovsky, April 1934; a striking detail for Soviet citizens was Prokofiev's jacket with that American novelty – a zip.

unaware of the deluge of disappointed reviews which followed its first night. Robert Brussel of *Le Figaro* wrote:

> *Those who have admired the Russian musician will search in vain throughout the choreographic poem … for anything reminiscent of the verve and caricature of* Chout, *of the vigorous scope of* Le Pas d'acier *or of the sentiment of* The Prodigal Son. *What a shame! We love him so much. Here in Paris he is practically a citizen … We hoped that the day he made his début on the stage of our National Academy of Music and Dance would bring us a great deal. We were mistaken … The music is some of the weakest M. Prokofiev has written.*

This is perhaps a rather unfair criticism, as the music of *On the Dnieper* is clearly in the same lyrical style as *The Prodigal Son*; it was also unreasonable to have expected a rehash of the styles of *Chout* or *Le Pas d'acier* within a 'realistic' rural context. But despite some strikingly expressive and lyrical passages, there are too many moments of vague, noncommittal writing and pallid imitations of Stravinsky for the ballet as a whole to make a strong impression. But Prokofiev did not lose faith in the work, and was certain that it would be appreciated at a later time.

Upon his return to Paris in February 1933, Prokofiev was a little alarmed to find neither official invitations to teach at Soviet conservatories nor any of the scores of new Soviet music he had been promised. The scores were meant not only to allow him to promote Soviet music, but were in lieu of payment of rental fees for his compositions performed in the Soviet Union (he had persuaded his publisher to accept this special arrangement since the Soviet government were no longer prepared to pay fees in foreign currency). Worried that the lack of Moscow deliveries might be a symptom of official disfavour, he had to be reassured by Myaskovsky that it was due only to tardy Soviet bureaucracy.

Prokofiev left Paris in April for a two-month visit to the Soviet Union. He gave only a few concert appearances – two in Leningrad, and two in Moscow – including the first Russian performances of his Third Symphony which, to Prokofiev's delight, was well received by the public. In Moscow he showed a piano score of his new *Symphonic Song* to Myaskovsky, who found it 'not entirely right for us … it lacks what we would call monumentality – a familiar simplicity and breadth of contour.'

Myaskovsky's reaction was all too symptomatic of a new artistic policy implemented by Stalin. In October 1932, Stalin had gathered several of the Soviet Union's leading writers to implement the new doctrine of 'socialist realism'. Soviet art, he said, was not only to be relevant to the everyday life of the Soviet people, but was also to 'point out what is leading it towards socialism.' In some ways socialist realism was a logical extension to what was already being done to Russia's past by Soviet historians: just as their political slant led them to select and even modify historical facts, socialist realism was a way of writing about the present, as if viewed by historians of the fully achieved Soviet State. This, in theory, meant that anything negative could be portrayed, so long as it was shown to be overcome by the cause of socialism. In practice, far greater emphasis was given to the positive aspects of the daily progression to the future Socialist State. Any artistic endeavour thought irrelevant to the aims of socialist realism – particularly anything abstract or 'personal' – was 'formalist'. In other words, it was considered anti-social and self-indulgent. Many writers and artists were to discover that any production or work of art not fully in accord with official policy, or which simply did not meet with the tastes of their 'leader and teacher' Stalin, was liable to be

branded 'formalist', resulting in a ban and quite often the arrest of
those responsible.

Inevitably it took some time before it was clear how socialist
realism might be applied to music. For the time being, though, it was
reasonably clear that what was required was an upbeat, 'monumental'
style – as in the epic 'socialist-realistic' novels by such writers as
Valentin Katayev and Nikolay Ostrovsky, or the 'wedding-cake'
architecture approved by Stalin. Myaskovsky's advice to Prokofiev was
to compose another ambitious piece specifically for a Soviet première,
something 'monumental, with definite personality and – don't be
angry, o horrors! – even cheerful'.

Prokofiev, who certainly thought the *Symphonic Song* was all these
things already, ignored his friend's advice and proceeded to score the
work. It did not meet with success in or out of the Soviet Union.
Soviet audiences (who first heard the work on 14 April 1934,
conducted in Moscow by Alexander Gauk) found it too introverted,
tuneless and chromatic, while the sophisticated Parisians thought it
old-fashioned and lacking the startling orchestral effects they so loved
in Prokofiev. It remains a little-known but interesting transitional
work, standing stylistically midway between the cool lyricism of
Prodigal Son and the dramatic, clear-cut melodic style of Prokofiev's
later symphonic works.

More successful was his next Soviet work – incidental music to
Alexander Tairov's *Egyptian Nights*. One of Moscow's most innovative
theatre directors, Tairov created a drama about Anthony and
Cleopatra based on three different texts: Bernard Shaw's *Caesar and
Cleopatra*, focusing on Cleopatra's youth, and Shakespeare's *Anthony
and Cleopatra*, concerned with her mature years, the two linked
together by a monologue from Pushkin's *Egyptian Nights* (from which
Tairov took the title for his drama). Its première on 14 December was
a brilliant occasion attended by Moscow's 'entire theatrical-musical
world'. After a run of seventy-five performances during the 1935
season, the production was suddenly axed by the cultural authorities
on the grounds that it was a 'formalist' production irrelevant to the
needs of the Soviet people.

Ironically, Prokofiev was particularly pleased with the suite he
derived from the incidental music. In an article published in *Izvestiya*
on 16 November 1934, entitled 'The Course of Soviet Music', he cited

both this and the suite from *Lieutenant Kizhe* as suitable for the new Soviet audience discovering concert music for the first time. Prokofiev was attempting to address the new requirements of socialist realism while accommodating his own developing style:

> *What we need above all is great music, i.e., music that will be in keeping both in conception and technical execution with the grandeur of the epoch. Such music would be a stimulus to our own musical development; and abroad too it would reveal our true selves … The composer must take into consideration the fact that there are thousands of people in the Soviet Union who are discovering music, people who, in the past, would have been resistant or indifferent to it, and it is this new situation that the Soviet composer must consider today.*

Prokofiev recognized that writing suitable music for such an audience was 'not so easy':

> *Above all, it must be melodious; moreover, the melody must be simple and comprehensible, without being repetitive or trivial. … The simplicity should not be an old-fashioned simplicity, but a new simplicity.*

Prokofiev argued that in order to create this 'new simplicity', a composer had first to discover a technique capable of creating 'great music' without turning to past styles, which could 'at the same time be challenging to an avant-garde musician'. Such a technique, by implication, would be flexible enough to enable a composer to write in a simple but not trivial style. Unfortunately Prokofiev's essay was to be deliberately misrepresented – by less talented Soviet composers jealous of his pre-eminence and unwilling to consider the idea of raising cultural standards – as upholding 'great music' that was élitist and anti-Soviet in character.

Before returning to Europe in late December, Prokofiev was approached by Sergey Radlov – now artistic director of the Leningrad State Academic Theatre of Opera and Ballet (formerly the Mariinsky Theatre) – with a new project. Recognized as the leader of Leningrad's avant-garde theatre, Radlov had staged the first Russian production of Prokofiev's *The Love for Three Oranges* in 1926, and Berg's *Wozzeck* in 1927. He also ran his own dramatic theatre, staging a number of

Shakespeare plays: *Othello* in 1932, then, in 1934, *Romeo and Juliet*.
No doubt this gave him the idea of commissioning a full-length ballet
on the famous love story. Radlov had already produced 'choreodramas'
with Prokofiev's friend Asafyev, who composed *Flames of Paris* (with
themes sent by Prokofiev from Paris), and *The Fountain of Bakhchisarai*.
The proposal to Prokofiev was of a ballet on Shakespeare's tragedy,
which would be produced at the State Academic Theatre.

But then, on 1 December, the Leningrad Party's First Secretary,
Sergey Kirov, was assassinated (almost certainly on Stalin's orders),
inaugurating what later became known as the Terror. Stalin used
Kirov's death as a pretext to begin arresting all his political opponents,
usually on trumped-up charges. The Leningrad State Academic
Theatre was promptly renamed the Kirov State Academic Theatre in
his honour, and its administration was drastically altered. Radlov was
among those who left; the projects he had proposed – including
Prokofiev's *Romeo and Juliet* – were shelved.

In late January, after touring Eastern Europe and Brussels, Prokofiev
returned to Paris, where he received a letter from Myaskovsky reporting
on his standing with the new Kirov management: 'In the circles of the
Leningrad Composer's Union … they fear you terribly and will do
everything they can to keep you out. Therefore [Asafyev] believes that
your projects for productions at the Mariinsky Theatre are built on
sand.' Despite this warning that his political stock – at least in
Leningrad – was rapidly falling, Prokofiev persisted in his identification
with Russia and his dream of returning there. The Soviet authorities in
turn were mindful of the propaganda coup of securing Prokofiev's
allegiance to the USSR, and courted him as they had already courted
Gorky, who had been persuaded to return from exile in 1931. Prokofiev
almost certainly received reassurance from Soviet officialdom that the
benefits he enjoyed as an internationally celebrated composer would
not be compromised by closer association with the Soviet Union;
furthermore, if he were to commit himself by moving his family and
taking full Soviet citizenship, he would be awarded a 'luxury'
apartment and no longer need to stay in hotels. Myaskovsky's veiled
warnings about jealous colleagues in Leningrad, rather than putting
Prokofiev off the idea of moving to the Soviet Union, persuaded him
to make his home in Moscow instead; by early 1935 his course was set.

In March that year he gave a recital at the Soviet Embassy in Paris,
and then left Paris for Russia. Having found a new home for *Romeo*

and Juliet at the Bolshoi in Moscow, he travelled up to Leningrad to work out the scenario with Radlov.

In the original scenario, the play's five acts of twenty-four scenes were divided into fifty-eight short episodes – even shorter than had been the norm with Diaghilev's ballets – with a descriptive dramatic title for each, such as 'The Street Is Awakening' and 'The Nurse Delivers Juliet's Note to Romeo'. The result was swift-flowing action, and the chance to create sharply contrasting moods in a short period. For the most part, Prokofiev and Radlov were true to the spirit of Shakespeare's original. But, unable to conceive how the poisoned lovers could dance, they changed the ending. Romeo was allowed to arrive a minute earlier thus finding Juliet still alive. But Prokofiev later reverted to the original tragic ending after someone remarked that his original music 'does not express any real joy at the end', and was assured by choreographers that Shakespeare's ending could be expressed in dance.

Inspired by the subject and delighted to be working with Radlov, Prokofiev composed *Romeo and Juliet* at phenomenal speed. He spent the summer and autumn of 1935 at Polenovo, a rural retreat for the staff of the Bolshoi; there he worked in a converted sauna, consisting of one room with a writing desk and a terrace overlooking the River Oka. The terrace had a large table, on which Prokofiev arranged sixteen chessboards to form one huge board, used for playing an inscrutably complex game. As well as chess, he played tennis, read, swam, walked in the forest and, above all, composed for about five hours a day.

It was a prolific summer for Prokofiev. He worked on *Romeo and Juliet*, and also on a second violin concerto – commissioned by a group of admirers of the French violinist Robert Soetens (who had taken part in the French première of the Sonata for two violins). In addition, he completed a set of twelve short piano pieces, *Music for Children*. In August he was joined by Lina and the boys. He was amused by the fuss and affection his sons inspired from his colleagues, and felt sufficiently benevolent to allow Oleg, then aged seven, to stay with him while he worked, provided he was absolutely silent. Oleg obediently sat at the edge of his desk and drew while his father composed. By the time the family left for Moscow at the beginning of October, the entire piano score of *Romeo and Juliet* was finished, and Prokofiev was able to start scoring at the equally extraordinary rate of about twenty pages a day. Just three days after they got back to Moscow, he played the piano score to the staff of the Bolshoi.

A radiantly happy Prokofiev
with Lina and their younger
son, Oleg, at Polenovo,
summer 1935

Romeo and Juliet marks the culmination of Prokofiev's dramatic art. In none of his earlier works had he drawn so convincing a gallery of characters. The most striking portrayal is that of Juliet, first presented as an excitable young girl (in a scherzando style familiar from the finale of his 'Classical' Symphony). But what follows is quite new for Prokofiev – a tender theme played by flute, with a richly coloured counter-melody from solo cello; it perfectly captures the guileless warmth of a girl on the verge of womanhood, her thoughts touching a new emotional depth. This same melody, pristine at its first appearance, reaches its most impassioned form in the final act when played by strings to extraordinarily poignant effect. This, notably, is Prokofiev's first sympathetic portrayal of a female character, only to be matched by his portrayal of Natasha in the later *War and Peace*.

It is of no surprise that Prokofiev was well able to encompass the more violent emotions of the play, but it is striking how differently he portrays the two fights: Mercutio's with Tybalt is jaunty and almost insouciant, with just the odd syncopated accent to suggest the vicissitudes of the fight; Romeo and Tybalt's fight, with Romeo out to avenge Mercutio's death, is impetuous, the relentlessly driven string semiquavers and sudden dissonant clashes suggesting the blind fury with which Romeo fights.

It seems the Bolshoi staff responded positively to what they heard, for the ballet was soon scheduled to be produced at the Bolshoi the following spring. Later in October 1935, Prokofiev took his sons and Lina to see one of Natalia Satz's productions at the Moscow Children's Musical Theatre. Although, according to Satz, Prokofiev and family first attended a performance that did not go well, they came back a week later to see another show and to meet Satz and the actors. Satz noticed how Prokofiev responded 'more spontaneously than his sons … If he liked something, he liked it a lot – if he didn't like it, he didn't like it at all.' The Prokofievs came to the theatre several more times, and Satz became quite friendly with Sergey. Eventually she was bold enough to ask him to write a piece specially for her theatre – it would become Prokofiev's best-known work.

On 25 October Prokofiev travelled back to Paris with his sons, leaving Lina alone in Moscow. From Paris he set off on a tour with the violinist Robert Soetens to Spain, Portugal and north Africa. In Madrid, Soetens gave the world première of Prokofiev's Second Violin Concerto. The work is often paraded as a paradigm of

Prokofiev and his sons prepare to board a trans-European train in 1935.

Prokofiev's 'new simplicity', but its more disquieting side has rarely been commented upon. True, the first movement had a rich-toned, lyrical second theme, and the central slow movement features one of Prokofiev's most charming, long-breathed melodies, floated over one of the most unpromisingly plain arpeggios ever to open a concerto movement. But there is also the first movement's brooding opening theme, its chromatic twist developed to increasingly sinister effect. And interspersed with the lyrical themes of both movements are more fleeting, haunted passages, which irresistibly recall similar moments in Prokofiev's sepulchral Third Symphony. Most sinister of all is the prominent role played by the bass drum, at its most menacing in the finale where its driving rhythm dislocates the movement's waltz rhythm and harries the soloist to the concerto's final sardonic cadence.

In the few weeks before and after his tour with Robert Soetens, Prokofiev was making preparations for his family's impending move from Paris. At a time when it was highly unusual for Soviet artists of any kind to be allowed to travel abroad, Prokofiev left Moscow again in late January 1936 to fulfil a number of concert engagements. Even in the absence of corroborating evidence, it is clear that Prokofiev had been officially granted special status and therefore privileges as one of the Soviet Union's leading cultural ambassadors. As such, he was given virtual *carte blanche* to tour the West, contrary to the current policy of minimizing contact between Westerners and Soviet citizens. There may also have been another, more sinister reason why Soviet officialdom allowed Prokofiev to go abroad at this critical stage before his final settlement in the Soviet Union: within days of leaving, a cultural storm broke that was to have a wide and pernicious effect on Soviet music.

7

Prokofiev and his family on
their return to Moscow, 1936

*Tragedies in hindsight look like farces. When
you describe your fear to someone else, it seems
ridiculous. That's human nature.*

Dmitry Shostakovich in *Testimony* recalling
life in the 1930s under the Terror

The Terror 1936–41

Until the morning of 28 January 1936 Dmitry Shostakovich had been the bright young hope of Soviet music. After the international success of his First Symphony and producing a number of film scores and incidental music, his career reached its zenith with the première in 1934 of his opera *Lady Macbeth of Mtsensk.* It was hailed in the Soviet Union and abroad, one Soviet critic claiming 'it could only have been written by a Soviet composer brought up in the best traditions of Soviet culture'. By 1936 it had enjoyed around 180 performances. Then, on 26 January, Stalin, with Vyacheslav Molotov and Andrey Zhdanov, came to see the opera at the Bolshoi; ominously, the three of them left before the end. Just two days later, Shostakovich found himself castigated in an article, 'Muddle Instead of Music', in the State newspaper *Pravda.* Almost certainly written on Stalin's orders, the article, which was unsigned, condemned Shostakovich's opera *Lady Macbeth of Mtsensk* as 'fidgety, screaming, neurotic music ...' and claimed that its tremendous international success was because it 'tickles the perverted tastes of the bourgeoisie'.

Pravda was not a paper to waste column space on musical matters. The implications of such an article, following as it did the recent persecution of some of the Soviet Union's leading writers for formalistic crimes, was clear: composers would now receive similar treatment in an exercise to cow individuality and make the arts subservient to the State. As if to confirm that Shostakovich would soon join the thousands arrested, a second article appeared a week later, attacking his ballet *The Limpid Stream.*

Early in February the Leningrad Union of Composers held discussions on the content of the two *Pravda* articles. Asafyev was forced by political expediency to admit that supporting Shostakovich's composition of *Lady Macbeth* had been an 'error of judgement'. Similar 'discussions' were held in Moscow at the House of Writers. The 23-year-old composer Tikhon Khrennikov not only joined the obligatory mud-slinging against *Lady Macbeth*, but also took the opportunity to attack Prokofiev. Wilfully distorting Prokofiev's published statements on the need for 'great music', Khrennikov accused him of having described Soviet music as provincial, and Shostakovich as being the only worthy contemporary Soviet composer. 'Prokofiev has tremendous influence over our young composers, and it is the same Prokofiev who made the statement only a year ago that he writes two kinds of music: one for the masses, the other ... may I ask, is it perhaps for posterity?'

Had Prokofiev known at first hand what was happening, he would have done everything in his power to leave the Soviet Union. But away on tour until early March, he probably heard only a circumspect account when he got back to Moscow, and seems to have persuaded himself that it was of no importance to his career. Shortly after his return, he was invited by Natalia Satz to see her company in their new venue in the former Nezlobin Theatre, now renamed the Central Children's Theatre. Prokofiev was not only in a good mood, but was delighted by her programme, so he was well primed when she telephoned him two days later and asked whether she could see him to propose a project.

Meeting Prokofiev in his rooms at the Hotel Nationale, Satz explained her idea. She envisaged a work intended to introduce young children to the instruments of a symphony orchestra, and encourage them to listen to and enjoy symphonic music 'in the same way as they read books'. She suggested 'a symphonic fairy tale with the musical development accompanied by, guided by, narration. The children could then hold onto the words like a handrail.'

Prokofiev took up this idea enthusiastically, even though Satz could only offer an embarrassingly modest fee. The only rocky moment in their collaboration came when Satz presented a scenario written by Nina Saksonskaya in rhyming couplets, which Prokofiev immediately rejected, berating her for her efforts: '... the balance between words and music in a work like this is very delicate. The words must know their place, otherwise they may lead the listener's attention astray, instead of helping their perception of the music.' In the end, Prokofiev wrote the story himself. His affinity with the world of fairy tale had already been demonstrated in *The Ugly Duckling* and *The Love for Three Oranges*, and the short stories he sometimes wrote in his spare time display a well-developed yet childlike inventiveness which he now put to use in composing his symphonic fairy tale, *Peter and the Wolf*. Its music was composed in just one week.

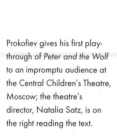

Prokofiev gives his first play-through of *Peter and the Wolf* to an impromptu audience at the Central Children's Theatre, Moscow; the theatre's director, Natalia Satz, is on the right reading the text.

Peter and the Wolf, Prokofiev's best-known and most popular work, remains the most successful and enduring introduction to classical music ever written for children. His ingenious musical tale's combination of humour, suspense and sheer bravado is perfectly pitched at a child's imagination – even offering a sly dig at adult authority in the form of Peter's grumpy old grandfather! Prokofiev's music is splendidly illustrative: the stealthy cat, for instance, is perfectly portrayed by the clarinet's playing staccato in its velvety low register; the duck's gawky oboe melody, first heard in the instrument's comfortable 'home' register, is compellingly transformed with her apparent demise into something utterly poignant simply by being played 'sadly and expressively' an octave higher.

To Prokofiev's Soviet audience, Peter was ostensibly a Pioneer, a junior member of the Young Communist League; but while Peter's rebellious stance towards his grandfather might appear to chime with the official canonization of Pavlik Morozov (a fourteen-year-old whose denunciation of his father to the authorities 'inspired' the founding of the Pioneers), Peter displays considerable loyalty to his animal friends and has an individual ingenuity in marked contrast to the blundering huntsmen (the state police?) who arrive late on the scene.

Prokofiev was invited to perform the work on the piano to a small group of children, with Satz narrating the text. Their informal performance was a great success; the children, who had sat quietly through the 24-minute work, clamoured for more, and Prokofiev had to play the final march another three times. Unfortunately Satz was too unwell to give, on 2 May, the first official performance of *Peter and the Wolf*, which, narrated by someone less adept at delivering the text sympathetically to the music, was not a success. It was only months later, when a special performance was mounted at the Central Pioneer Palace for the benefit of visiting journalists and dignitaries, that the work was truly launched; Lina and the boys were in the audience, and participated in the rapturous reception which assured *Peter and the Wolf*'s tremendous, worldwide reputation.

Prokofiev was now able to welcome his family into an 'almost luxurious' apartment. Situated on Zemlyanoy Val (later renamed Chkalov Street after the heroic air-force pilot), a wide and busy section of road that encircles Moscow, it was in an imposing, typically graceless building given over to those who had performed cultural or other services to the Soviet state: many distinguished artists, including the pianist Heinrich Neuhaus, the violinist David Oistrakh and the poet Samuil Marshak have lived there.

This apartment block on Chkalov street was the Prokofievs' Moscow home from 1936.

The Prokofievs' second-floor apartment consisted of four comfortable if basic rooms, including a study and dining room. Furniture and household goods were imported from Paris, as well as a new Förster piano, sent free of charge from Czechoslovakia. Prokofiev was ecstatic. He embraced Lina, saying, 'I am so happy, that we are finally here!'

His joyful state of mind was reflected in the *Russian Overture* completed that year, a heady brew of mischief mixed with nostalgia. Genuine Russian folk-dance themes are combined with his own free paraphrases of lyrical Russian folk songs to create one of his most exuberant scores. Restless and frenetic, the overture rapidly spins one idea after another, eventually reaching a broad theme that rises nobly in Prokofiev's most ardent string scoring. The joyous energy of the overture is unprecedented in Prokofiev's work, and its orchestration is the most colourful and telling since *Chout*. In comparison with this fizzing score, the expressions of joy in Prokofiev's later Soviet works seem at times forced or artificial.

That summer Prokofiev retreated once more to the artists' colony at Polenovo. When not swimming to keep cool in what was unusually hot weather, he worked on musical adaptations of three works by Alexander Pushkin. All had already been made into famous Russian operas (Tchaikovsky's *The Queen of Spades* and *Eugene Onegin*, and Mussorgsky's *Boris Godunov*), and now Prokofiev had been commissioned to set the works to music for the centenary of Pushkin's death. One was a film score for *The Queen of Spades*, to be directed by Mikhail Romm; *Eugene Onegin* and *Boris Godunov* were stage adaptations needing incidental music. But all these Pushkin projects were ultimately aborted, as nearly all the directors involved came under attack for the formalist style of their work. *The Queen of Spades* was scrapped after a new official policy demanded that only films on contemporary themes were to be produced. *Eugene Onegin* was more directly quashed by official order: its director Tairov, whose *Egyptian Nights* had been so successful, was forced to cancel this new project, and by the end of the year his theatre was closed down. Meyerhold likewise had to abandon his production of *Boris Godunov*, though he was to struggle to maintain his theatre for several more years. (To have had so much music fail to reach performance must have been disheartening for Prokofiev. Loath to let it go to waste, he was to make extensive use of the cancelled scores in his later works: most of the dance numbers from *Eugene Onegin* were to resurface in his magnum opus *War and Peace*, while extensive stretches of *Boris Godunov* were reused in *Semyon Kotko* and *Ivan the Terrible*.)

In the autumn Prokofiev returned with his family to Moscow. As well as presenting his Pushkin scores to the various directors, he attended the première of the first suite from his ballet *Romeo and Juliet*. He had been frustrated by the failure to stage the ballet at either the State Academic Theatre or the Bolshoi (the Bolshoi having dropped the ballet by early 1936, most probably because of its lack of socialist realist content), so had arranged the suite, including the now well-known Balcony Scene and Death of Tybalt, to give his music an airing on the concert platform. Ironically, it was at the Bolshoi that the suite was first heard on 24 November 1936.

Only days later, Prokofiev once again exercised his privileged status by leaving Moscow for a three-month concert tour of Europe and the USA. Lina joined him in Paris about a month later, after what Prokofiev described to Myaskovsky as 'passport problems' when leaving the Soviet Union, testimony of how exceptional this trip was at a time when very few Soviet citizens were being allowed to cross the Russian frontier.

While in Paris, he enjoyed performances of Stravinsky's *Jeu de cartes* and Milhaud's early opera *Christophe Colomb*. He then appeared in Bordeaux, Lausanne and Prague before sailing with Lina to New York on 6 January 1937. The USA tour included performances of the Third Piano Concerto in Chicago and St Louis, two further concerts in Boston with Koussevitzky and the Boston Symphony Orchestra, and the inevitable recital at the Soviet Embassy in Washington. At the end of his tour, Prokofiev, in an extraordinarily tactless display of his special privileges, purchased a new streamlined, blue Ford and had it shipped back to Moscow. Private cars were an almost unheard-of luxury in the Soviet Union, and Prokofiev had to defend himself against understandably jealous criticism in a speech to the Union of Composers: 'I have spent much time in the West, but this does not mean I have become a "Westerniser".'

The very appearance of Prokofiev and his wife was striking, even shocking, in the context of the drab existence of most Muscovites. The pianist Sviatoslav Richter, then twenty-two, encountered the Prokofievs in the street near their apartment: 'His clothes were checkered all over, with bright yellow shoes and a reddish-orange tie.' Evidently little had

Prokofiev with his two sons, c. 1937; the man in the background was Oleg's Russian tutor, who told the boy of better days in pre-revolutionary Russia.

changed in Prokofiev's sartorial tastes since his 1909 graduation from the St Petersburg Conservatory – yellow shoes included! This gross display of Western-style wealth, coupled with Prokofiev's brusque manner (often interpreted as patronizing or arrogant), provoked a natural resentment among several of his colleagues. Understandably, many were all too eager to see him fall from grace.

Despite her relative privileges, Lina had difficulty adjusting to the new life in Moscow. She had left all her friends in western Europe and, as an only child, badly missed her mother (her father having died the previous year). Furthermore, she and her husband had to cope with what were, by Western standards, chronic shortages of basic necessities. They came to rely on trips to the West not only to maintain Lina's wardrobe but to procure such essentials as music manuscript paper. The boys, too, had their problems. Throughout the late 1930s, Sviatoslav and Oleg changed schools several times. They initally attended a special school for foreign children and children of Soviet citizens who had been living abroad – mostly those of diplomats. Instruction was in English – hence Prokofiev's brag to Vernon Duke that his sons were attending 'a fine English school in

Moscow'. But after a year the school was closed, as by 1937 most of the pupils' parents had been arrested. At his subsequent school Oleg remembers being taunted by fellow-pupils as a 'composer's son', as classmates could see that he and his brother were privileged. This was rubbed in when one or two from the class came to visit their apartment and saw Oleg's comic books and toys from Paris.

Back in Moscow Prokofiev felt it necessary not only to defend himself against accusations of being a bourgeois westerner, but to attack what seemed to him to be an unchecked growth of provincialism within the Union of Soviet Composers (USC). On 9 April he made a speech at a meeting of the USC, in which he belatedly added his voice to the ongoing debate over 'formalism' as exemplified by Shostakovich's now officially banned opera *Lady Macbeth*. Although there was considerable interest in Soviet music in the West, said Prokofiev, there was a real danger that people abroad would find composers in the Soviet Union still 'chewing over old things'.

> *We are striving ahead in all spheres of the Soviet economy. Politically we are not only contemporary, but the country of the future ... Why then do our comrade musicians imagine that they alone can feed on yesterday's bread and rotten beef?*

Aware that much of the progress of Stalin's Five Year Plans was due to professional engineers from abroad, Prokofiev suggested that his fellow composers should take note of Western opinion – 'it would be wrong to ignore that which could help us advance.' Attempting to redefine the USC's bug-bear 'formalism' according to his own terms, Prokofiev argued that the struggle against formalism should not be 'a struggle against the perfection and improvement of technique', and attacked 'lazy-minded or uncultured comrades' for welcoming socialist realism as a way of 'writing without any clever philosophizing'; he saw this as lowering the standard of their musical culture. Prokofiev had very rarely used folk song in his own works, but nevertheless he had to address the now official prescription that composers should use Russian folk song (particularly in the officially approved 'song opera' form of music-theatre). 'If one compares the arrangement of delightful folk songs in *Boris Godunov* with Dzerzhinsky's opera [*Tikhii Don*], one is amazed at the way we have started throwing around the precious folk song instead of developing it carefully and lovingly.' He suggested that a more sensitive treatment and development of folk song, allied with respect for musical technique, would lead to a development of an indigenous style. But whether his irreverent *Russian Overture* exemplified his argument was debatable, and, unfortunately, his reference to Dzerzhinsky's *Tikhii Don* was a reckless attack on an opera that had been officially approved by Stalin himself. In the circumstances, it is unsurprising that Prokofiev found it hard to get his music performed over the next year.

More surprising was Prokofiev's own survival during Stalin's policy of terror, in which anyone at all might be arrested and charged with crimes against the state. On 11 June 1937, the purges reached their zenith; leading members of the Red Army Command were charged with treason, including Shostakovich's patron and protector, the civil-war hero Marshal Tukhachevsky. Chastened by these events and possibly by the difficulties he encountered in getting his music performed, Prokofiev toned down his arguments in a *Pravda* article at the end of 1937. In this he cunningly turned a main tenet of socialist realism – that socialist art should further the cause of the future communist state – to his own use:

The search for a musical idiom in keeping with the epoch of socialism is a worthy, but difficult task for the composer [...]

It is something like shooting at a moving target: only by aiming ahead, at tomorrow, will you avoid being left behind at the level of yesterday's needs. All attempts to 'play down' to the listener not only inherently underestimate his cultural maturity and the development of his taste – they also contain an element of insincerity. And music that is insincere cannot endure.

Even given Prokofiev's extraordinary status as a privileged Soviet artist, these were still brave words. Alas, they were scarcely matched by any of his works performed that year. Of the Three Romances to poems by Pushkin, the one work of Prokofiev's performed (by Lina in a radio broadcast on 20 April) to commemorate Pushkin's centenary, only the setting of 'Pine Trees' is at all remarkable, its lean piano-writing and chilly discords a foretaste of the opening movement of the Eighth Piano Sonata. But the other two are pallid imitations of Tchaikovsky songs without a memorable melody between them.

That summer of 1937, the Prokofievs rented the second floor of a *dacha* in Nikolina Gora, a small settlement about thirty miles west of Moscow. There Prokofiev worked for two months completing a huge cantata commemorating the twentieth anniversary of the Bolshevik Revolution. Written out in over 250 pages of full score, it requires no fewer than 500 performers, including a symphony orchestra, military band, percussion group, an accordion band and two mixed choirs – one amateur, one professional. Prokofiev had probably worked on this mammoth project for longer than just that summer. His friend Pierre Suvchinsky was heavily involved in its early stages, trawling the works of Marx, Lenin and Stalin for suitable texts to set, and the two may have held consultations during one of Prokofiev's tours through Paris.

Far from glorifying the heroes of the Bolshevik revolution, the strident, horror-filled music which opens the 'October' cantata presages some terrible calamity. The texts themselves paint a deeply unflattering portrait of the Bolshevik leaders: Lenin candidly admits, 'We don't have the people on our side,' and his words 'we shall strip the capitalists of everything, even their boots' are set to loud, angular music. Following the movement representing the Revolution itself, the bland, major-key music, to which the female chorus sings of 'cold, hunger, typhus and devastation', is bitterly ironic. And the opening of the final movement – supposedly celebrating the new Soviet Constitution – is no glorious apotheosis, but something horrible and doom-laden.

For many Soviet intellectuals, Stalin's most cynical act was to have Bukharin, one of the party's leading political thinkers, draft the Soviet Constitution, only to present it as his own work – and then have Bukharin arrested. When Prokofiev set Stalin's speech (made late in 1936) inaugurating the Constitution, therefore, it is no surprise to hear ominous, jarring notes heralding the opening phrase – 'As a result of following the path' ('V rezul'tate proydennovo puti'), declaimed to a pointedly liturgical-style harmonization; Stalin delighted in dignifying his speeches with religious phraseology. Further, should anyone miss the satirical point, there is a sudden downward plunge at the word 'puti' ('path'), set against a grating bass dissonance, a wry comment on Stalin's route to the impressively worded but essentially ineffectual Constitution. After this opening line, Prokofiev reverts to a grandiose choral peroration, clearly not wishing to risk disturbing party bosses and hoping the caustic opening was enough to make his point.

When he showed his completed work to some of his colleagues, they were intensely wary. Perhaps fortunately for Prokofiev it never reached performance. This may have been due more to the ludicrous circumstances of its audition before the Arts Committee rather than to anything subversive being noticed. Presenting his work to the musically illiterate panel, Prokofiev had to approximate the effect of the cantata's gargantuan scoring on a piano while singing the choral parts in his far from mellifluous voice (a bass-baritone liable to suddenly shoot up into falsetto). The committee, bemused by the recondite musical style used to set classic Bolshevik texts, politely but firmly refused to allow the cantata to be performed.

To have laboured over such a large score only to be told that it would not be allowed performance must have been a great blow (even though it seems extraordinary that Prokofiev should have expected any other outcome). He kept the cantata, but, unlike the Pushkin works, scarcely plundered it for later scores. The one exception is a theme from the purely orchestral 'symphony', which he used later in his *Ode to the End of the War*.

Prokofiev's demoralization was soon obvious to Lina: 'gradually he was changing – his manners, his taste. He began to dress later, loaf around in a dressing-gown.' This was in marked contrast to Prokofiev's one-time habit of getting up early, then exercising or taking a brisk walk before settling down to compose for at least three hours. Lina, who had long tolerated her husband's moods, now felt less able than ever to help him. Her own career as a singer, which Sergey had done much to shore up during their life in the West, had foundered and died with their move to the Soviet Union. She was now dependent on Prokofiev for her well-being; her position, now that even her husband's confidence in his fortunes within the Soviet Union had been shaken, was little short of desperate.

That winter Prokofiev completed a new cantata, *Songs of Our Days*, setting verses on such worthy subjects as the (enforced) collectivization of the peasants into modern *kolkhozy* (collective farms), the perils of being a frontier guard, and in the longest song, *A Twenty-Year-Old*, how a resourceful Young Communist rescues a little girl from a burning building. Even the cultural authorities were embarrassed by the cycle's banalities, one critic delicately suggesting 'To be simple and at the same time remain himself proved too difficult for the composer. Much in the cycle is pale and lacking in individuality.' It was a cruelly ironic verdict in light of Prokofiev's earlier warnings about the dangers of writing music that would prove 'provincial'.

Early in 1938, Sergey and Lina left Moscow for an extended tour of Europe and the USA, leaving the boys in Myaskovsky's care. This was to be their final tour together, and Prokofiev's last trip abroad. Apart from letters he wrote at the time, Prokofiev left no record of this tour, so it is uncertain what concerts, if any, they gave in Czechoslovakia. They may possibly have stopped long enough to attend a performance of one of Janáček's operas, since traces of the Czech composer's style can be heard in Prokofiev's subsequent operas, particularly in *Semyon Kotko* and *War and Peace*.

Their first known concerts took place in Paris, and, after performing in England, the Prokofievs crossed the Atlantic. Prokofiev played in nine cities in what seems to have been a successful tour of the States. But all his émigré friends noticed a change about him: Nicolas Nabokov saw a 'profound and terrible insecurity' in place of his usual breezy demeanour. Victor Seroff, author of *Sergei Prokofiev – a Soviet Tragedy*, has claimed that Prokofiev was under NKVD surveillance and on account of this avoided his former close friends. A hostess in Colorado, at whose house Prokofiev spent ten days while giving concerts with the Denver Symphony, found him a terrible 'grouch' who hardly spoke to anyone. He only snapped out of his gloom when she took him to see the recently released Walt Disney feature-length cartoon, *Snow White and the Seven Dwarfs*.

Prokofiev enjoyed himself more in Los Angeles and spent much time visiting the studios. He met Walt Disney, and the film director Rouben Mamoulian organized a banquet in his honour. Nathan Milstein, who was staying at the same hotel, has said that Prokofiev was negotiating a film music deal; Prokofiev was indeed tempted to stay in Hollywood, but his sons were in Moscow and he could not change his plans. This held true even when Vernon Duke's agent managed to land a most enticing offer for Prokofiev from a Hollywood studio, including a salary of $2500 a week. 'That's nice bait,' Prokofiev responded, 'but I won't swallow it. I've got to go back to Moscow, to my music and my children.'

He invited Duke to go shopping with him at Macy's – a necessary part of stocking up before returning to the Soviet Union and its chronic shortages. Duke later recalled:

Sergey Eisenstein, the
legendary Soviet film
director, in 1926

Although he wouldn't admit it, Serge enjoyed himself hugely in the store – he loved gadgets and trinkets of every description. Suddenly he turned to me, his eyes peculiarly moist, his voice even gruffer than usual: 'You know, Dima, it occurred to me that I may not be back for quite some time … I don't suppose it would be wise for you to come to Russia, would it?' 'No, I don't suppose it would,' I answered, smiling bravely, my happiness abruptly gone.

Indeed, Prokofiev's hopes to return to America in 1939 were to be thwarted by the Soviet authorities.

Back in Moscow by May, Prokofiev was approached by the great film director, Sergey Eisenstein, to compose music for *Alexander Nevsky*, a particular honour as this was to be Eisenstein's first film in sound. A former pupil of Meyerhold, Eisenstein had, like Prokofiev, spent time in the West. On his return in 1932, he had been dismayed by the increasing regimentation of the Soviet film industry. The state in turn regarded him with suspicion, both for his period in the decadent West, and for his attack on the policies of the RAPP, made before he left the Soviet Union. Although the RAPP had been banned, its members were still active and on the watch for any deviation from the new policy of socialist realism. Over the next four years Eisenstein's attempts to cut his own individual path had been thwarted at every turn, and in 1937, at the height of the cultural purge, he was accused of formalistic experimentation in his still incomplete film *Bezhin Meadow*. One of his greatest admirers in the industry, the cinematographer Vladimir Nilsen, was arrested, never to be seen again. Fearing that he himself would soon meet the same fate, Eisenstein sought to pre-empt any attack by writing an essay of self-criticism – 'The Mistakes of *Bezhin Meadow*'.

The Russian film industry was relatively young and could ill afford to lose trained personnel. Stalin, who appreciated cinema's value as an instrument of propaganda, was certainly aware of this, and the industry came off comparatively lightly during the purges of 1937. Even so, Eisenstein, in desperation, sought help and was advised by his friend, the writer Isaak Babel, to write personally to Stalin asking for another chance. Boris Shumyatsky, head of the film trust *Soyuzkino*, then offered Eisenstein two projects. The one Eisenstein chose was *Alexander Nevsky*, based on the real-life medieval prince of

Novgorod who defeated the Teutonic Knights (and was later canonized in the sixteenth century by Stalin's hero, Ivan the Terrible). As Eisenstein later confessed, he chose that project since 'nobody knows much about him, and so nobody can possibly find fault with me.'

Alexander Nevsky was intended to convey a direct anti-Nazi message, and Eisenstein's political advisors instructed him that his new film had to be patriotic, less intellectual than his earlier films, and aimed at the widest possible audience. The film's production was planned along lines similar to the steep schedules Stalin's Five Year Plans had imposed on industry, and was completed in an astonishing five months. The first sequence shot, the 'Battle on the Ice' in fact took place on a plain outside Moscow at the height of a heatwave. Crushed asphalt, glass and white sand had to be used to represent the snow and ice on Lake Chud.

Eisenstein, in a remarkable demonstration of his trust in Prokofiev and the degree to which he was prepared to treat him as an equal partner, invited him to write the music for the opening shots of this battle, through the charge of the Teutonic Knights, up to the headlong clash of arms between forces – even before he had finally edited that section of film. Prokofiev watched the rushes for the battle scene twice, then composed over six continuous minutes of music which so astonished Eisenstein that subsequently, in his seminal text *The Film Sense*, he cited the sequence as a perfect fusion of film and music. Eisenstein was unusual in allowing Prokofiev's music to be a 'foreground' participant in the drama: in the charge sequence, 'natural' sound is entirely absent and the soundtrack is completely given over

The famous 'Battle on the Ice' scene from Eisenstein's film *Alexander Nevsky*, for which Prokofiev composed the music

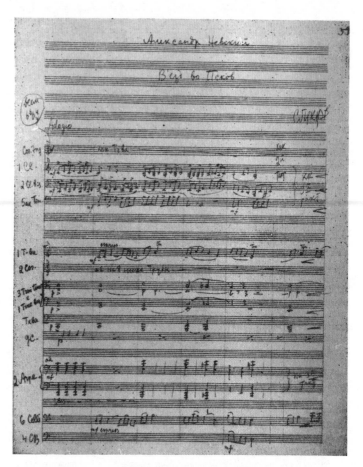

Prokofiev's original score for
the film sequence
Alexander's Entry into Pskov
from *Alexander Nevsky*

to the music until the final clash of arms. And with the Teuton
capture of Pskov, the knights mow down Russian civilians and throw
children into a roaring bonfire in almost total silence: the pathos is
expressed through Prokofiev's plaintive string writing.

Even before Eisenstein had finished editing, Stalin demanded to see
the film. The summons came at night, as was typical, and Eisenstein's
assistants had to whisk the film away while the director slept in the
cutting room. It came back with Stalin's approval, but the relief
Eisenstein and Prokofiev must have felt was tempered by noticing that
a whole reel was missing (it had been left by Eisenstein on the
Moviola ready to finish editing the following day); fearful of the
possible consequences of including material 'withheld' from Stalin's

vetting, they had simply to discard ten minutes of film. Likewise the soundtrack had been in an unfinished state: as it had been officially approved, one scene in the final print retained the provisional music soundtrack (used as guidance during the editing process), with a piano playing rather than the organ specified in the score.

In the summer of 1938, while staying in Kislovodsk, Prokofiev first met the woman who was to effect a profound change to his life: Maria-Cecilia Abramovna Mendelson. Known to everyone as Mira, she was then twenty-three years old and a student at the Literary Institute in Moscow. Lina later recalled receiving a letter from Sergey that summer in which he jokingly mentioned 'a young Jewess who is chasing me. She calls herself a poet.' Shy and provincial (like most Russians of her generation she had never been abroad), Mira nevertheless had a passionate love of literature. Perhaps more importantly, she had grown up under the Soviet regime, and therefore had a far better feel for its cultural and political mores than Prokofiev did. The composer was probably flattered by Mira's attention, and also recognized that she could be useful as a literary collaborator; he may well have believed that she would be able to indicate which topics and literary texts suitable for musical setting were likely to be approved by the cultural authorities. (At this point most of his Soviet works had failed to gain approval, often failing to reach performance.) There is no reason to believe that Prokofiev had anything but a professional interest in Mira at this stage; indeed, things may have stayed that way but for the terrible sequence of events that were to unfold the following year.

Back in Moscow Prokofiev supervised a rehearsal of his new Cello Concerto with the cellist Berezovsky. This was a work Prokofiev had taken five years to compose, having been persuaded to start by the great cellist Gregor Piatigorsky (like Prokofiev, an émigré from the Soviet Union, he played with the Berlin Philharmonic before moving to the USA to pursue a solo career). Prokofiev – who had never been greatly attracted to the cello – did not bother to conceal his distaste for Piatigorsky's suggestion. To being shown Dvořák's Cello Concerto as encouragement, Prokofiev is said to have responded, 'You should not keep this stuff in the house. It smells.' But he finally relented and began to make sketches in the summer of 1933. It was laborious, and only the continued promptings of Piatigorsky and, above all, Myaskovsky ensured the work's completion. He now found himself rehearsing the work with Berezovsky, a far less talented cellist, and

vented his frustrations on him, as Richter, who had worked with
Berezovsky on the concerto, witnessed:

> *Prokofiev was businesslike, but not pleasant. Berezovsky's questions*
> *probably irritated him. I was pleased that his demands coincided with my*
> *views. He wanted that which his music demanded – nothing more!*
> *Berezovsky had a tendency for sentimentality, and he couldn't find a place*
> *to use it anywhere.*

The work combines cello writing of restrained lyricism with sombre,
not always clearly delineated orchestration. Despite muted anguish
from the brass and woodwind in the central movement, and, in the
final movement, pained chromaticism punctuated with moments of
some beauty, the concerto's terse style overall created a subdued
quality that failed to appeal to the Soviet audience at its first
performance. Piatigorsky himself gave the American première of the
work in 1940.

That winter, Prokofiev started composing a violin sonata from
sketches he had made earlier that year. The bleak, tragic tone of the
work (finally completed some eight years later) probably reflects
something of his darker feelings during that time. Between 1936 and
1938 around seven million Russians had been arrested, several cultural
figures included, of whom the writer Osip Mandelstam was the most
famous. Most were sent to the Gulag as slave labour, but up to half a
million public figures were shot. No one could avoid the sense of
endless dread, once defined by the writer Alexander Solzhenitsyn as
'black Marias at night and demonstrations by day'. Prokofiev must
have been aware of how close Eisenstein had been to arrest.
(Eisenstein's reprieve seemed assured when *Alexander Nevsky* was first
screened on 1 December to great public success: Stalin reportedly
clapped Eisenstein on the back afterwards saying, 'Sergey, you're a
good Bolshevik after all!') Prokofiev's thoughts turned to his friend
Meyerhold, now much vilified and struggling to make a living after his
theatre was closed. He had been taken on as an assistant by
Stanislavsky, head of the Opera Theatre, and became its director on
Stanislavsky's death. Prokofiev, determined to allow Meyerhold to share
in his public success, abandoned his violin sonata with the intention of
repeating the formula that had worked so well for *Alexander Nevsky* –
writing an anti-German opera for Meyerhold to produce.

As early as 1933 Prokofiev had expressed his wish to write a Soviet
opera, but had complained about the lack of a suitable subject: 'while
much space is given in our plays and libretti to a satirical, caricature-
like portrayal of the negative hero, little is said about the positive and
heroic type, or – if at all – it is done too schematically …' He
eventually turned for advice to Alexey Tolstoy, a writer who like
Prokofiev had been an émigré before returning to Russia, who
suggested a story published in 1937 by Valentin Katayev: *I Am a Son of
the Working People*. Although written in an orthodox socialist realist
style, the novel's Ukrainian setting would have appealed to Prokofiev,
reminding him of his childhood home. The novel's charm resides in its
local colour, with extensive use of Ukrainian dialect and meticulous
descriptions of peasant village customs. Semyon Kotko, a young
Ukrainian peasant, returns home during World War I having been
demobbed from the Russian army by the Revolution. The father of his
sweetheart Sofya, Tkachenko, is a *kulak*, a 'capitalist' peasant
enterprising enough to farm his own holdings. (The understandable
resistance of the *kulaks* to the seizure of their property by the state
meant that they had been the victims of a systematic policy of
extermination by the Bolsheviks over two decades.) Needless to say,
Tkachenko is painted as an unscrupulous murderer, all too ready to
collaborate with the invading German army. He wants to have nothing
to do with Semyon, and when the Germans capture the village he
forces his daughter to marry the son of the former landowning family.
Semyon attempts to rescue Sofya only to be himself captured, before
local partisans retake the village and free the lovers.

Having found his subject, Prokofiev got in touch with Meyerhold,
who was deeply touched by Sergey's offer to write the opera for his
company even without a contract. In composing *Semyon Kotko*,
Prokofiev reverted to the Mussorgskyan style of prosody he had last used
in *The Gambler*, but now, unlike the earlier work's modernistic style,
married his prosody to a more restrained, deliberately accessible musical
language. This compromise may have been partly due to political
pressure, but Prokofiev was also genuinely interested in creating a new
style of folk opera. Glinka had similarly once wanted to write music the
Russians would 'feel at home with', while Janáček had created in *Jenůfa*
an opera of melodic prosody interspersed with folk choruses.

Such comparisons only underline the lack of zest and a sluggishness
in Prokofiev's new operatic style, which all too faithfully reflects the

Prokofiev in February 1939, during the composition of his opera *Semyon Kotko*

plodding, uninspired novel on which *Semyon Kotko* is based. Even his attempts to enliven proceedings with humorous touches – the two old men are sung by ponderous *bassi profundi* – are rather stolid, lacking the light streak of devilry to be found in his best works; the characterization of the villains, too, lacks subtlety. Yet Prokofiev does capture Tkachenko's self-importance, and there is great charm in his portrayal of the courtship of the young lovers, most effortlessly at the beginning of Act Three when Sofya is comforted by Semyon after a nightmare she has had.

By 8 April 1939 Prokofiev was able to play through almost the entire first two acts before a small group composed of Myaskovsky, Katayev and Meyerhold. He had completed the entire piano score of the opera by 28 June, and left for Kislovodsk (where Mira Mendelson was also on holiday) to complete the orchestration. In this, he had the assistance of Pavel Lamm and Derzhanovsky, who worked from his detailed short score. The actress, Serafima Birman, happened to be in Kislovodsk and witnessed Prokofiev playing tennis, noting an 'inexhaustible passion for the game' on the composer's part. 'He took defeat hard and was delighted with victory.' Only days later Birman received a letter from Moscow asking her to take over the production of *Semyon Kotko*; Meyerhold had been arrested by the NKVD on the morning of 20 June. The coincidence of Birman's presence in Kislovodsk with Prokofiev at this time raises the question of whether she had been planted, and how much she knew of what was happening. These thoughts certainly crossed Prokofiev's mind. It is hardly surprising that Birman found Prokofiev distant and 'unfairly critical' throughout their collaboration.

Prokofiev had every reason to fear the worst for Meyerhold, one of his truest and most eloquent champions. Too many people had disappeared over the past few years, and Meyerhold had run foul of the cultural authorities too often for him to be likely to reappear, except possibly as an abject defendant in one of Stalin's notorious show trials. This never happened: Meyerhold, though tortured by the NKVD, refused to incriminate his colleagues. After a travesty of a trial held *in camera*, he was finally shot on 2 February 1940, although this was to be kept a secret for decades. Less than a month after Meyerhold's arrest, two men broke into the flat of his wife, the actress Zinaida Raikh, and stabbed her repeatedly, including through both eyes, a signature of the criminal underworld. It seems likely that

Raikh's fate had been sealed when searches by the NKVD discovered draft letters she had written in protest at her husband's treatment, addressed to Stalin and the chief prosecutor Vyshinsky.

Prokofiev, isolated in Kislovodsk and with the prospect of having to collaborate with a young actress whom he had every reason to mistrust, must have felt very alone and vulnerable. He may have unburdened himself to Mira and asked her advice; in any case, his next few compositions ostensibly emphasized his loyalty to the Soviet government. One was a song to a text by Mira, 'Bravely Forward', a paean to the Red Army and to the Soviet system. Then, back in Moscow, Prokofiev was 'asked' by officials from the All-Soviet Union Radio Committee to write a work celebrating Stalin's sixtieth birthday.

Zdravitsa, sometimes subtitled 'Hail to Stalin' in English, was written in a climate of fear. Prokofiev knew that merely to be associated with someone who was arrested could mean that his turn would be next. Having had his earlier mass songs damned for being pallid and unmemorable, he forced himself to write a celebratory work with at least one good tune. He finally settled on a Mussorgskyan melody – later called by a non-partisan listener 'one of the fairest and noblest melodies in all music' – with which to open the cantata. To this blissfully yearning theme the chorus sings:

My life has now blossomed like the cherry trees in the spring.
Oh, the sun shines, it plays among the bright drops of dew!
Stalin brought us this brightness, warmth and sun.
You will know, my beautiful son, that his warmth comes to you over
  forests, over mountains.

The cantata was interspersed with bucolic choruses, all lavishly scored, which extolled the Russian country people's pastoral contentment and Stalin's paternal care. The work was a great official hit, broadcast on loudspeakers 'in all the squares and streets of Moscow'. Oleg recalls how, aged eleven, he was walking the streets in winter, 'the wind whirling snowflakes over the dark, gloomy asphalt, and then suddenly I heard this music being played through loudspeakers. I ran home and announced: "Papa, they're playing you in the streets through loudspeakers!" But he was quite indifferent; the matter was never discussed again.'

Prokofiev's mood that winter was understandably grim. Having forced himself to compose a cheerful evocation of the nirvana Stalin

wanted everyone to believe he had created, he now expressed his true
feelings in an extraordinary trilogy of piano sonatas. Although the
trilogy is often erroneously known as the 'War' sonatas (two being
completed during the 'Great Patriotic War' when Nazi Germany
invaded the Soviet Union), the first of them, his Sixth Piano Sonata,
was in fact completed by spring 1940, over a year before the Soviet
Union was truly involved in World War II. The sonata's opening is
one of the most ferocious ever written: an A-major chord instantly
negated by the bass leaping up Prokofiev's once favourite *diabolus in
musica*, the tritone (but now sounding more menacing than in any of
his early piano works). This howling motif is followed by a wanly
lyrical C-major theme, which recurs throughout the following
development section, struggling to be heard through grinding
dissonance; at one point the pianist is even directed literally to punch
note clusters in the bass. The brittle, sardonic second movement
reveals a contained misery in a halting treble melody which
persistently breaks into high notes of hysteria. Calm returns in the
third movement – 'in the tempo of a slow waltz': Prokofiev often
resorted to old dance forms to express a wistful nostalgia and memory
of more civilized times. The scherzo-like finale anticipates the second
movement of his later Fifth Symphony. Its overall effect is
exhilarating, if also grimly purposeful.

Over the winter of 1940, Prokofiev was involved with rehearsals for
the Kirov production of *Romeo and Juliet*, belatedly scheduled after –
to the embarrassment of the cultural bureaucrats – a highly successful
production had been mounted at the provincial Czech city of Brno.
Recent events had made Prokofiev guarded and gruff, and the
choreographer Lavrovsky found him far from easy to work with: 'Sergey
Sergeyevich responded to my suggestions – necessitated by dramatic
considerations – with great difficulty and extreme unwillingness.'
Prokofiev's temper worsened as he saw the Kirov dancers struggling to
cope with the syncopated rhythms and often subtle chamber-scoring of
his ballet. Galina Ulanova, who was to become legendary in the role of
Juliet, recalls that when she and her Romeo had to explain that the
music at the beginning of Act Three was too quiet for them to hear,
Prokofiev roared at them: 'I know what you want – you want drums,
not music!' By late December it was all Lavrovsky could do to stop the
Kirov troupe from boycotting the production.

A scene from the Bolshoi production of Prokofiev's *Romeo and Juliet*, with Galina Ulanova as Juliet; she initially had little enthusiasm for either the music, with its difficult rhythms, or its moody composer, but eventually came to value the role of Juliet above all others.

The first night, 11 January 1940, took place with Leningrad in blackout due to the Soviet Union's war with Finland. Prokofiev, Lina and Radlov had to grope their way along the canals to the Kirov Theatre. Much to everyone's surprise, the production was a tremendous success. The state journal *Soviet Art* wrote, 'The success of *Romeo and Juliet*, a production of rare beauty, content and interest, is not just an ordinary success for Leningrad ballet, it is a success for all of Soviet choreography, and a testament to its colossal creative and ideological growth.'

Prokofiev was officially honoured shortly afterwards when in early February he was elected vice-chairman of the Board of the Moscow Union of Soviet Composers. Months later, he played his newly completed Sixth Piano Sonata to fellow musicians at Pavel Lamm's apartment. Among those who attended this play-through was Sviatoslav Richter, who was so impressed by what he heard that he vowed to play the sonata:

The remarkable clarity of style and structural perfection of the music amazed me. I hadn't heard anything like it before. The composer, with barbaric audacity, breaks with the ideals of the Romantics and includes the shattering pulse of the twentieth century in his music.

Rehearsals for *Semyon Kotko* continued, but were not without their problems. The Nazi–Soviet pact, signed on 23 August 1939, had caused what Katayev described as 'diplomatic unpleasantries': the opera's Germans had to be changed into an unnamed occupying force. Prokofiev, wishing to give his opera the best possible chance of a proper hearing, tried to prepare his audience with an introductory essay. Aware that few operas apart from the standard warhorses – such as *Ivan Susanin* (formerly known as *A Life for the Tsar*) and *The Battle for the Commune* (also known as *Tosca*) – had reached the Soviet stage since the condemnation of Shostakovich's *Lady Macbeth*, Prokofiev defended his very different operatic style as appropriate for 'a new people, new feelings, a new life [requiring] new means of expression'. At the same time he provided reassurance to his audience, using a tactic similar to one he used in 1916 before the scheduled production of *The Gambler*. This time, instead of citing Mussorgsky, he paraphrased a well-known letter by Tchaikovsky, which stated that 'when a person goes to an opera he wants not only to hear but to see.' Prokofiev identified two types of aria, both found in Tchaikovsky's *Eugene Onegin*: the 'Lensky type', which holds up the action while the singer takes centre stage, and a second type which carries the action along, exemplified by Tatyana's Letter Scene. Prokofiev therefore led his readers to believe that he had made use of the latter type in order to give dramatic flow to his opera – a disingenuous claim, as 'dramatic flow' had, of course, been intrinsic to Prokofiev's operatic style even before the Soviet Union's creation, and so had not been adopted specifically for his Soviet audience. The opening night of *Semyon Kotko* on 23 June was a muted affair. The company, after losing their original director, and after all the vicissitudes involved with the production, was demoralized. But Richter, who made a point of attending several performances, became convinced by *Semyon Kotko* of Prokofiev's genius.

Even before *Semyon Kotko*'s first night, Prokofiev had chosen a new operatic subject. He abandoned patriotic Soviet works, using instead a farce by Sheridan, *The Duenna*, set in eighteenth-century Spain. *Betrothal in a Monastery* – as Prokofiev titled his new opera – was a psychological retreat after the fraught sonatas and the portentous style of *Semyon Kotko*. He worked with Mira that spring on the libretto, he himself translating most of the prose text, and Mira providing verses for the songs specified in the libretto. Their relationship, by now, had developed beyond a professional level. Shebalin's wife, Alissa, caught

The final scene from *Betrothal in a Monastery*, where young love triumphs over adversity

sight of the two walking down a street in Moscow one day, and was struck above all by Prokofiev's radiantly happy expression.

Betrothal in a Monastery was composed at extraordinary speed between July and September 1940. The plot, as Prokofiev recognized, was very much in accordance with the *opera buffa* style of Rossini. It concerns two pairs of young lovers who overcome the opposition of their elders to their marriage, and all ends happily except for the avaricious Jewish fishmonger, Mendoza, who is bamboozled into marrying the penniless but resourceful Duenna. Like Rossini, Prokofiev concentrated on creating psychologically convincing characters, rather than the fantastical fairy-tale archetypes of his previous comic opera *The Love for Three Oranges*, so developing further the warmly lyrical style of *Romeo and Juliet*. The result is one of his most charming works, with gentle, rather than his once typically acidic, humour. There are moments of ardent lyricism, such as the serenade the young Antonio sings beneath the balcony of his beloved Louisa; his aria becomes a potent motif for young love throughout the opera.

While Prokofiev's relationship with Mira blossomed, his marriage with Lina became increasingly strained. Even the most self-sufficient people are unlikely to be able to tolerate the kind of terrible pressure and stress Prokofiev was undergoing without needing calm, unconditional companionship. Lina, more than Prokofiev, was uprooted from everything she had held dear, and so was in no condition to offer the support he desired. One does not need to look further than Mira Mendelson's evident devotion to Sergey, and her calm, unaffectedly affectionate manner, to understand what drew Prokofiev to her.

Well before he met Mira, however, Prokofiev's relationship with Lina had become an unequal partnership. There is no doubt that Prokofiev had been genuinely in love with Lina at their marriage, and it appears that Lina never fell out of love with him: to the end of her life, she spoke admiringly of his genius as a composer, and his honourable character. Unfortunately for Lina, Prokofiev had fallen out of love with her some time before. This is quite clear from the often contemptuous treatment he gave her even in the West (in his book *Old Friends, New Music* Nicolas Nabokov describes an excruciating scene between husband and wife during one of Prokofiev's *tours gastronomiques*). Years later, Prokofiev told a friend that compared to Mira, Lina was like 'a beautiful desert' – a devastatingly cruel description of a relationship that no longer nourished him. Lina had been a useful partner for Prokofiev while they were still in the West: with good looks, a gregarious nature and social grace, she had helped smooth relations between her forthright husband and his more sophisticated Western colleagues. Soviet Russia, on the other hand, had little or no use for such bourgeois graces; political acumen was not only more valuable, but could mean the difference between 'freedom' or arrest. Lina was totally out of her depth, but was unable, or unwilling, to recognize this.

The marriage reached breaking-point early in 1941. In March Prokofiev came home to the Chkalov Street flat, telling Lina he had much work to do and to make sure he was left undisturbed. Possibly he wanted a more extreme form of his rigorous Parisian schedule where callers were kept at bay while he did his morning work: closed performances of *Betrothal* were due to take place from May at the Stanislavsky Musical Theatre, and after the problems of *Semyon Kotko*'s production Prokofiev wished to ensure that his new opera was trouble-free. Adding to his workload was a new ballet commissioned by the Kirov in the wake of the tremendous success of *Romeo and Juliet*: this was to be *Cinderella*, to a scenario written by Nikolay Volkov (who had written scenarios for Asafyev's *Flame of Paris* and *Fountain of Bakhchisarai*). Lina, however, understood, or convinced herself, that her husband was in hiding from Mira. Over the next ten days Mira telephoned several times, but Lina always fended her off by saying that Prokofiev was out. Mira, in increasing desperation, left messages in the apartment's post box.

In an attempt to lighten Prokofiev's mood, Lina threw a party – with champagne, vodka and caviar – and invited all his musician friends. As she later recalled, 'he was like a fury; people congratulated him and he would scowl.' Prokofiev may have been infuriated by what lay behind the party (that Lina was trying to counter rumours about his relationship with Mira), but it is as likely that he was simply angry that Lina had forced this party upon him when he was trying to work in total peace.

Lina and Sergey's last few days together were stormy and unpleasant. Neighbours heard loud arguments from their apartment. One morning late in March, Prokofiev finally left his wife and two sons (who were then aged twelve and sixteen). Sviatoslav saw his father with suitcase in hand and, on asking where he was going, was told, 'I'm going because it may save a life.' Prokofiev had apparently heard that Mira had tried to take her own life.

Prokofiev joined Mira in her parents' apartment. It was a distinct step down from the 'luxury' apartment on Chkalov Street: they shared one room which served as bedroom, living room, dining room and Prokofiev's study, while Mira's parents lived and slept in a room next door; the kitchen and bathroom were communal, shared with several other apartments. These living conditions were, however, better than those of many Muscovite families, and Prokofiev fortunately got on well with his new 'parents-in-law'. Prokofiev and Mira were to live as man and wife until his death, though Prokofiev was never divorced from Lina, and continued sending financial support towards his sons' living expenses. Even so, Prokofiev referred to Mira as his 'wife' from this time onwards and, in those of his scores for which she provided texts, credited her as 'Mira Mendelson-Prokofieva'.

In late March, Prokofiev spent some time in Sochi, a resort on the Black Sea coast, where he finished the second act of *Cinderella*. In an interview by a local paper, he made clear that he would make concessions to a more conventional ballet style: 'I conceive it as a classical ballet with variations, adagios, *pas de deux*, and so on.' Possibly he had made this decision in the face of the initial bewilderment and hostility *Romeo and Juliet* had met from its dancers. But he was clearly reluctant to relinquish the greater psychological depth of his protagonists: 'I see Cinderella not only as a fairy-tale character, but also as a real person, feeling, experiencing, and moving among us.' Just how real Cinderella was to Prokofiev may be gauged by the fact he took a principal theme from *Eugene Onegin*, originally associated with Tatyana, to represent Cinderella's longing for a happier life. Significantly, he composed the first two acts of *Cinderella* immediately after leaving Lina for Mira.

On 23 April Prokofiev celebrated his fiftieth birthday. Myaskovsky had reached his sixtieth birthday three days earlier, and *Sovetskaya Muzyka* devoted a special edition to the two composers. Prokofiev was commissioned to write a short autobiography, which he provided in a masterly summary of the detailed childhood autobiography he had been working on since June 1937. A substantial first part was published in the special edition of *Sovetskaya Muzyka*. It covered the period up to Prokofiev's graduation from the St Petersburg Conservatory and concluded with his outline of the main traits of his music. In this, Prokofiev objected strongly to to the label 'grotesque', which had all too often been applied to his music – 'I would prefer my music to be described as "scherzo-ish" in quality, or else by three words describing various degrees of the scherzo – whimsicality, laughter, mockery.'

That summer he and Mira rented a *dacha* in Kratovo, outside Moscow, where Prokofiev continued his autobiography and his work on *Cinderella*. Both projects were soon to be forcibly postponed, as the Soviet Union's unlikely alliance with Nazi Germany came to a sudden and ignominious end.

8

Soviet machine gunners
battle to recapture
Sevastopol, 1944; the Great
Patriotic War freed Soviet
artists and composers from
the need to be relentlessly
upbeat and legitimized
expressions of tragedy.

*The history of music has yet to evaluate what
was achieved at Ivanovo. Many Soviet classics
were produced there in a stimulating, heady
atmosphere conducive to creative invention. As
we worked, we played our compositions for each
other, sought advice and exchanged opinions. It
is a remarkable fact, but while we were at
Ivanovo our work seemed to progress without
any hitches. Were we influenced by nature and
our surroundings? Or was it the feeling of
victory round the corner? Or simply that we
were getting properly fed? The war drew us
together in an atmosphere of unity.*

Aram Khachaturian recalling the summer of
1943 spent at the House of
Creativity and Rest, Ivanovo

The Great Patriotic War 1941-5

'On June 22, a warm sunny morning,' Prokofiev recalled, 'I was sitting at my desk when suddenly the watchman's wife appeared, looking greatly upset. "The Germans have invaded us," she gasped. "They say they're bombing our cities."'

The German armies had found the Soviet Union poorly prepared. By the time news of the invasion broke in Moscow, the German army was racing eastwards along a front more than a thousand miles long. Twelve hundred Soviet aircraft were burning, most of them destroyed on the ground by enemy bombing. It was twelve days before Stalin, who on receiving news of the invasion had locked himself in his office, refusing to see anyone, finally broadcast to the nation and appealed directly to his 'dear friends, brothers and sisters' to defend their Motherland.

Soviet composers were expected to do their bit to increase morale by producing patriotic songs and marches. Prokofiev wrote Seven Mass Songs to appease the cultural bureaucrats, but before long he approached them with a more congenial project. *War and Peace*, Russia's epic novel, had been a favourite book of Prokofiev's from childhood; according to Lina, he had considered writing an opera on it since 1935. More recently, Mira had started reading the novel to Prokofiev during his afternoon rest period: when she read the final reunion between Natasha Rostov and her mortally wounded fiancé Prince Andrey Bolkonsky, Prokofiev remarked upon the scene's operatic quality. By 12 April 1941 he had written a brief outline libretto, which focused on the idea of a 'spiritual resurrection' through the miracle of love. This is clearly manifested in the development of Prince Andrey, who at the opera's start is jaded and disillusioned, but is redeemed in the end by the love between himself and Natasha. Since his return to the Soviet Union, Prokofiev had shown particular interest in dramatic plots involving world-weary or cynical men confronted by passionate love from guileless young women: *Romeo and Juliet* and the incidental music to *Eugene Onegin* had been early

Natasha Rostov and Prince Anatol in Prokofiev's opera *War and Peace*; Prokofiev had initially intended the opera to focus on Natasha and her various suitors, but Germany's invasion of Russia forced him to create a more epic and blatantly patriotic work.

examples. *War and Peace* was to be his most penetrating exploration of the theme of rejuvenation through life-affirming love.

With the official demand for patriotic works, Prokofiev seized what seemed the ideal opportunity to make a serious start on the opera. Inevitably, the Nazi invasion moulded Prokofiev's treatment of the plot: '... those pages recounting the Russian people's struggle against Napoleon's hordes in 1812 and the expulsion of the French armies from Russian soil seemed especially close. It was clear that precisely those pages should lie at the basis of the opera.' Additionally, the time-consuming nature of working on so grandiose a scale provided Prokofiev with the perfect excuse to avoid writing the kind of banal music for mass consumption to which he so objected. It must have been with considerable relief that he received the project's go-ahead from the Soviet Committee on Artistic Affairs (or Arts Committee).

But then came a more immediate concern. With Moscow under constant bombardment and in imminent danger of falling to the Germans, the Arts Committee decided to evacuate Moscow's leading artistic figures. Prokofiev went to see Lina to discuss his family's evacuation, but when Lina learnt that Mira was to join them, she refused to have anything to do with Sergey's plans. If she had hoped her refusal would force him to chose between his family and his young paramour, her gamble failed. Prokofiev simply left and packed several works in progress to take with him, including the Seventh and Eighth Piano Sonatas, the Violin Sonata, two acts of *Cinderella* and the almost completed libretto of *War and Peace*.

On 8 August Prokofiev and Mira joined a group of Moscow Conservatory professors (including Myaskovsky and Pavel Lamm), actors from the Moscow Art Theatre and other 'artistic labourers' on board a special four-car train which pulled out of the capital on an overcast evening. Their destination, Nalchik, was capital of the Kabarda-Balkar Autonomous Republic in the foothills of the Caucasus. Prokofiev and Mira were to be based there for the next three months.

Many evacuees were housed in a large sanatorium, overlooking the Elbrus Mountain slopes – the highest in Europe – and the grandiose panorama of the Bezengis snow wall. Prokofiev and Mira, however, were initially housed with the family of the local Minister of Culture before being moved into a hotel where they shared one small room. Prokofiev soon settled into a regular routine of composition: within three months he had written the first six scenes – nearly half – of *War and Peace*, his Second String Quartet, the dutiful but uninspired suite for orchestra *The Year 1941*, and several mass songs to texts by Mira.

The Second String Quartet was written following a suggestion from the chairman of the Nalchik Arts Committee that the evacuated composers write musical works that made use of local Balkar and Kabardinian music. (After the war Stalin exiled the Balkars from their homeland for having collaborated with the Germans; their existence was wiped from all Soviet publications, including all mention of Prokofiev's use of their folk music.) The quartet's first movement is launched with deliberate, almost insolent crudity, which has tempted some writers into believing that the work was written under protest. The charming central movement, by contrast, opens with gently mournful cello followed by an insouciant, folk-like melody on the violin with pizzicato accompaniment; an infectiously strutting Kabardinian dance tune dominates the bittersweet finale. (Many of the quartet's folk themes also appear in Myaskovsky's contemporaneous Symphony No. 23.)

Prokofiev's happiness was obvious to long-standing friends who were with him. They noticed a marked softening in his character, a new openness and kindness. Mira would invite the Lamms and Myaskovsky to their cramped hotel room for tea; when Prokofiev had been living with Lina in their Moscow apartment such informal gatherings had been rare.

While still composing his quartet, Prokofiev learned that he and his colleagues had to pack, ready for evacuation. The Germans had captured Rostov-on-Don just 200 miles away, and were now within striking distance of Nalchik. Late in November Prokofiev, Mira and other distinguished refugees were crammed onto a railway carriage, travelling further along the Caucasus range. They arrived next morning in Tbilisi, capital of Georgia.

Tbilisi was a cosmopolitan city that blended Russian culture with influences from Europe and nearby Turkey. Prokofiev is said to have spent much of his free time attending performances at Tbilisi's conservatory, opera house and theatre; that winter and spring he saw productions of Shakespeare, Balzac and Sheridan, heard both European and Georgian opera, and attended symphonic concerts of Beethoven, Tchaikovsky, Skryabin and Shostakovich. He himself toured Caucasian cities, giving what were to be his final public piano recitals.

Winter in Tbilisi was unusually cold; under wartime rationing, Prokofiev and his colleagues were allocated rations for white-collar workers, less than half that allocated to manual workers. They had to supplement their meagre allowance with highly priced goods from the market. Prokofiev, so various witnesses testify, learnt to sharpen his haggling abilities, but poor nutrition meant that his health steadily deteriorated.

He spent much time in the city's library researching the war scenes of *War and Peace*, studying Napoleon's campaign and searching for folk and military songs of the period. Progress on the opera was such that when Eisenstein wrote early in 1942 asking him to collaborate on his new film epic *Ivan the Terrible* Prokofiev was able to write back at the end of March: 'Your letter arrived at precisely the right moment. Am finishing up the last bars of *War and Peace*, so very shortly I'll be ready to submit to your bondage.' By April he had finished the piano score and sent it off for evaluation by the Arts Committee in Moscow; their endorsement was essential before any state opera house could produce the work.

On 2 May he completed his Seventh Piano Sonata. It would first be performed just over eight months later by Richter in Moscow's Hall of the Home of the Unions on 18 January 1943. According to Richter, the audience at its première 'perceived the spirit of the composition as if it

were reflecting everything with which they lived, just as they did when
they heard Shostakovich's Seventh Symphony for the first time'. The
parallel drawn by Richter between the two works is more interesting
than it may at first appear. Shostakovich's symphony had been first
performed in Moscow on 29 March 1942. Although its famous
'invasion' theme is usually taken to represent the invading Nazi forces,
much of the work was conceived before the German invasion of
Russia; the conductor Yevgeny Mravinsky, who knew this, described
the theme as 'a universalized image of stupidity and crass tastelessness'.
In making the theme something terrible and cataclysmic,
Shostakovich created a damning portrait of Stalin's wilful destruction
of Leningrad's intelligentsia. Similarly, Prokofiev had sketched most of
the Seventh Sonata's main themes in 1939, well in advance of the
German invasion and at the height of Stalin's purges. Between the
sonata's demonic first and final movements is a deceptively calm
central movement: its opening, suave melody is, significantly, derived
from the opening of a song by Schumann – *Wehmuth* ('Sadness') – in
Liederkreis, Op. 39, the text of which runs: 'I can sometimes sing as if
I were glad, yet secretly tears well and so free my heart. Nightingales
... sing their song of longing from their dungeon's depth ... everyone
delights, yet no one feels the pain, the deep sorrow in the song.'
Prokofiev's movement reaches an impassioned climax with tolling bell-
like chords before closing resignedly with the Schumann quote. The
State, fortunately, missed such fine points. The tremendous public
and critical success which greeted the sonata's slow movement and
exhilarating seven-beats-to-a-bar finale earned the work a Stalin Prize,
and it was soon exported as cultural propaganda to the USA.

    Evidence that Prokofiev's music was increasingly valued for its
morale-boosting properties could be seen in the fortunes of the now
revived *Alexander Nevsky* cantata, which became something of a
rallying cry during what became known as the Great Patriotic War.
On 5 April the seven-hundredth anniversary of the Battle on the Ice
was marked by a special complete performance of the cantata by the
Sverdlovsk Philharmonic Orchestra, with excerpts from Konstantin
Simonov's poem 'The Battle on the Ice' read between the third and
fourth movements. Choruses from the cantata, particularly 'Arise,
People of Russia', were regularly broadcast and Eisenstein's film was
used to raise morale in, among other places, Sevastopol during its

siege. But by the summer of 1942 the Russian counter-offensive had petered out: none of its main objectives, including breaking the siege of Leningrad, had been achieved. The Germans counter-attacked and by the summer had captured Sevastopol. The Soviet government was careful to minimize news of this disaster, but rumour inevitably trickled through of the German advance. Against this background, Prokofiev worked on a new cantata, *Ballad of an Unknown Boy*.

It set a poem by a popular Soviet writer, Pavel Antokolsky; the story, based on a true-life incident, concerns a boy whose mother and sister have been killed by the German invaders, and who, in revenge, lobs a grenade into a German staff car. *Ballad of an Unknown Boy* is less populist than *Nevsky* and, unlike many of Prokofiev's other works specifically 'inspired' by the war such as *The Year 1941*, it is a genuinely felt piece with recognizable Prokofievian traits, such as the insistent bass ostinato that underpins the tenor's narration halfway through the ballad. Yet there is also a tender lyricism, notably in the writing for the soprano when she expresses compassion for the boy's broken childhood.

In May Prokofiev and Mira finally left the Moscow group of evacuees to join Eisenstein, setting off on their long journey to Alma-Ata, capital of the central Asian state Kazakhstan, near the Chinese border. With the war, both the Moscow and Leningrad film industries had been evacuated to this provincial town. Prokofiev and Mira were pleasantly surprised to find it so attractive, set against the background of a distant mountain range, with wide streets framed by rows of poplars ('it would be like a summer resort if not for the asphalt,' Prokofiev wrote to Myaskovsky). Settled in a hotel room, Prokofiev made an almost immediate start on Eisenstein's *Ivan the Terrible* (the filming of which had started a month earlier), as well as working on several other film scores.

While in Alma-Ata, Prokofiev received the Arts Committee's verdict on *War and Peace*. Their 'advice' was to strengthen obvious contemporary analogies, boost the mass heroism of the Napoleonic War and tone down the genre episodes depicting the aristocracy in time of peace. They also questioned Prokofiev's decision to begin the opera with a lyrical scene (involving Prince Andrey being charmed by Natasha's rhapsodizing over the spring night). Since the committee's endorsement was needed before any state opera house could produce the work, Prokofiev had no choice but to revise accordingly. Rather

Prokofiev and Eisenstein at
Alma-Ata, 1942, where they
collaborated on Eisenstein's
epic film *Ivan the Terrible*

than injure the charming opening scene, Prokofiev wrote a weighty
Epigraph for chorus that could precede it: representing the Russian
people, the chorus sings a stern warning to all who dare invade 'our
Mother Russia'.

Eisenstein gave some characteristically striking suggestions for
Prokofiev's revisions: for 'Moscow Aflame', in which the Russian
people set fire to their capital rather than let it fall intact to
Napoleon's forces, he suggested that actors from the French theatre
might be seen fleeing the fire in make-up and costume. He also
suggested that 'The French Retreat' be given a 'more belligerent'
send-off; in response, Prokofiev created a 'howling and whistling'
orchestral prelude.

By the autumn, the war was turning decisively in Russia's favour. In
one of the most destructive battles ever, the Germans suffered a major
defeat in Stalingrad, with thousands of troops killed or captured.
Moscow was now considered safe, and Prokofiev and Mira returned in
December, staying at the Nationale Hotel. One of Prokofiev's first
tasks was to try to persuade the authorities to allow a performance of
his revised *War and Peace*. The opera was given an official hearing at
the Composers' Union, where it provoked conflicting opinions. Many
of those present considered it impossible to translate Tolstoy's epic
novel into opera, and were unconvinced by Prokofiev's attempt. But in

that session Prokofiev gained an ardent supporter in Samuil Samosud, a conductor then working for the Bolshoi Theatre. He arranged a private hearing of both *War and Peace* and *Betrothal in a Monastery* for the Bolshoi Theatre staff the following January.

Prokofiev himself presented *War and Peace*, trying 'without much felicity' to sing the vocal parts as he played the piano reduction of the score. Again the opera failed to impress many of its listeners, who, according to Samosud, considered the difficulties it posed insurmountable; but the smaller scale and obvious charm of *Betrothal in a Monastery* led to the tentative proposal of a production at the Bolshoi Annexe the following season. Most of the Bolshoi company, however, were still scattered over the Soviet Union due to the war, making it impossible to finalize any definite production plans. Not to be put off, Samosud spent the next few months trying to arrange productions of both operas, in particular to involve Eisenstein as director for *War and Peace*.

It is not known whether Prokofiev attempted to see Lina and his sons during the two months he spent in Moscow. Possibly he was too involved with Mira, and too daunted by the prospect of an emotionally fraught meeting. Certainly neither Sviatoslav nor Oleg saw their father again during the war. With their mother they had suffered the privations of those who stayed in Moscow during the air raids and bombardment by the German forces. Lina's rejection of the official offer of evacuation meant that they lost their only chance of escaping Moscow. The blue Ford Prokofiev had left behind was confiscated by the Soviet authorities. Lina, like many others who had opted to stay in Moscow, fell under suspicion: 'Those who were left, it was rumoured, were those who were going to welcome the Germans,' she later recalled.

Oleg and Sviatoslav, seeking to understand their father and his sudden abandonment of his family, spent much time looking through his property. In Prokofiev's library were books by H. G. Wells, including the *Outline of History* Prokofiev had so relished while living in France, D. H. Lawrence and his favourite living 'Western' author, Vladimir Nabokov. There was also his great record collection – some of the fragile 78s sadly broken, but still enough for the boys to enjoy the music their father had once listened to regularly: Debussy's *Prélude à l'après-midi d'un faune*, scenes from Mussorgsky's *Boris Godunov* and Rachmaninov's Second and Third Piano Concertos.

Early in February Prokofiev and Mira returned to Alma-Ata. There
they received the news that, for the first time, Prokofiev had been
awarded a Stalin Prize, for his Seventh Piano Sonata. He had been
conspicuously absent from previous lists of prize-winners, which had
included Myaskovsky and Shostakovich. Even now, his work was only
awarded 'second class', first class being presented that year to Shebalin's
'Slavonic' Quartet. But as Myaskovsky pointed out, 'the important
thing was to break the ice, and, it seems, it has now been broken.' And
indeed, before the year was out Prokofiev had been awarded the Order
of the Red Banner of Labour and the title Honoured Artist of the
Russian Soviet Socialist Republic.

By April the orchestration of *War and Peace* was complete, and
Prokofiev began to revisit *Betrothal in a Monastery* and introduce some
changes. He planned to finish the symphonic suite from *Semyon Kotko*
(having already made sketches) and also to complete the Eighth Piano
Sonata, one movement of which had been written. The Eighth Piano
Sonata, the last of the so-called 'War' trilogy and dedicated to Mira, is
the longest and also the most understated of the three. Precisely
because of this, it is also the most haunting in effect. The first
movement starts deceptively with a placid series of themes, the merest
touch of chromatic colouring in each creating a disquieted atmosphere;
this culminates in a quietly played, sustained dissonant chord in the
bass while a music-box-like theme unhurriedly plays in the treble. The
movement reaches a nightmarish climax as the two main themes from
the exposition are crushed by chromatic scales and grating dissonances
before subsiding to a passage strongly reminiscent of Ravel's piano
work *Scarbo*. Then, most disturbingly, the placid opening exposition
returns, note for note the same as before. (Prokofiev had begun the
movement in 1939, after Meyerhold's arrest, which Shostakovich
described as 'one of the terrible signs of the age, a man had disappeared
but everyone pretended that nothing had happened' – a comment
horribly apposite to the movement's character.)

A deceptively calm minuet follows, borrowed from the jettisoned
incidental music to *Eugene Onegin*. In its original context, the minuet
had heralded Onegin's recognition of Tatyana, now transformed into a
princess. Given the sonata's dedication to Mira, there might be
something symbolic in Prokofiev's inclusion of this music. The
progress of the glittering toccata of the finale is interrupted by a

brutally hammered-out middle section in 3/4 time; sounding like a popular dance tune played by a clumsy amateur pianist, this is in fact a scarcely recognizable variant of the second movement's minuet theme. This dies away to the chilly reprise of the musical-box theme before the toccata inevitably returns, winding up to a ferocious conclusion.

In June Prokofiev revisited the evacuated Kirov company in their temporary home at Perm (then called Molotov). The company was now interested in staging *Cinderella*, and Prokofiev discussed with them possible productions of both this ballet and *Betrothal in a Monastery*, which he was now revising in the light of the Bolshoi audition earlier that year. While in Perm, Prokofiev completed a Flute Sonata he had been planning over several years (later to become much better-known as Violin Sonata No. 2, recast in this form at the suggestion of the violinist David Oistrakh.) Although it is on the surface a sunny and carefree work, the sonata hints at a more uneasy mood: the third movement, in particular, is a striking parallel to the third movement of the not yet completed First Violin Sonata, not only having some of the same bleak mood but even similar material. And there may be more than mischief in the finale's deliberate parody of mechanistic piano exercises; a Soviet critic once suggested, within Prokofiev's hearing, that 'music should get more and more mechanized' to reflect the growing industrialization of the Soviet Union. A number of Prokofiev's works of this period – for instance, the First Violin Sonata (completed after the Second) and the Eighth Piano Sonata – have the piano part parodying commissars of culture as amateur pianists, demonstrating their 'culture' with inept attempts to take the lead or to imitate an earlier musical idea.

Prokofiev spent much of the rest of 1943 completing *Cinderella*, the orchestration of which was not completed until late spring 1944. In October 1943 he and Mira returned to Moscow, where they remained until the end of the war. Prokofiev had hoped for a production of *War and Peace* at the Bolshoi by the end of the year, but the delayed reunion of the company meant that this had to be postponed. A concert performance under Samosud was planned for December, but at the last minute Samosud was, without explanation, relieved of his duties at the Bolshoi.

Recent evidence suggests that Samosud's dismissal was due to Stalin's semi-official policy to purge cultural institutions of 'cosmopolitan' elements – in other words, Jews. A memorandum from the head of the Central Committee's Propaganda and Agitation Department to the Secretariat of the Central Committee (17 August 1942) had cited the 'unacceptable clogging' of the Bolshoi Theatre by 'primarily Jewish' aliens. In order not to offend the Soviet Union's Western allies, the effects of this policy were cloaked by such gestures as awarding Stalin Prizes to its victims (Samosud was to be awarded two such prizes in the following years). Meanwhile the director of the Bolshoi, as Prokofiev wrote to Eisenstein, had been instructed to revive the traditional repertoire, so *War and Peace* was dropped; 'to pacify me, they'll produce *Cinderella*.'

It was possibly the unsettled circumstances of war which made the Kirov in Leningrad similarly postpone their production of *Betrothal* indefinitely. Even so, composers such as Kabalevsky and Dzerzhinsky did not encounter similar problems in having less significant works staged. First performances of some of Prokofiev's other works did, however, take place. On 7 December the Flute Sonata was performed by Nikolay Kharkovsky and Sviatoslav Richter. Then on 21 February 1944 came the première of *Ballad of an Unknown Boy* conducted by Alexander Gauk.

Composed when Soviet fortunes were at their bleakest, the work almost certainly suffered from being performed just when the Soviet armies were beginning to drive back the Germans. Reactions to the work ranged from cautious to hostile. In the plenary session, held in late March by the Organization Committee of the Composers' Union in order to assess work by Soviet musicians during the war, Shostakovich was one of the more moderate critics of the *Ballad*: 'Prokofiev possesses an astonishing gift for illustrating text, and in his enthusiasm to realize his work, he has neglected organic unity and musical form.' He had made similar criticisms of Prokofiev's *Alexander Nevsky* cantata; his comments on the *Ballad*, a far more sophisticated work, were probably made on the basis of a single hearing. In contrast to many of his colleagues, who were all too eager – on account of jealousy – to extend criticism to Prokofiev the man, Shostakovich made a point of praising other works by Prokofiev – the Seventh

Piano Sonata, the Flute Sonata and even *War and Peace*. Prokofiev himself was not uncritical of Shostakovich's works, disparaging his Eighth Symphony, for instance, for its paucity of ideas, its length and lack of 'a clear, melodic line'.

One beneficial consequence of the meeting of the Composers' Union was an invitation to all composers to stay that summer at a new 'House of Rest and Creativity' set up by the Composers' Union at Ivanovo. Prokofiev was one of many who spent time at what had originally been a nobleman's country estate. Composers and their families were each given a room in the main building and provided with working studios on the grounds. For wartime, the conditions were unique: the estate, a collective poultry farm until shortly before then, now offered ideal, peaceful working conditions and the stimulus that professional colleagues could provide. Well fed and relieved – now that the war's tide had turned in Russia's favour – the composers that summer were in convivial mood; many would remember the time with particular nostalgia.

While before the war Lina had noticed her husband physically deteriorating, by this summer of 1944 Prokofiev had regained his habit of rising early, taking breakfast, then leaving the dining room at nine to walk across the fields to a nearby village where he had his studio. There he worked in the morning before taking lunch; the rest of the day was then devoted to less intellectually demanding activities. He took part in some sport during his spare time, playing volleyball with his colleagues.

Some have claimed that Prokofiev deliberately snubbed Shostakovich that summer, which suggests that, despite his apparent contentment, he was still capable of sulking and had not forgiven what he must have considered a presumptuous attack at the Union's plenary session. Prokofiev had an abiding fondness for his *Ballad of an Unknown Boy* and later told Nestyev sadly that it had been 'trampled to death'.

For Prokofiev it was a productive summer. He completed his Eighth Piano Sonata, composed settings of Twelve Russian Folk Songs, and started what was to be his most widely admired symphony – the Fifth. This symphony particularly seems to capture his ambivalent mood that summer. The Eighth Piano Sonata and Fifth Symphony have some common characteristics – both are in B flat

A gathering of leading Soviet Composers, 1946; left to right: front row – Aram Khachaturian, Gadjibekov, Shostakovich, Glière and Prokofiev; second row – Shaporin, Kabalevsky, Dzerzhinsky, Koval, Mouraiev

major and contain a preponderance of slow, meditative lyrical music – but the symphony's sometimes biting sarcasm is almost entirely absent from the piano work.

Much of the Fifth Symphony's musical argument is through tonal conflict rather than thematic development, although many of the themes go through unmistakable transformations of character. Most striking is that undergone by the whimsical scherzo theme which launches the second movement: after the central trio section, the scherzo theme returns, but as a sinister, stalking procession of sneery-toned, muted brass. The slow movement opens with a soothing melody floated above disquieted arpeggios; after a second theme on the strings (not unlike the love music from *Romeo and Juliet*, but contorted with anguish), the arpeggios return, now grown into something monstrous. The symphony's finale has often been portrayed as an evocation of uninhibited joy – but the music is as double-edged as the finale of that other famous Soviet Fifth Symphony, by Shostakovich. The braying laughter from the strings is not genuine mirth but something forced and inane, and motorized rhythms increasingly overwhelm the music until its chilling final few bars, when most of the orchestral fabric is whipped away to spotlight a quartet of string players. Usually thought of as the heart of an orchestra, they are dramatically seen playing a mindless, mechanistic ostinato – such, Prokofiev suggests, is the heart of all this 'merriment'.

Prokofiev was back in Moscow by early October, and gave a play-through of his newly completed sonata at the Composers' Union. Richter, who was present, noted that Prokofiev's once forceful and reliable piano technique had suffered some deterioration: 'His hands dragged somehow.' On 16 October, a concert performance of eight scenes from *War and Peace* was given with piano accompaniment at the Moscow Actor's Club, conducted by Konstantin Popov. Though well received, the performance failed to encourage any opera house to take up the project and Samosud, who had now been deprived of his post at the Bolshoi, was in no position to persuade them to change their minds. To add to Prokofiev's disappointment, the Kirov and Bolshoi productions of, respectively, *Cinderella* and *Betrothal*, both scheduled for that autumn, were postponed yet again.

Prokofiev then worked at orchestrating his Fifth Symphony and at finishing the music for the first part of *Ivan the Terrible*. By now he and Mira had their own apartment at No. 11/13 Mozhaisk Road (today called Kutuzov Prospekt), and he was able to work in relative privacy. Sadly he still saw very little of his sons. According to Lina, 'He wouldn't have them visit, he didn't want them to meet her [Mira]. He was ashamed somewhere, he was decent enough – he was really a very decent person.' Prokofiev only saw the boys when he came to their apartment, usually to sort out financial arrangements, or – as Oleg recalls – once to vet a potential art teacher for him. This distressed Lina, who tried to invite her husband to come to lunch or dinner because the boys 'were at an age when they needed really a father more than a mother.'

On 30 December, two premières signalled a change in Prokofiev's fortunes. One was of the Eighth Piano Sonata, performed in the Great Hall of the Conservatory by Emil Gilels. The other was the first public screening of the first part of Eisenstein's *Ivan the Terrible*. Both events were popular and critical successes. Just two weeks later, on 13 January, Prokofiev conducted the première of his Fifth Symphony. The rest of the concert was directed by Anosov, who conducted *Peter and the Wolf* and the 'Classical' Symphony. Richter witnessed the striking moment when Prokofiev prepared to launch his new symphony:

> *When Prokofiev mounted the podium and silence set in, artillery salvos suddenly thundered. His baton was already raised. He waited, and until the cannon fire ceased, he didn't begin. There was something very significant, very symbolic in this. It was as if all of us – including Prokofiev – had reached some kind of shared turning point.*

The rugged lyricism of the symphony and the apparent hilarity of its finale whipped the audience into a frenzy. In just two weeks it

Prokofiev rehearsing an orchestra, c. 1945; his final appearance as a conductor was at the première of his warmly received Fifth Symphony in Moscow, 13 January, 1945.

seemed that Prokofiev had sealed his reputation as a leading composer in the Soviet Union. To celebrate his new-found success and their resettlement in Moscow, Prokofiev and Mira threw a house-warming party at their new apartment.

Only days later, Prokofiev had a sudden attack of dizziness leading to a serious fall. The fact that neither Mira nor any of his close associates can agree where or when this happened may suggest that he had had at least one previous accident from bouts of dizziness, perhaps as early as October (when Richter had noted Prokofiev's sluggish performance at the piano), but had been reluctant to publicize the fact. In any event, on this occasion Prokofiev suffered such severe concussion that he had to be taken to hospital. Kabalevsky, returning from a trip to Finland, visited him there:

He lay completely motionless ... From time to time he could not recognize the people he was talking with, and would lose consciousness. In a weak voice he asked a few questions about my visit with Jean Sibelius, complaining bitterly about the enforced break in his own working routine. I went away from him with sad thoughts. It seemed this was the end.

Kabalevsky's fears were to prove premature. But the vicissitudes of Prokofiev's next few years, involving both his health and his career, would be such that a very different sort of epitaph might have been written had his life ended at this point, just when his reputation was at its greatest and most unsullied.

9

Drawing of Prokofiev by his
son, Oleg, in 1948; in that
year Prokofiev's reputation was
savaged by Stalin's henchman,
Zhdanov, and several of his
major works were banned from
performance.

*A theme is an elusive thing – it comes, it goes,
and sometimes never returns. Some of my critics
might say, no doubt, that the more themes of
mine that never return, the better.*

Sergey Prokofiev interviewed by
Musical America, 28 September 1918

Winter Bonfire 1945–53

Spring came late in 1945, but the mood in Russia was euphoric. Soviet troops entered Berlin in April, and on 8 May the German command surrendered. Prokofiev, who would have relished the spectacular Victory Parade held in Moscow's Red Square the following day, could only receive second-hand accounts from visitors to the sanatorium at Barkhiva, in the countryside outside Moscow where he was recuperating.

Although his health had improved over the winter, he was increasingly frustrated by the restrictions imposed by his doctors: no work of any kind, no excitement, no reading, no wine and no cigarettes (which he had come to rely upon for relaxation during the war). Prokofiev had disregarded at least some of these orders, composing a new aria for General Kutuzov in *War and Peace* to be inserted in the scene 'Before the Battle of Borodino'. Originally, the scene's main focus had been on the bravery and morale of the Russian army, who accordingly sing a noble refrain. But the General, officially regarded as a precursor to the great modern strategist Stalin, had to be given a very bold entry in this, his first scene – a quiet appearance would not do. Prokofiev accordingly provided a stately aria for him, in which he sings about the greatness of the Russian people.

In June Prokofiev was able to travel to Moscow and attended an almost complete concert performance of *War and Peace* by the Moscow Philharmonic conducted by Samosud, in the Great Hall of the Conservatory. Samosud recalled the occasion:

An unusual holiday atmosphere reigned in the hall. It was already summer, but the performance attracted literally the entire cultural elite of the capital … They gave Prokofiev a genuine ovation, and he was very moved. Observing the conflicting feelings of his doctor, an important Moscow professor, was amusing. A sincere music lover, the doctor was unable to conceal her interest in Prokofiev's opera. At the same time, she was saying to us, with unfeigned anxiety, 'What is he doing! He should be at home in bed, not here getting excited for nothing.'

In reply, someone recalled the line from Ostrovsky, 'You don't die from happiness.'

Prokofiev spent that summer with Mira at Ivanovo: during walks through the woods, he would write down musical themes, and talk about music, his plans for the future, and possible subjects for new compositions. 'If he didn't have his little notebook with him,' Mira recalled, 'he would write the themes down on a scrap of paper, on a cigarette package, a medicine box, or a used envelope. Later, he would try out on the piano what he had written down, and then include it in his organized music notebook.' Prokofiev was now allowed by his doctor to compose, but was under strict medical orders to avoid excitement. Aware of his fiercely competitive nature, his doctor forbade him even to play chess. Mira also did her best to reduce his other commitments. When Eisenstein wrote begging Prokofiev to complete 'The Dance of the *Oprichniki*' so that he could continue filming *Ivan the Terrible*, it was Mira who wrote back from Ivanovo:

He tried to work, but recently he has had several nosebleeds, which disturbed the Moscow professor treating him ... She strictly prohibited work for the moment. Sergey Sergeyevich very much wants to do that dance for you, but it is unlikely he will get to it soon, especially since it would demand intense concentration. He, too, is eager to work and is enduring this enforced inactivity with great difficulty.

Ivanovo's peaceful atmosphere was, however, most beneficial to Prokofiev: 'The air is marvellous, the food is tasty, and my health has significantly improved – at least my head aches only rarely.' By late August he had managed to sketch out an orchestral *Ode to the End of the War*, and had almost completed two sections of his Sixth Symphony. He also started what was to be his last completed piano sonata, the Ninth.

Back in Moscow by early autumn, Prokofiev and Mira exchanged their apartment on Mozhaisk Road for rooms adjoining Mira's father's apartment (her mother had died during the war). Prokofiev was now able to write the *oprichniki* dance, enabling Eisenstein to film his striking sequence using Agfa colour film which had been taken from the captured German army.

Early in October, Samosud conducted the first complete (concert) performance of *War and Peace* in its original form of eleven scenes. He hoped to stage the opera at the Maly Theatre in Leningrad, and was working on this with the director, Boris Pokrovsky. Both Samosud and Prokofiev agreed that the opera should be divided and staged on two consecutive evenings, first 'Peace', then 'War'. With this plan, Samosud passed on Pokrovsky's suggestion that Prokofiev should add a scene to the 'Peace' half – a grand New Year's Eve ball in which Natasha first meets Prince Andrey. It was duly composed in Ivanovo over the winter of 1945–6, and Prokofiev kept in regular correspondence with Samosud about the Maly Theatre production throughout.

On 12 November, in Moscow's Tchaikovsky Hall, Samosud conducted Prokofiev's *Ode to the End of the War*, the first such 'celebratory work' to be heard after the war. It is scored for a huge orchestra, with expanded brass section, a large woodwind section, four pianos and eight harps; there are no violins, violas or cellos, but double the usual complement of double basses. The resulting sound is dark-toned, steely and as the musicologist Hans Swarsenski strikingly describes it, evocative of 'the glitter of parades on a sunny day, the uniform and heavy steps of marching troops over the pavements of immense squares'. Given its extraordinary forces, the *Ode* did not enter the standard repertoire.

Much more successful was *Cinderella*'s first production at the Bolshoi. Consciously modelled on Tchaikovsky's evening-long ballets, such as *Sleeping Beauty*, *Cinderella* lacks something of the impudent zest of Prokofiev's best ballets, such as *Chout* or even *Romeo and Juliet*; it nonetheless has considerable charm with some vivid character pieces and dances, such as the ebullient mazurka in Act Two. Prokofiev was pleased with Galina Ulanova's interpretation of the heroine, but found the Bolshoi's lavish décor at odds with the ironic tone of the music, and was irritated by the way his score had been coarsened by those who believed the original was 'too transparent' to be effective. (They had added percussion parts and among other changes rescored an oboe solo for trumpet.) He was much happier with the Kirov's more elegant production of *Cinderella*, which opened in early April 1946. With the Bolshoi production of *Cinderella*, however, the fortunes of Prokofiev's dramatic works changed for the better; by late 1946 *Betrothal in a Monastery*, *Romeo and Juliet* and, above all, the first part of *War and Peace* had all reached the stage.

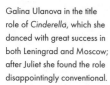

Galina Ulanova in the title role of *Cinderella*, which she danced with great success in both Leningrad and Moscow; after Juliet she found the role disappointingly conventional.

Prokofiev had already received official confirmation of his standing as a leading Soviet composer when, in late January 1946, recipients of the year's Stalin Prizes were announced: Prokofiev won two first-class prizes, one for the Fifth Symphony and the Eighth Piano Sonata, and the second for *Ivan the Terrible*, Part One. Eisenstein was also awarded a first-class Stalin Prize for *Ivan*, and a party was held early in February in his honour to celebrate the award and the completion of the second part of the film. During the party, the fêted film director suddenly collapsed from a heart attack. Prokofiev visited him frequently at the Kremlin Hospital in the following months, and was distressed to find his friend weak and apparently resigned: 'It's all over,' Eisenstein told him. 'Only the postscript remains.' Prokofiev answered that Eisenstein in that case should write his memoirs – a gruff but kindly meant suggestion: he himself had returned to writing, or rather dictating to Mira, his hugely detailed autobiography – a kind of therapy, perhaps, for the fear he felt about his own poor health.

Prokofiev's fifty-fifth birthday on 23 April 1946 was celebrated by friends and colleagues with nearly a month of special events and concerts of his music. Most exciting for Prokofiev was the stage première on 12 June of the first half of *War and Peace* at Leningrad's Maly Theatre, including the newly written second scene – the Grand Ball. After attending the highly successful first few performances, Prokofiev left Leningrad assured that the second part would be staged the following season. The production enjoyed considerable popularity with Leningrad audiences, and by March the following year, *War and*

The curtain-call for the first, highly successful staged production of Part One of Prokofiev's *War and Peace*; Prokofiev and Mira stand on either side of the conductor Samuel Samosud.

Peace had been performed at the Maly Theatre fifty times, an enormous number for any new opera.

Although the director, Boris Pokrovsky, later accepted blame for the opera's elephantine length – necessitating its split into two parts – the German invasion had done as much to force Prokofiev to accentuate the war elements and so increase its length. Besides, at least one of the scenes Pokrovsky asked Prokofiev to add – the war council at Fili – gave the opera's 'war' part an epic weight and focus lacking in its original version. This was, arguably, at the expense of Prokofiev's original intention of focusing the drama on the love between Andrey and Natasha; but in its original form, despite some powerful scenes, the opera was over-episodic and excessively reliant on the audience's knowledge of Tolstoy's novel. Even in its final form there are some loose threads – for example, in scene six Natasha, in despair, takes poison, and she is not seen again until scene twelve when she inexplicably turns up at Andrey's deathbed.

This is none the less Prokofiev's most ambitious and also his greatest opera. Of over sixty characters, at least fourteen are well-rounded portraits. Although it could not encompass the entire fabric of the novel, the opera gives an extremely good impression of its drama and diversity: there is the enchanting duet by Natasha and her cousin Sonya to the spring night, the seedy braggadocio of Anatol's scheming to abduct Natasha, the cold menace of Marshal Davout as Russian prisoners are dragged off to be shot, and Pierre emotionally beside himself as he declares his love for Natasha. These portraits, and the extreme vividness of almost every scene (only the final scene, in which the chorus sings a hymn of victory, feels manufactured rather than a natural culmination to the drama), somehow create an opera greater than the sum of its parts.

In July Prokofiev was awarded yet another Stalin Prize, first class, this time for *Cinderella*. Having now won 300,000 rubles' worth of Stalin Prizes in one year, on top of all the earnings he was gaining with performances of his ballets and other works, Prokofiev decided to purchase his own private *dacha*. This decision was probably also due to his last, less than ideal stay at what had formerly been a haven in Ivanovo. The cellist Rostropovich, who first stayed at the House of Creativity and Rest over the winter of 1945–6, recalls how Shostakovich's young son Maxim 'used to run up and down the corridors shouting and screaming, and I think that Prokofiev was longing to box his ears. He used to slink out of his room and hiss, "Can't you be a bit quieter?"'

Prokofiev and Mira Mendelson at Nikolina Gora, 1946; after his split from Lina, Prokofiev was to refer to Mira as 'my wife'.

Prokofiev bought a property in Nikolina Gora, a small, modest wooden *dacha* which had belonged to a well-known soprano. It stood within a wood of pines, forty-two kilometres west of Moscow, with an attractive view over the Moscow River. But the *dacha* had been neglected, and Mira, her father and Prokofiev all worked to make it habitable. Prokofiev particularly enjoyed equipping it with gadgets. He took a childlike delight in the electric lamps he had fixed on either side of the porch, making it a personal ritual to switch them on when receiving guests or when seeing them off. He also loved to sit out on the porch, admiring the trees and the plants outside; eventually he had the porch enclosed in glass so that he and his guests could sit there even in cooler weather. Among Prokofiev's guests were his sons, who started to come for extended visits at Nikolina Gora, developing a civil, if never intimate, relationship with Mira.

During his first summer there, Prokofiev finally completed his First Violin Sonata. Many of its main themes had been sketched in 1938, but the sonata had been shelved when other projects such as

Alexander Nevsky took up his time. Its sombre mood may now have appealed to him as a repository for his darker thoughts, perhaps partly in connection with his grief over Eisenstein's debilitated state. Additionally, in February that year, Stalin had implied that there would be no relaxation in cultural policy after the exhausting war effort.

Prokofiev invited Myaskovsky and David Oistrakh, who had helped revise his Flute Sonata for violin and piano, to hear the new sonata. Prokofiev, as was usual when introducing a new work to his colleagues, briefly described each movement before playing through the entire work on the piano. 'It seemed to me that on this occasion he played somehow with great restraint, even timidity,' Oistrakh later recalled. 'Even so, the music itself made an enormous impression – one had the feeling of being present at a very great and significant event.' When Prokofiev had finished, Myaskovsky, deeply moved, called it 'a thing of genius' and kept asking, 'Don't you realize what you have written?'

Even after Prokofiev's last three piano sonatas, the First Violin Sonata is a powerfully expressive and startlingly beautiful work. Prokofiev had told Mira that he was inspired to start writing the work in Kislovodsk, where he heard a trio sonata by Handel. Possibly the opening piano writing and the trills with which the violin enters may have originated from what he heard, but their purpose and effect is quite different from anything Handel might have conceived. It is furtive and edgy at first; the violin blossoms for a moment of intensely lyrical and anguished melody before retreating into wary, introverted writing, turning over seemingly private thoughts, including a quotation of the First String Quartet's chilly end. The violin's mood is mirrored by the dark, brooding piano part, which eventually resolves into cool, chiming chords (the impression of church-like harmonies reinforced by a low bass octave left resonating like an organ pedal point); above this *freddo* (cold) scalic passages on the violin rush up and down through virtually its entire compass – Prokofiev told Oistrakh to make it sound 'like the wind in a graveyard' (a literal allusion to the several million Russians arrested and the hundreds of thousands shot in the late 1930s when the sonata was originally conceived).

A brutal second movement follows: despite the violin's heroic second theme, the piano's bludgeoning octaves often seem on the verge of beating the violin part into submission. The third movement

is contrastingly fine-textured; often there are no more than one or two
unsupported melodic lines, with an almost continuous and steady run
of quiet semiquavers. Against this the violin, muted throughout,
sounds its plangent lament. The finale launches with a vigorous dance
which alternates – not always predictably – beats of 5, 7 and 8.
Increasingly the movement's progress is disturbed by galumphing,
ferociously loud bass octaves, which menacingly take up an
inconsequential three-crotchet idea that had signed off the central
section. This basso idea is heard at several points, often at rhythmic
odds with what is otherwise going on; at times, in its evident fury, it
stomps clumsily up and down three notes until forcing a return of the
finale's opening, the violinist's nerves seemingly so ragged by this point
that semiquavers jitter vaguely around the theme.

This bullying bass motif is a graphic example of what the pianists
Yevgeny Kissin and Andrey Gavrilov have identified as a 'Stalin motif'.
They have found similar motifs in the three so-called 'War' sonatas.
The significance of such symbolism becomes most evident as the bass
pounds out its three-crotchet idea to herald the return of the 'wind in
the graveyard' scales. Even if such symbolism is discounted, one
cannot ignore the protesting misery with which the violin winds down
before coldly resuming the scales, and its quiet yet anguished final few
bars. It is ironic that this tragic masterpiece was to earn Prokofiev his
fifth Stalin Prize in June 1947.

Encouraged by his friends' response to this sonata, Prokofiev
devoted his energies to composing his Sixth Symphony. His Soviet
biographer, Nestyev, has claimed that many of the symphony's themes
had been composed before the Fifth Symphony – that is, during
World War II. Given the political situation of the period when
Prokofiev worked on the Sixth Symphony, however, it is probable that
he had in mind events more recent than the carnage of war.

Oleg recalls that on one of Prokofiev's visits to Lina and the boys in
Chkalov Street, he told her, 'My dear, you're seeing too many
foreigners. You must be careful!' Lina, now fifty years old but looking
many years younger, enjoyed going out, and regularly mixed with
foreign diplomats and their families. She refused to see any harm in
such behaviour. She was not alone in this; in the optimistic
atmosphere of the immediate post-war period, several leading Russians
unwittingly placed themselves in jeopardy with the Soviet authorities

by socializing with foreign dignitaries. Prokofiev himself had taken advantage of this brief period when Russia and her wartime allies seemed to be drawing together in co-operation and friendship: in the spring and summer of 1946 both Vernon Duke and Pierre Suvchinsky received telegrams from Prokofiev with news of himself and friends they knew in Russia. But Prokofiev now sensed a new period of political oppression.

On 14 August 1946, the Central Committee issued a 'Resolution on the Journals *Star* and *Leningrad*'; these two Leningrad literary magazines were banned for the 'anti-patriotic' crime of publishing writings by Akhmatova and Zoshchenko, authors representative of 'the reactionary cult of the old St Petersburg'. This was the first salvo against the intelligentsia, whom Stalin wished to silence before plunging the country into another insane round of purges. Andrey Zhdanov, the boorish Governor of Leningrad, was entrusted with the task of cowing the Leningrad writers into subservience.

Zhdanov summoned a meeting of all writers, and personally attacked Akhmatova from the platform as 'a demented gentlewoman dashing to and fro between her boudoir and her confessional – half-nun, half-harlot, mingling prayer with fornication'. His ignorance or blatant disregard of basic facts was all the more horrifying given the executive power that lay behind him: none of his audience had forgotten the horrors of the late 1930s. Akhmatova and Zoshchenko, the latter condemned as a 'literary hooligan', were banned from publication and stripped of their union membership and ration cards. Akhmatova left the hall in dignified silence, while a devastated Zoshchenko tearfully tried to buttonhole friends who, terrified of being associated with an enemy of the people, studiously avoided him.

Prokofiev had set Akhmatova's verse before the Bolshevik revolution, and was horrified by her fate. Zhdanov then struck closer to home, turning his attention to the film industry. Even before then, Stalin had asked to see Eisenstein's *Ivan the Terrible*, Part Two, and watched the film in the company of Bolshakov, Minister of Cinematography. An eyewitness recalls that Bolshakov was unrecognizable on his return: 'his right eye was half-closed, there were red spots on his face and after what he had gone through he was incapable of saying anything further for the rest of the day.' Stalin had called the film a 'nightmare', menacingly telling Bolshakov, 'We could

Andrey Zhdanov, Governor of Leningrad, took charge of savaging the intelligentsia after the Patriotic War.

never quite get around to you during the war, but now we'll give you the full treatment.'

For Stalin, everything was wrong with the film. Ivan the Terrible's *oprichniki* – with their all too obvious parallel to Stalin's own NKVD – were portrayed by brutishly unpleasant music. Feodor's bloodthirsty aria was launched with shrieking whistles and giddily rushing string scales strongly reminiscent of those that accompanied the ecstatic release of violence in *Seven, They Are Seven*. It was bad enough seeing the child Ivan entering in oversized regal garments to an ironic woodwind march; worse to see the fully-grown Ivan humiliatingly pleading with Philip, Metropolitan of Moscow, before capitulating and promising to suppress his *oprichiniki*. Stalin, who closely identified with Ivan, reacted with fury that the Tsar should be shown as putty in the hands of others, uncertain of his right to judge his people. The final straw was the Fiery Furnace charade, staged by Ivan's aunt in a manner which recalled the 'mousetrap' play in *Hamlet* too closely for Stalin's comfort.

Late in August the cultural bureaucrats turned on Eisenstein, only recently released from hospital. *Ivan the Terrible*, Part Two, they said, 'betrayed his ignorance of historical facts by showing the progressive bodyguards of Ivan the Terrible – the *oprichniki* – as a degenerate band rather like the Ku Klux Klan, and Ivan the Terrible himself, who was a man of strong will and character, as weak and indecisive, somewhat like Hamlet.' Prokofiev was certainly affected by the terrible stress of this period. Through much of the early winter he was plagued by headaches and nosebleeds, and spent days in bed under strict instructions not to compose. He complained to Mira about his forced inactivity: 'Don't they understand that I compose music in my head anyway?' he said, fretting that his head was filling with ideas which might, without pen and paper, disappear irretrievably.

Once he was allowed to compose again, Prokofiev worked on his Sixth Symphony, perhaps hoping that its abstract nature would shield it from opprobrium. Following official 'advice', he also revised the second part of *War and Peace* to include a scene where Kutuzov confers with his generals on how to defend Moscow. He was too ill to attend the Kirov première of *Betrothal in a Monastery* on 3 November. After its long delay before reaching the stage, it now enjoyed tremendous popular and critical success. Shostakovich, writing in *Sovetskoe iskusstvo*,

A scene from Eisenstein's film, *Ivan the Terrible, Part Two*, 1945; the film drew dangerous parallels between Ivan and Stalin – behind the Tsar can be seen his hooded *oprichniki*, precursors of Stalin's secret police.

described it as 'one of Prokofiev's most radiant and buoyant works' and compared it to Verdi's *Falstaff* in its wit and humanity.

That winter Prokofiev completed his Sixth Symphony. Its first movement, lasting around fourteen minutes, is one of his longest sonata movements, second only to that of the Eighth Piano Sonata. Despite its wealth of material and its sometimes shocking contrasts, this is a most masterfully constructed movement. Its drama is as compelling as its argument is inexorable. Speaking of the work almost a year later, Prokofiev told his Soviet biographer, Nestyev: 'Now we are rejoicing in our great victory, but each of us has wounds which cannot be healed. One has lost those dear to him, another has lost his health. This must not be forgotten.' That he had in mind the loss of his own health, and certainly that of Eisenstein's, seems more plausible than the suggestion that the Symphony was intended to exorcize images of wartime carnage that Prokofiev never saw at first hand. At rehearsals, according to Nestyev, Prokofiev 'called particular attention to the effect of the asthmatic "wheezing" of the French horns in the development of the first movement.' The 'wheezing' particularly suggests a graphic portrayal of the hypertension which led to Prokofiev's fall, winding down as it does to a throbbing pedal note. Tied in with this is a profound realization of his own mortality; the sense of time running out is graphically spelt out by a ticking piano and bassoon ostinato.

More menacing is the first movement's coda, where dark forces just below the surface seem to be represented by low brass instruments. These forces are felt throughout the symphony, breaking through in the middle of the central movement and finally, after the mindless bustle of the finale, emerging in full and horrible triumph at the symphony's end. Just before this terrible apotheosis, the orchestra gives a final howl of anguish, which is no mere recollection of war's horrors, but a cry of outrage against the injustices of the post-war Soviet Union.

In July 1947, the second part of *War and Peace* was shown in dress rehearsal to prominent musicians and cultural authorities. The end of each scene was greeted with often tumultuous applause. Yet before the opening night, the theatre's management was instructed – in a manner that made discussion impossible – to remove several of the most important scenes; these included the sardonic portrait of Napoleon during the battle of Borodino, and the colourful tableau of Moscow on fire. Samosud and Prokofiev, confronted by these unexplained objections, refused to cut the scenes, pointing out that the opera would become incomprehensible without them. But the bureaucrats were not to be denied, and the production had to be cancelled. It was a shot across the bows, warning Prokofiev that his halcyon era with the authorities was coming to an end.

That summer at Nikolina Gora Prokofiev wrote no new works of worth. He revised his Fourth Symphony, orchestrated his Sixth and dashed off two blatantly political works: a *Festive Poem*, subtitled 'Thirty Years' (the thirtieth anniversary of the Bolshevik revolution) for symphony orchestra, and *Flourish, O Mighty Land* – a cantata for mixed chorus and orchestra to a text by a state-approved poet, Yevgeny Dolmatovsky. This relatively humdrum work was symptomatic of Prokofiev's sitting tight while working out his next move.

Deciding that the best way to reingratiate himself as a composer of opera was to find an unambiguously Soviet subject, Sergey, with Mira, spent time identifying a suitable contemporary source for operatic treatment. They considered Nikolay Ostrovsky's *How the Steel Was*

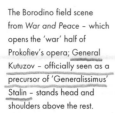

The Borodino field scene from *War and Peace* – which opens the 'war' half of Prokofiev's opera; General Kutuzov – officially seen as a precursor of 'Generalissimus' Stalin – stands head and shoulders above the rest.

Tempered and Fadeyev's *Young Guard*, both ultra-orthodox novels in the officially approved socialist realistic style, but Prokofiev found them too blatantly propagandist for his taste. Officials from the Kirov Theatre then suggested Boris Polevoy's novel *The Story of a Real Man*. Based on a real-life event, the story concerns a Soviet fighter pilot, Alexey Meresyev, who, shot down and wounded behind enemy lines, manages to crawl back to Soviet territory. As a result of frostbite, his legs are amputated, and the rest of the story concerns his struggle, with the loving support of his fiancée Olga, to overcome his sense of futility and self-pity, rejoin his comrades by learning to walk again with false legs, and ultimately fly again.

Although Prokofiev had originally chosen the subject for political convenience, there is reason to believe that he found *The Story of a Real Man* genuinely appealing. Like Alexey, Prokofiev felt he was fighting against great odds – his poor health, and the machinations of shadowy officials – in order to prove himself a worthy Soviet citizen. Ultimately, of course, he simply wanted to be left to compose in peace and get due recognition for his work, but reintegration seemed a necessary first step.

At the same time he wrote two non-political works: one was the Sonata for unison violins, which was ostensibly bright and cheerful (although there is a bitterly sarcastic undertow in the first movement's brusque coda); the second was a more intimate work, the Ninth Piano

Sonata, which he completed by early autumn 1947. It was to be almost four years before its première.

On 11 October 1947, the Sixth Symphony received its first performance at the Great Hall of the Leningrad Philharmonic, conducted by Yevgeny Mravinsky. Prokofiev was well enough to attend, and witnessed the storm of applause that broke at the work's end. News soon spread of his major new symphony, and tickets for its first Moscow performance sold out a fortnight before the concert. The British journalist Alexander Werth recalled meeting the musicologist Grigory Shneyerson on the stair to the concert hall, 'I heard it in Leningrad,' said Shneyerson excitedly. 'It is wonderful; better than the usual Prokofiev. It is philosophic, has the depth of Shostakovich. You'll see!'

Within a week, the air of euphoria had quite evaporated. Stalin had attended the première at the Bolshoi of Vano Muradeli's opera *The Great Friendship*. The opera was intended as a tribute to Stalin's native Georgia, but the Soviet leader was incensed by its unwitting glorification of Commissar Ordzhonikidze, an old political rival, and stormed backstage to confront the composer and the Bolshoi's director, Leontyev. After the visit Leontyev had a heart attack, and days later his death was casually mentioned by the Moscow press.

In the backlash that followed this incident, several musicians were arrested. Others were urged to reconsider their choice of programmes for their performances. Richter, scheduled to play Prokofiev's Ninth Piano Sonata early in January, had to make a last-minute substitution of Schubert with no explanation given. All this was a mere prelude to the conference of musicians Zhdanov called that month. Prokofiev, who knew what was likely to occur, had no intention of going. Oleg visited his father at this time, and saw Prokofiev arguing with Mira's father Abram, who was urging him to attend the meeting. Prokofiev claimed he was suffering from flu and could not possibly go. Finally, despite Prokofiev's vehemence, Abram persuaded him it would be folly not to attend.

No official record remains of what, if anything, Prokofiev said at the meeting. But there have been unofficial accounts of Prokofiev being truculent and refusing to respect Zhdanov and his associates. The most persistent story is that Prokofiev was reprimanded for turning his back on Zhdanov when the latter was addressing the

conference. Another account has Prokofiev arriving late for the first
day's session, wearing a medal awarded by the Royal Philharmonic
Society of London – rather than any of his Stalin prizes. Overcome by
the room's heat, he dozed off in his chair and had to be called to order
by Chkiriatov, a member of the session's board: 'Comrade Prokofiev,
you are disturbing the meeting. If comrade Zhdanov's proposals are
not to your liking, no one is preventing you from leaving!' Prokofiev
accordingly got up and left the room. Whatever did happen, the
authorities did not wish it to be known that so high-profile a figure
had held the sessions in contempt. All mention of Prokofiev's
attendance was struck off the minutes of the meeting, so misleading
a number of his biographers, who claim that illness prevented him
from attending.

It is difficult to say how much difference his attendance and
behaviour on that first day made to his reputation: probably very
little. The agenda was clearly set by Muradeli, whose opera had been
the cause of Zhdanov's 'informal sessions'. Called to account for the
formalism of his opera, Muradeli confessed his crime, but then
blamed (it seems by prearrangement) the 'big four' of Soviet music –
Prokofiev, Shostakovich, Khachaturian and Myaskovsky. Through
their pre-eminence in the Composer's Union, Muradeli claimed, the
'big four' had infected all young Soviet composers with their formalist
doctrine. Zhdanov then provocatively suggested that, despite the
pretensions of the 'big four', many honest composers had
'conscientiously tried' to copy Russian classical music (that is, music
by such nationalist composers as Glinka and Tchaikovsky, though it is
doubtful whether Zhdanov would have known any of their work); as
chairman of the meeting he wanted to protect those good Soviet
composers from the contempt of the highbrows. It was a clear
invitation to all those lesser talents who resented the success of the 'big
four' to have their say. Zhdanov drew a parallel with Shostakovich's
Lady Macbeth of Mtensk by quoting extensively from 'Muddle Instead
of Music'. He also claimed that Muradeli's new opera had attracted
especial interest, because no new Soviet operas had been composed in
the previous ten years. One may imagine Prokofiev's reaction to
having three of his operas effectively wiped from the record!

Zhdanov's comments paved the way for further attacks on the
Soviet Union's four leading composers by their less talented and

successful colleagues, led by Khrennikov, Vladimir Zakharov and Belyi: their ire was aimed particularly at Shostakovich and Prokofiev.

Although Prokofiev had left before the end of the sessions, there was to be no avoiding their consequence. On 10 February 1948 the Central Committee published its official resolution, 'On the Opera *The Great Friendship* by Muradeli'. A full summary was given of Zhdanov's speeches, attacking Muradeli's opera and the 'anti-people formalism' of which it was said to be symptomatic. Significantly, nothing was published of the arguments by those composers brave enough to have protested at Zhdanov's denouncement of the 'big four'.

The resolution was enough to strike terror into the Composers' Union. The 'big four' were sacked from the USC's directorate, and a week of meetings was held from 17 February, presided over by Khrennikov, the USC's new Secretary General. In the course of the meetings Khrennikov sought by all means to sully the reputations of the 'big four', deliberately ignoring their unequivocal achievements and popular successes, and highlighting their 'failures'. Systematically examining Prokofiev's output, he stigmatized the Sixth Symphony, along with the *Ode to the End of the War* and the *Festive Poem*, as worthless, even evil, works. The three great piano sonatas – Six, Seven and Eight – were proscribed; all the ballets Prokofiev had written abroad – *Chout*, *The Prodigal Son*, *On the Dnieper* and *Le Pas d'acier* – were 'evil products of bourgeois tendencies'; also banned were the opera *The Fiery Angel*, and the Third and Fourth Symphonies and the Fifth Piano Concerto. To ensure everyone present at the meetings was quite clear about the cosmopolitan origins of the insidious formalism he was rooting out, Khrennikov made a point of trashing such leading foreign composers as Messiaen, Jolivet, Hindemith, Berg, Menotti and Britten.

Prokofiev avoided these meetings, using ill-health as his excuse. His friend Eisenstein had died just a week before they started. Demoralized and incapable of facing the lambasting he expected from the committee, Prokofiev retreated to Nikolina Gora and sent a letter addressed to Khrennikov, which he requested 'be made public at the assembly should you deem it necessary'. The letter was subsequently widely published by the Soviet authorities as evidence that Zhdanov's attack on Soviet musicians had now been endorsed by one of his leading victims. Several Western commentators, shocked by what appeared to be Prokofiev's humiliating capitulation, have suggested that he was virtually dictated the letter by higher authorities (or possibly by Mira's father Abram), or that he did no more than sign the letter written on his behalf.

Certainly the letter contains politically expedient nods towards the Central Committee's Resolution, describing it as invaluable 'because it has pointed out that the formalist trend is alien to the Soviet people, that it leads to impoverishment and decline in music, and has clearly shown to us the goal which we must strive to achieve as the best way to serve the Soviet people'. But the tone of the main body of the letter is unmistakably that of Prokofiev:

> *I have never neglected the importance of melody in my work, as melody is the fundamental element of all music. Over the years, I have worked at improving the melodic quality of my compositions.*
>
> *To create a melody that is instantly understandable and to ensure that that melody remains original is very difficult for a composer, especially if his listener is not initiated to music. From this point of view, composing more elaborate melodies remains easier.*
>
> *Often the composer, while working at length at a melody, is not aware that in the process he is making it sophisticated, complicated and, in fact, losing its simplicity. For myself, I recognize that I have fallen into this trap. This is why one must remain vigilant, to ensure the melody has a natural simplicity without becoming banal or plagiaristic. But this is easier said than done …*
>
> *I should equally recognize that often I have also fallen into the trap of atonality …; but I must admit with pleasure that for some considerable time already I have established a tonal style, since I have quite understood that one may compare the structure of a work of tonal music with that of a monument built on solid foundations, while the structure of an atonal work rather resembles a sandcastle.*

Prokofiev's letter went on to explain that his use of atonality in certain works had simply been to create spectacular contrasts with the tonal elements. He then attempted to prepare the way for the reception of his new opera *The Story of a Real Man* by repeating, in effect, the paraphrase of Tchaikovsky's letter he had used in 1940 to justify his use of *arioso*, rather than full-blown aria, in order to carry the action forward.

If Prokofiev had hoped by this letter to prove his personal loyalty to the Soviet regime and his credentials as a Soviet composer, the authorities soon made it clear that this was beside the point. Prokofiev's letter, in its emphasis on 'compliance' to the Resolution (albeit on his own terms), did attempt to appease, but the new masters – chief among them Khrennikov – could not forgive Prokofiev his pre-eminence and international prestige. They were determined to break him and remake him on their own terms, and they soon found a way.

Lina, despite Prokofiev's warnings, had recklessly continued to see friends and associates from the West. She had also sought permission for herself and her sons to visit her mother in France, but her requests were denied. By early 1947, Stalin's increasingly xenophobic policies meant that friendship or even acquaintance with any foreigner was a punishable offence. Lina's desire to travel abroad had effectively become a heinous crime. She became aware that she was being followed, but it seems she believed that the simple expedient of shaking her pursuers off her trail was enough. Then on 20 February, when in bed with a cold, Lina was lured from her apartment by a phone call from a friend, asking her to come and collect a package at a prearranged meeting place. It was a trap: while she was waiting for the friend, a black car drew up and a man forced her in. She was driven to the Lubyanka, the notorious NKVD prison on Dzherzhinsky Square. There she was charged with 'spying and betrayal of the Motherland' (a charge based solely on her constant contact with Western diplomats) and sentenced to twenty years in Siberia's labour camps. She was never able to telephone her sons to tell them where she was. It was five years before she saw them – and she was never to see her husband again.

On the day of her arrest, NKVD agents came to the Chkalov Street apartment. Sviatoslav and Oleg watched in terror as they carried out a search. Not only were several papers concerning Prokofiev's life and works confiscated, but also many valuables that took the agents' fancy. Lina's jewellery, Prokofiev's piano, family photographs and mementos, Sviatoslav's postcards with pictures of fallen Soviet leaders – all were taken. The collection of 78s was shoved into sacks and dragged down the stairs, crashing into the walls in such a way that Sviatoslav could only assume they were all broken in transit.

When the all-night search was finally over, Sviatoslav and Oleg set out to find their father at Nikolina Gora. With no buses running due to black ice, they had to walk sixteen kilometres to his *dacha*. The door was opened by Mira who, without a word, fetched Prokofiev, still in his dressing gown. Told of Lina's arrest, he asked his sons to wait while he went in to get dressed. Prokofiev asked about everything, including the search. 'Overawed, he stayed silent,' Sviatoslav later recalled. One can only imagine Prokofiev's terrible sense of guilt and, even worse, his realization of how utterly powerless he was.

The savaging by the Central Committee, Eisenstein's death and Lina's arrest affected Prokofiev's ongoing composition of *The Story of a Real Man*. That his heart was not in the scenes in which Alexey proves his fitness for Soviet life seems clear from the reuse of a jaunty march composed over four years earlier, and the rumba to which Alexey dances (finally convincing the doctors of his fitness to return to the front) is crude and noisy. Only the final duet between Alexey and his fiancée, Olga, rings true: Prokofiev was aware, at least, of his unfailing support from Mira.

The entire score was completed by mid August. On 3 December *The Story of a Real Man* was auditioned at the Kirov. (Prokofiev's doctors allowed him to attend the play-through only on condition that he did not stay for the discussion which followed.) He was dismayed by the standard of the performance, complaining afterwards to Samosud that he did not recognize his own music. It was fortunate that he did not stay to hear what his colleagues had to say. No direct record was made of their discussion, but it is likely that a fair reflection was given by the official statement, prepared by Tikhon Khrennikov, published by the Central Committee on 21 December 1948:

> *The new opera of Prokofiev, produced in Leningrad, shows serious defects from the ideological and artistic point of view. Prokofiev's music is in direct contradiction to the text and dramatic action. The Soviet spectator is outraged to see the pilot, a hero of the war, depicted as a grotesque marionette. Almost the entire opera is constructed on an unmelodious musical declamation and the few songs introduced by the author cannot save the situation …*

This was final, brutal confirmation that Prokofiev had been forgiven nothing and was still to be branded an enemy of the Soviet people. With the exception of the Cello Sonata, performed on 1 March 1950 by

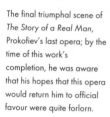

The final triumphal scene of *The Story of a Real Man*, Prokofiev's last opera; by the time of this work's completion, he was aware that his hopes that this opera would return him to official favour were quite forlorn.

two of his most steadfast champions, it was to be almost exactly two years before any new work of his was allowed to be performed in Russia.

After the discussion which followed the audition of *The Story of a Real Man*, Kabalevsky went to see Prokofiev in his room at the Hotel Astoria. Huddled in a blanket, Prokofiev was working on his new ballet *The Stone Flower*. He refused to discuss the opera. Just a day after, the Maly Theatre gave a concert performance of the second part of *War and Peace*. Again Prokofiev attended but did not stay for the discussions which followed. This time the performers passionately defended the work, but their voices had no decision-making power. Once again the officials present condemned the work, so consigning it once again to cold storage. Prokofiev was naturally in despair. Typically he attempted to bury himself in his work, and composed *The Stone Flower*, the plot of which had been suggested to him by Lavrovsky (choreographer of the first Russian production of *Romeo and Juliet*). Lavrovsky and Mira worked together to create the scenario: a stonecutter, Danilo, is betrothed to Katerina, but in his pursuit of artistic perfection – in the form of a flower carved out of malachite (a stone with a distinctive green colour derived from its copper ore) – he is ensnared by the Mistress of the Copper Mountain. It is only Katerina's selfless love for Danilo that saves him, as the Mistress takes pity and releases him to his true bride.

Prokofiev's own devotion to artistic perfection and his experience of Mira's devoted love meant he could empathize with the story.

Interestingly, he insisted on the inclusion of a brutal character, the clerk Severyan, who is portrayed with lugubrious, low-registered and sinister music. Severyan's crass tastes and lifestyle are revealed in his taste for popular gypsy-style music; Prokofiev apparently found this exceedingly hard to write, despite Lavrovsky's own attempts to demonstrate the steps of the dance and even to sing the kind of melody required. Prokofiev began to play a variation on this melody, but abruptly stopped and begged Lavrovsky to have the windows closed: 'I simply cannot allow such sounds to come out of Prokofiev's home.' Most strikingly, Prokofiev has Severyan dance wildly to a Russian folk song called *The Monk*. Prokofiev had in the past used liturgical references to portray Stalin and his aides, writing in a quasi-liturgical style for the sinister *oprichniki*, or for Stalin's speeches in the 'October' Cantata. It is perhaps not too fanciful to see his use of *The Monk* as a private code to suggest that the crass Severyan represents Stalin himself.

By the end of March 1949 he had completed the score. But the officials who came to its audition criticized the ballet for being 'sombre, heavy [and] undanceable'. Prokofiev worked sporadically at the score over the last four years of his life – it would only reach performance a year after his death.

In Prokofiev's last years, Mira, for the sake of his health, had to protect him in almost every way. She answered the telephone and dealt with all his correspondence. The two years following Prokofiev's condemnation by the Union of Soviet Composers were desperate. Despite Mira's support, it is quite possible that Prokofiev would have suffered a total collapse in his creativity but for his friendship with the young Rostropovich. The two first met in late 1947, when the cellist performed the neglected Cello Concerto. Prokofiev had been so struck by his performance that he went backstage to congratulate him afterwards (something he rarely did), and promised to rewrite the concerto specially for him. Rostropovich subsequently seized every opportunity to remind Prokofiev of this promise. Finally, Prokofiev was moved to start a work for Rostropovich when he heard him give the première of Myaskovsky's Second Cello Sonata, less than three weeks before the Central Committee's resolution of February 1948.

Prokofiev's own Cello Sonata was in some ways a kind of limbering up for his retackling of the Concerto. It is a understated, almost old-fashioned-sounding piece: but for the slightly tortuous solo cello

Prokofiev's final ballet, *The Tale of the Stone Flower*: here the stonecutter, Danilo, dances in thrall to the Mistress of the Copper Mountain.

melody which opens the work, and the passing bitter harmonies in the otherwise cheeky second movement's central section, the work could be called quite untroubled, even abstract. Rostropovich and Richter performed the sonata at a closed meeting of the Composers' Union on 6 December 1949. Its amiable tunefulness caused no offence; presumably, too, Prokofiev's enemies thought the work unlikely (by its genre) to be a popular success, and so allowed its public performance early the following year. Prokofiev was able to attend this, although he had been so ill that winter that he had been confined to the Kremlin Hospital for six weeks. Richter, visiting Prokofiev, found him weak, his voice 'as insulted as it could possibly be'. The doctors had refused to let him compose and had even removed all his manuscript paper. Undaunted, Prokofiev seized any paper napkins that came his way and wrote musical ideas on them, hiding them under his pillow.

By the summer Prokofiev was sufficiently recovered to be able to return to Nikolina Gora. There he worked on a large-scale cantata, *On Guard for Peace*, commissioned by the All-Union Radio Committee. The text was by Samuil Marshak, a popular Soviet children's writer who had also written the narrative for *Winter Bonfire*, a charming portrayal of Soviet Pioneers on a day-trip to the country, which Prokofiev composed in late 1949. *On Guard for Peace*, however, was no

simple exercise in writing music for children: its pacifist theme
accorded with Stalin's programme of mobilizing Soviet artists and
intellectuals into a so-called 'struggle for peace'. Just as Soviet artists
and composers had been expected to provide morale-boosting works
to support the 'Great Patriotic War', now they were expected to
provide music for this new cause. The official status of the *On Guard
for Peace* commission meant that the work had to be planned under
the direct supervision of Alexander Fadeyev, leader of the Writers'
Union since Zhdanov's literary purge.

Joint first performances of *Winter Bonfire* and *On Guard for Peace*
were held in the Hall of Columns on 19 December 1950. The occasion
marked a turning point: such was the official success that Prokofiev
was awarded a Stalin Prize, second class, for both works. It was a
rehabilitation of sorts, and other new works by Prokofiev would
subsequently reach performance, although very much in fits and starts.

While *Winter Bonfire* has plenty of unaffected charm, *On Guard for
Peace* is one of the most overly sentimental works in Prokofiev's
output. There are hints of a more rugged style in the opening section
which concerns the ravages of World War II, but the Soviet officials
singled out for praise the mawkish central section concerning Soviet
youth. This section's centrepiece is a lullaby sung by a mother to her
child (or Mother Russia to her people), assuring him that 'Your life,
your house, your motherland are guarded by your friends all over the
country.' The Lullaby was such a hit that it was exported to the West
via the great dramatic mezzo-soprano, Irina Arkhipova, who sang it on
tour. (No one, it seems, noticed that woven into the Lullaby was a
quotation from another mezzo-soprano aria, Saint-Saëns's 'Printemps
qui commence', in which Delila seduces Samson before handing him
over to the Philistines. Prokofiev, with his reputation savaged and his
health poor, felt only too keenly the hypocrisy with which he had been
lured back to his motherland.)

More felicitous was his return to the Cello Concerto. In revising
the work, he clarified its character and form, a number of subsidiary
themes found in the original work were dropped and the main themes
developed. He benefited from Rostropovich's technical advice,
replacing passages less idiomatic for the soloist with more brilliant or
lyrical ones. Thematic contrast was sharpened, most strikingly in the
central movement: here the sardonic scherzo themes stand in sharp

Prokofiev with the young
cellist, Mstislav Rostropovich,
in his Moscow apartment,
c. 1950

relief to the soloist's warmly lyrical second theme; Prokofiev expanded
this theme, providing initially gentle string tremulandos as
accompaniment (rather than the busy scherzando counterpoint of the
original), so making its anguished distortion at the movement's end
the more horrifying. Prokofiev also heightened the effect of another
theme – a thin, chromatically tortured wail from the woodwind – by
sharpening its rhythmic attack, reinforcing its orchestration with
trumpets and placing this now baleful howl immediately after the
lyrical theme's first appearance.

Rostropovich and Richter had to present the new version of the
concerto to the Composers' Union prior to arranging its
performance, Richter playing the orchestral part at the piano. The
play-through provoked what Rostropovich subsequently described as
a 'great scandal': Zakharov, who had been a leading voice against
Prokofiev early in 1948, was outraged as he realized that a subsidiary
theme in the finale was a 'distortion' of one of his popular themes.
(When Rostropovich told Prokofiev about this, the composer
replaced it with an innocuous waltz but told Rostropovich to replace
the original theme when the scandal had simmered down.
Significantly, when Prokofiev came to write the finale of his Cello
Concertino he wrote an even more grotesque arrangement of
Zakharov's theme into it.) Despite the vociferous disapproval
expressed by Zakharov and others, the Union allowed Rostropovich
and Richter to go ahead and arrange a performance. Rostropovich has
since suggested that the Union was afraid to stop the performance,
since the fame of the two young performers involved could stir up a
national scandal if they were thwarted. Besides, Prokofiev's opponents
believed that Prokofiev was in a no-win situation: either the work

would be a success, in which case the authorities could take credit for 'instructing' Prokofiev (just as they had taken credit for the success of Shostakovich's Fifth Symphony in 1937), or it would flop, giving them further licence to attack him.

Even so, Rostropovich and Richter could only arrange the performance by employing the Moscow Youth Orchestra, with Richter conducting for the only time in his career. The première took place on 18 February 1952: Prokofiev attended, but could only acknowledge the applause by standing up from his seat, being too weak to climb onto the platform. He was persuaded after the performance to make further revisions to the work – mainly, it seems, to the orchestral writing: the result, entitled Symphony-Concerto, would not be heard until 9 December 1954, in Copenhagen. (It was not to be heard in Moscow until over two years after that.)

Prokofiev spent his final years close to poverty – described by Rostropovich as being 'near to hunger'. The young cellist was horrified that a leading Soviet composer should be so shabbily neglected, and on one occasion burst into Khrennikov's office and shamed him into giving Prokofiev a grant of 5,000 rubles. Even so, Prokofiev had to continue wooing official approval before he could get any substantial works performed: hence the expert but drab orchestral work *The Meeting of the Volga and the Don*, written in 1951 to celebrate the completion of a major canal built at Stalin's instigation that linked the two rivers.

The last work Prokofiev heard performed before his death was his Seventh Symphony, written at the behest of the Children's Radio Division. Although a far cry from the drama of the Symphony-Concerto, let alone the preceding Sixth Symphony, it cannot be dismissed as insipid. The Seventh appears to be a typically soulful and lyrical Russian symphony, such as Kalinnikov might have written. But beneath the placid surface lie darker emotions: in the first movement a noble melody which would have been at home in *On Guard for Peace* is followed by a ticking glockenspiel tune which plays against jarring, sinister background melodies; the second movement's sudden high-pitch notes and numbed central section undermine the apparently carefree mood created by the sparkling orchestration. The poignant third movement is a heartbroken recollection of a more civilized past: variations on a yearning theme from Prokofiev's *Eugene Onegin*

Prokofiev with his sons Oleg and Sviatoslav, c. 1950; Prokofiev saw far more of them after the arrest of his wife, Lina, in 1948.

incidental music give way to a mournful cor anglais solo that might have been composed by Rimsky-Korsakov. The effect is like a nostalgic flick through an album of bygone styles, all beyond any hope of revival.

The bustling finale seems ready for an upbeat end when the first movement's noble melody reappears. Almost inevitably, the ticking glockenspiel theme also returns, but chromatically twisted, creating a sense of hopeless misery. The symphony was originally to have wound down on this desolate theme, but Prokofiev was advised – by Samosud, according to Rostropovich – to write a much more upbeat end in order to win a first rather than a third class Stalin Prize. Prokofiev told Rostropovich he did so in order to gain the much needed 100,000 rubles: 'But Slava, you will live much longer than I, and you must take care that this new ending never exists after me.'

With his worsening illness, Prokofiev and Mira had to spend more time in Moscow: Nikolina Gora was too cold in winter for Prokofiev, and he had to be within easy reach of his doctors. Aware that he had not long to live, to the very end he tried to forestall the inevitable by planning and working on future compositions. Early in 1953, after suffering a long bout of influenza, he suddenly asked Mira to write down a list of projected compositions. She tried to protest, telling him to save his energy, but eventually humoured him and took down from his dictation the following list:

Op. 132 Concertino for violincello and orchestra, in three movements.
Op. 133 Concerto No. 6 for two pianos and string orchestra, in three
    movements.
Op. 134 Sonata for violincello solo, in four movements.
Op. 135 Fifth Sonata for piano, new version, in three movements.
Op. 136 Second Symphony, new version, in three movements.
Op. 137 Tenth Sonata for piano in E flat.
Op. 138 Eleventh Sonata for piano.

Only the revision of the Fifth Sonata was to be completed. To Mira's distress, she found him each morning more depressed: when she asked if he felt pain anywhere, he told her, 'My soul hurts.' Mira began to think that a break in their *dacha* in Nikolina Gora would cheer Prokofiev up. On the evening of 5 March, she was in the sitting room giving instructions to a woman to prepare the *dacha* for their visit when Prokofiev suddenly appeared, staggering, in the doorway. Mira jumped up and supported him back to his room. As she helped him onto a divan, Prokofiev apologized for having startled her. The doctor was called, but within an hour Prokofiev had lost consciousness.

Prokofiev died at around 9 o'clock that evening. By a terrible irony, his death preceded that of Stalin's by just fifty minutes – both died of a brain haemorrhage. The dictator's death so overshadowed Prokofiev's that it was days before the Soviet people received official notification of the composer's death. His funeral was attended by just over forty of his surviving friends and colleagues, who battled through police barriers and a dreary cold, winter's day to attend the service held at the Composer's Union. There were no flowers – they had all been taken for Stalin's funeral. Sviatoslav Richter laid a single pine branch on the coffin. David Oistrakh, who was also present, played two movements from Prokofiev's First Violin Sonata – the first, with its 'wind in a graveyard' scale passages, and the mournful third movement, its running semiquavers seeming to presage the melting snow with its promise of spring.

Epilogue

After Stalin's death Sviatoslav and Oleg, who heard that some people incarcerated for crimes against the state were being released, did all they could to secure their mother's freedom. On her release in 1957, Lina spent several years struggling to gain her rights as Prokofiev's widow. But Mira's selfless care of Prokofiev and her subsequent promotion of his life and work (she helped to establish the Prokofiev Music School, and organized his manuscripts into an archive for scholars) was so admired by Prokofiev's colleagues that Shostakovich is said to have been horrified at Lina's desperate attempts to reclaim her rights and discredit Mira. (Mira died of a heart attack in 1968.) Lina's existence was further hampered by Khrennikov, who, after realizing that foreign royalties were still accruing on Prokofiev's work, started posing as her personal friend, and, where possible, arranging for royalties to be paid care of himself. Lina was finally permitted to return to the West in 1972, following Oleg (who had married the English art historian Camilla Gray and settled in London in 1971). She died in London on 3 January 1989, bequeathing a sum of money and several personal documents of her husband's in order to set up the Prokofiev Foundation. Through this the Prokofiev Archive in London's Goldsmith's College has been established; it houses an invaluable collection of Prokofiev's correspondence between 1922 and 1936.

Fifty years after his death, the dust has yet to settle regarding Prokofiev's reputation. The fraught political circumstances under which he worked for the last seventeen years of his life certainly played a part in obscuring his achievement. When the British journal *Tempo* produced a special 'Prokofieff Number' in 1949 (the year after Prokofiev had been publicly attacked by Zhdanov and Khrennikov), the published worklist had several striking omissions, reflecting Soviet officialdom's reluctance to publicize the recently disgraced composer: these included the Ninth Piano Sonata, the Sixth Symphony, the Sonata for unison violins and the scores for *Ivan the Terrible*. Add to these *War and Peace* and the Symphony-Concerto, and one has an almost complete list of those of Prokofiev's major works which even today are yet to make a definite impression on the concert-going public outside Russia.

Only works given the widest exposure – not simply performed several times – tend to win a place in the regular repertoire. The Fifth Symphony was exported as a triumphant example of Soviet symphonism, at the height of the East–West alliance against Nazi Germany, and so was seized upon by dozens of leading conductors who then, perhaps most crucially, went on to commit their interpretations to disc (more than 30 are available at the time of writing). By contrast, the Sixth Symphony barely squeaked into the West following its condemnation by Zhdanov, and has since been recorded scarcely more than half-a-dozen times.

It is unfortunate that Prokofiev's prolific output, coupled with the difficulties until recently of obtaining scores of several of his major Soviet works, has hampered attempts by several Western writers and scholars to give a balanced overview and therefore assessment of Prokofiev's standing as a composer. This situation was compounded rather than clarified by the first full-length biography, written by the Soviet musicologist Israel Nestyev. Though Nestyev initially started his biography (in the 1940s) with his subject's cooperation, he was driven by the political events of 1948 to join the chorus of condemnation against Prokofiev's 'formalist crimes', a stance which inevitably skewed his assessment of Prokofiev's music (in favour of accessible lyricism, while branding expressionistic passages in the Sixth Symphony as 'artificial' and 'contrived'). Prokofiev has been 'marketed' to post-war audiences largely through journalists and writers of programme notes who have taken their lead from this necessarily lopsided account of Prokofiev's career.

Prokofiev's reputation suffered further from the kind of evolutionary view of musical history fashionable in the 1960s, a time when to be earth-shakingly 'revolutionary' was almost more important than to be truly creative. Direct comparisons were made with Stravinsky, who appeared the more important composer, not least for his revolutionary *The Rite of Spring*, recognizably a masterpiece by any standard; its innovative polyrhythms, aggressively percussive harmonies and tremendous visceral impact cruelly underlined the crudities of Prokofiev's atypical *Scythian Suite*. Prokofiev's reputation among early twentieth-century critics (particularly in Tsarist Russia) as a shocking *enfant terrible* in fact backfired on him; despite his use of 'audacious' harmonies, he was demonstrably more conventional than Stravinsky, as he worked within a well-defined musical syntax. Showing Prokofiev up as a 'sham modernist' only reinforced prejudices about his supposed superficiality.

Over the last twenty years, however, there has been a remarkable sea-change in contemporary music, so affecting our perceptions of musical history. The apparently unassailable bastion of twelve-tone compositional method – the central tenet of post-Webernian modernism promoted in the post-war West by Stockhausen, Boulez and, in a startling volte-face, Stravinsky – has been abandoned and replaced by an extraordinary plurality of methods and styles. The idea of a coherent avant-garde and the credibility of the idea of 'musical progress' has simply collapsed. In the wake of this, the reputations of 'non-progressive' composers, or those who did not clearly belong to any particular school or trend, are being reassessed. Prokofiev is one of many composers to benefit from this process, and his gifts beyond an ability to create dozens of distinctive melodies are now more readily recognized. Most significantly, it is clear from taking a broader perspective that arguing the relative merits of Prokofiev's and Stravinsky's work through direct comparison is specious: though they were both Russians who worked briefly together under Diaghilev, from World War I onwards they were working along quite different, though equally valid, paths.

Prokofiev was above all a dramatic, or 'expressive', composer, and as such was profoundly Russian (while Stravinsky, by the 1940s, was busily trying to deny that music could express anything at all, and became increasingly virulent in his 'jealous' hatred, as his friend Robert Craft described it, of his homeland). Until recently the very concept that music could be 'expressive' or even 'descriptive' would have been considered improper in musicological circles unless dressed up as 'extra-musical meanings'. Today, though, there is growing recognition among musicians and musicologists that this expressive tradition not only played a vital part in such 'abstract' works as Shostakovich's symphonies, but can be traced back to Tchaikovsky's famous cycle. In this light, the Earl of Harewood's description of Prokofiev's opera *War and Peace* as being in the grand epic tradition of Mussorgsky's *Boris Godunov* or Borodin's *Prince Igor* no longer appears to be special pleading but seems a sensible affirmation of the Russian tradition within which he worked.

It is true that Prokofiev, a rebellious student who outraged his professors with his radical harmonies, did not initially regard himself as belonging to a 'Russian' school. But while he reacted against the academic 'nationalist' style represented by Rimsky-Korsakov and Glazunov, he fully embraced the innovations of that greatest of Russian nationalists, Mussorgsky, whose declamatory approach to word-setting profoundly influenced all Prokofiev's operas from *The Gambler* onwards and virtually all the songs he set until his return to the Soviet Union.

Prokofiev also paid increasingly open tribute to Tchaikovsky, not only playing his music but, with his return to Russia, gently parodying him in his Pushkin-inspired works, his ballet *Cinderella*, and in *War and Peace*. Almost certainly it was the example of Tchaikovsky's symphonies that led to Prokofiev's greatest achievement, not only to forge a compositional style that reconciled Tchaikovsky's refined, expressive melody with Mussorgsky's radical approach to harmony and word-setting, but to make this flexible enough to attempt a truly symphonic approach that reached its culmination in his Sixth Symphony.

Diaghilev, in his time one of the great arbiters of what was *le dernier mot* in music and art, once reproached Prokofiev for flirting with too many styles of music. Yet arguably it was this very diversity, and the prolonged struggle through the 1920s to find his voice, that ultimately enriched Prokofiev's language and enabled him to write the handful of truly great pieces – the last few piano sonatas, his First Violin Sonata and the Sixth Symphony – which continue to speak powerfully and profoundly today.

Classified List of Works

Even discounting those works Prokofiev did not manage to complete by the end of his life, his list of opus numbers runs to over 130; at least another hundred works could be added if one were to include all his juvenilia and those works he composed while a student at the St Petersburg Conservatory. This number seems less daunting when one realizes that at least a quarter of Prokofiev's output consists of revisions of earlier works, or even simply arrangements of piano works for orchestra or vice versa. In the following list cross-references indicate where one work is derived from another (such as a symphonic suite arising from a 'parent' ballet); inter-relationships between two works are also explained within a single entry. Details of a work's first performance (fp) are given where known.

Stage Works

Opera

The Giant (Velikan), opera in one act, libretto by Sergey Prokofiev (1900). fp (private family performance) summer 1900

Desert Islands (Na pustïnnïkh ostrovakh), opera, libretto by Sergey Prokofiev (1900–02). Incomplete

A Feast in Time of Plague (Pir vo vremya chumï), opera in one act based on Alexander Pushkin's verse drama (1903, revised 1908–9)

Undine, opera in four acts, libretto by M. Kilstett after a narrative poem by De La Motte Fouqué (1904–7)

Maddalena, Op. 13, opera in one act, libretto by Magda Lieven and Sergey Prokofiev from Lieven's play (1911–13), orchestration completed by E. Downes. fp (broadcast) London, 25 March 1979

The Gambler (Igrok), Op. 24, opera in four acts, libretto by Sergey Prokofiev from a story by Fyodor Dostoyevsky (1915–17; revised 1927–8). fp Brussels, 29 April 1929 (see also Orchestral)

The Love for Three Oranges (Lyubov k tryom apelsinam), Op. 33, opera in four acts, libretto by Sergey Prokofiev after Vsevolod Meyerhold's adaptation of a play by Carlo Gozzi (1919). fp Chicago, 30 December 1921. March and Scherzo arranged for piano (see also Orchestral)

The Fiery Angel (Ognennïy angel), Op. 37, opera in five acts, libretto by Sergey Prokofiev from the novel by Valery Bryusov (1919–23, revised 1926–7). fp (excerpts only) Paris, 14 June 1928; (complete) Paris, 25 November 1954

Semyon Kotko, Op. 81, opera in five acts, libretto by Sergey Prokofiev and Valentin Katayev from Katayev's novel *I Am a Son of the Working People* (1939). fp Moscow, 23 June 1940 (see also Orchestral)

Betrothal in a Monastery (Obrucheniye v monastïre, The Duenna), Op. 86, opera in four acts, libretto by Sergey Prokofiev, with verses by Mira Mendelson-Prokofieva, from the play *The Duenna* by Richard Brinsley Sheridan (1940–1). fp Leningrad, 3 November 1946 (see also Orchestral)

War and Peace (Voyna i mir), Op. 91, opera in five acts, libretto by Sergey Prokofiev and Mira Mendelson-Prokofieva, from the novel by Leo Tolstoy (1941–3, revised 1946–52). fp (first part only) Moscow, 16 October 1944; fp (revised version, first and second parts) Moscow, 8 November 1957 (see also Orchestral, and Piano)

Khan Buzay, opera, libretto by Sergey Prokofiev and Mira Mendelson-Prokofieva (1942–). Incomplete

The Story of a Real Man (Provest' o nastoyashchem cheloveke), Op. 117, opera in four acts, libretto by Sergey Prokofiev and Mira Mendelson-Prokofieva from the novel by Boris Polevoy (1947–8). fp (closed performance) Leningrad, 3 December 1948; (staged) Moscow, 8 October 1960

Distant Seas (Dalyokiye morya) planned as Op. 118, opera, libretto by Sergey Prokofiev after play by V. A. Dïkhovichnï (1948–). Incomplete

Ballet

Ala i Lolli, Op. 20, scenario by Sergey Gorodetsky and Sergey Prokofiev (1914–15). Incomplete (see also Orchestral)

Chout, (Skazka pro shuta, The Buffoon), Op. 21, scenario by Sergey Prokofiev from folk tales by Alexander Afanasiev (1915, revised 1920). fp Paris, 17 May 1921 (see also Orchestral)

Trapetsiya (Trapeze), Op. 39, scenario by Boris Romanov (1924). fp Berlin, autumn 1925 (see also Quintet in Chamber/Instrumental)

Le Pas d'acier (Stal'noy skok, The Steel Step), Op. 41, scenario by Georgy Yakulov and Sergey Prokofiev (1925–6). fp Paris, 7 June 1927 (see also Orchestral)

The Prodigal Son (L'enfant prodigue), Op 46, scenario by Boris Kochno (1928–9). fp Paris, 21 May 1929 (see also Orchestral)

On the Dnieper (Na Dnepre, Sur le Borysthène), Op. 51, ballet, scenario by Sergey Prokofiev and Serge Lifar (1930). fp Paris, 16 December 1932 (see also Orchestral)

Romeo and Juliet, Op. 64, ballet, scenario by Sergey Radlov, Adrian Piotrovsky, Leonid Lavrovsky and Sergey Prokofiev after play by William Shakespeare (1935–6). fp Brno, 30 December 1938 (see also Orchestral and Piano)

Cinderella (Zolushka), Op. 87, ballet, scenario by Nikolay Volkov after the folk-tale (Charles Perrault's edition) (1940–44). fp Moscow, 21 November 1945 (see also Orchestral, Chamber/Instrumental and Piano)

The Stone Flower (Skaz o kammenom tsvetke), Op. 118, ballet, scenario by Leonid Lavrovsky and Mira Mendelson-Prokofieva after Pavel Bazhov's *The Malachite Box* (1948–53). fp Moscow, 12 February 1954 (see also Orchestral)

Incidental Music for Theatre and Film

Lieutenant Kizhe (Poruchik Kizhe), music for film based on a story by Yury Tynianov, directed by Alexander Faintsimmer (1933) (see also Orchestral and Vocal)

Egyptian Nights (Evipetskiye nochi), incidental music for drama based on plays by Alexander Pushkin, William Shakespeare and George Bernard Shaw (1934). fp Moscow, 14 December 1934 (see also Orchestral)

The Queen of Spades (Pikovaya dama), Op. 70, music for (uncompleted) film based on the novella by Alexander Pushkin, directed by Mikhail Romm (1936)

Boris Godunov, Op. 70b, incidental music for play by Alexander Pushkin (1936). fp Moscow, April 1957

Eugene Onegin (Evgeny Onegin), Op. 71, incidental music for Alexander Tairov's dramatization of Alexander Pushkin's verse-novel (1936). fp London, 1 April 1980

Hamlet, Op. 77, incidental music for play by William Shakespeare (1937–8). fp Leningrad, 15 May 1938 (see also Piano)

Alexander Nevsky, music for film directed by Sergey Eisenstein (1938). fp 1 December 1938 (see also Choral)

Lermontov, music for film directed by Alexander Gendelstein (1941–2) (see also Orchestral and Piano)

Tonya, music for film directed by Abram Room (1942)

Kotovsky, music for film directed by Alexander Faintsimmer (1942)

Partisans in the Ukrainian Steppes (Partizanï v stepyakh ukrainï), music for film directed by Igor Savchenko (1942)

Ivan the Terrible (Ivan Groznïy), Op. 116, music for two-part film directed by Eisenstein (1942–6). fp (Part 1) 30 December 1944; (Part 2) September 1958

Orchestral

Symphony in G (juvenile work) (1902)

Symphony 'No. 2' in E minor (1908). fp St Petersburg, 23 February 1909. Withdrawn (see also Piano)

Sinfonietta in A major, Op. 5 (1909, revised 1914–15). fp Petrograd, 24 October 1915. Further revised version, Op. 48 (1929). fp Moscow, 18 November 1930

Dreams (Snï), Op. 6, symphonic poem for orchestra (1910). fp St Petersburg, 22 November 1910

Autumnal Sketch (Osenneye), Op. 8, sketch for orchestra (1910, revised 1915 and 1934). fp Moscow, 19 July 1911; (1915 version) Petrograd, 8 October 1916

Piano Concerto No. 1 in D flat major, Op. 10 (1911–12). fp Moscow, 25 July 1912

Piano Concerto No. 2 in G minor, Op. 16 (1912–13, revised 1923). fp Pavlovsk, 23 August 1913; (revised version) Paris, 8 May 1924

Violin Concerto No. 1 in D major, Op. 19 (1915–17). fp Paris, 18 October 1923

Scythian Suite, Op. 20, suite from the ballet *Ala i Lolli* (1914–15). fp Petrograd, 3 January 1916

Symphony No. 1, 'Classical', in D major, Op. 25 (1916–17). fp Petrograd, 21 April 1918

Piano Concerto No. 3 in C major, Op. 26 (1917–21). fp Chicago, 16 December 1921

The Love for Three Oranges, Op. 33a, symphonic suite (1919, revised 1924). fp (revised version) Paris, 29 November 1925

Symphony No. 2 in D minor, Op. 40 (1924–5). fp Paris, 6 June 1925

The Buffoon, Op. 21b, symphonic suite from *Chout* (1920). fp Brussels, 15 January 1924

Le Pas d'acier, Op. 41a, symphonic suite (1926). fp Moscow, 27 May 1928

American Overture, Op. 42a, for chamber orchestra (1926). fp Moscow, 7 February 1927. Arrangement for full orchestra, Op. 42b (1928). fp Paris, 18 December 1930

Symphony No. 3 in C minor, Op. 44 (1928). fp Paris, 17 May 1929

The Prodigal Son, Op. 46a, symphonic suite (1929). fp Paris, 7 March 1931

Divertimento, Op. 43 (1925–9). fp Paris, 22 December 1929. Arranged for piano (1938)

Symphony No. 4 in C major, Op. 47 (1929–30). fp Boston, 14 November 1930. Revised version, Op. 112 (1947). fp (broadcast) London, 11 March 1950

Four Portraits, Op. 49, symphonic suite from the opera *The Gambler* (1931). fp Paris, 12 March 1932

Andante for string orchestra, Op. 50b, from String Quartet in B minor (1930)

Piano Concerto No. 4 in B flat major, Op. 53, for left hand (1931). fp West Berlin, 5 September 1956

Piano Concerto No. 5 in G major, Op. 55 (1932). fp Berlin, 31 October 1932

Symphonic Song (Chant symphonique), Op. 57 (1933). fp Moscow, 14 April 1934

On the Dnieper, Op. 51a, symphonic suite (1933). fp Paris, 1934

Cello Concerto No. 1 in E minor, Op. 58 (1933–8). fp Moscow, 26 November 1938

Overture on Hebrew Themes, Op. 34b, arrangement for symphony orchestra of Op. 34 for clarinet, piano and string quartet (1934). fp Moscow, 30 November 1934

Andante, Op. 29b, arrangement of second movement of Piano Sonata No. 4 (1934). fp Leningrad, 13 February 1958

Lieutenant Kizhe, Op. 60, suite from film score (1934). fp (broadcast) Moscow, 21 December 1934

Egyptian Nights, Op. 61, symphonic suite from the incidental music to the play (1934). fp (broadcast) Moscow, 21 December 1934; (concert) Moscow, 22 December 1934

Violin Concerto No. 2 in G minor, Op. 63 (1935). fp Madrid, 1 December 1935

Romeo and Juliet, Op. 64a, suite no. 1 (1936). fp Moscow, 24 November 1936

Romeo and Juliet, Op. 64b, suite no. 2 (1936). fp Leningrad, 15 April 1937

Peter and the Wolf (Petya i volk), Op. 67, musical tale for children with narrator and orchestra (1936). fp Moscow, 2 May 1936

Four marches for military band, Op. 69 (1935–7). fp (first march only) 1937

Russian Overture, Op. 72, with quadruple woodwind (1936). fp Moscow, 29 October 1936. Revised with triple woodwind (1937)

Summer Day (Letniy den), Op. 65b, children's suite for small orchestra (1941). fp (broadcast) Moscow, 1946

Semyon Kotko, Op. 81a, symphonic suite (1941). fp Moscow, 27 December 1943

Symphonic March in B flat major, Op. 88 (1941)

March in A flat major, Op. 89b, for military band, after No. 2 of Seven Mass Songs, Op. 89 (1941)

The Year 1941 (1941–y god), Op. 90, suite for orchestra (1941). fp Sverdlovsk, 21 January 1943

March in B flat major, Op. 99, for military band (1943–4). fp (broadcast) Moscow, 30 April 1944

Symphony No. 5 in B flat major, Op. 100 (1944). fp Moscow, 13 January 1945

Romeo and Juliet, Op. 101, suite no. 3 (1946). fp Moscow, 8 March 1946

Ode to the End of the War, Op. 105, for eight harps, four pianos and orchestra of woodwind, percussion and double basses (1945). fp Moscow, 12 November 1945

Cinderella, Op. 107, suite no. 1 (1946). fp Moscow, 12 November 1946

Cinderella, Op. 108, suite no. 2 (1946)

Cinderella, Op. 109, suite no. 3 (1946). fp (broadcast) Moscow, 3 September 1947

Waltz Suite, Op. 110, from *War and Peace, Cinderella* and *Lermontov* (1946). fp Moscow, 13 May 1947

Symphony No. 6 in E flat minor, Op. 111 (1945–7). fp Leningrad, 11 October 1947

Thirty Years (Tridtsat' let), Op. 113, festive poem (1947). fp Moscow, 3 October 1947

Two Pushkin Waltzes, Op. 120 (1949). fp (broadcast) Moscow, 1952

Summer Night (Letnyaya noch), Op. 123, suite for orchestra from the opera *Betrothal in a Monastery* (1950)

Symphony-Concerto, Op. 125, for cello and orchestra, a reworking of Cello Concerto No. 1, and briefly known as Cello Concerto No. 2 (1950–2). fp Moscow, 18 February 1952. Further revised and given its present title (1952). fp Copenhagen, 9 December 1954

Wedding Suite, Op. 126, from *The Stone Flower* (1951). fp Moscow, 12 December 1951

Gypsy Fantasy, Op. 127, from *The Stone Flower* (1951). fp Moscow, 18 November 1951

Ural Rhapsody, Op. 128, from *The Stone Flower* (1951)

Mistress of the Copper Mountain, Op. 129, from *The Stone Flower.* Never realized

The Meeting of the Volga and the Don (Vstrecha Volgi s Donom), Op. 130, festive poem for orchestra (1951). fp (broadcast) Moscow, 22 February 1952

Symphony No. 7 in C sharp minor, Op. 131 (1951–2). fp Moscow, 11 October 1952

Cello Concertino in G minor, Op. 132 (1952). Completed by Rostropovich and Kabalevsky. fp (cello and piano) Moscow, 29 December 1956; fp (cello with orchestra) Moscow, 18 March 1960

Piano Concerto No. 6 for two pianos and strings (1952). Incomplete

Choral

Two Choral Songs, Op. 7, *The White Swan* and *The Wave,* for women's voices and orchestra, texts by Konstantin Balmont (1909–10). fp (*White Swan* only) St Petersburg, February 1910

Seven, They Are Seven (Semero ikh), Op. 30, for tenor, chorus and orchestra, text by Konstantin Balmont (1917–18, revised 1933). fp Paris, 29 May 1924

Cantata for the Twentieth Anniversary of October ('October' Cantata), Op. 74, for symphonic orchestra, military band, accordion band and two choruses, texts by Marx, Lenin and Stalin (1936–7). fp (omitting movements setting Stalin texts) Moscow, 5 April 1966

Songs of Our Days (Pesni nashikh dney), Op. 76, suite for soloists, mixed chorus and orchestra (1937). fp Moscow, 5 January 1938

Alexander Nevsky, Op. 78, cantata for mezzo-soprano, mixed chorus and orchestra, text by Sergey Prokofiev and V. Lugovskoy (1939). fp Moscow, 17 May 1939

Zdravitsa ('Hail to Stalin'), Op. 85, cantata for mixed chorus and orchestra (1939). fp Moscow, 21 December 1939

Ballad of an Unknown Boy (Ballada o malchike, ostavshemsya neizvestnïm), Op. 9, cantata for soprano, tenor, chorus and orchestra, text by Pavel Antokolsky (1942–3). fp Moscow, 21 February 1944

Sketches for National Anthem of the Soviet Union, texts by S. V. Mikhalkov and El-Registan, and National Anthem of the RSFSR, text by S. P. Shchipanchev, Op. 98 (1943–6)

Flourish, O Mighty Land (Rastsvetay, moguchiy kray), Op. 114, cantata for the thirtieth anniversary of the Great October Socialist Revolution, for mixed chorus and orchestra, text by Evgeny Dolmatovsky (1947). fp Moscow, 12 November 1947

Soldiers' Marching Song, Op. 121, text by Vladimir Lugovskoy (1950)

Winter Bonfire (Zimniy koster), Op. 122, suite for narrators, boys' chorus and orchestra, text by Samuil Marshak (1949–50). fp Moscow, 19 December 1950

On Guard for Peace (Na strazhe mira), Op. 124, oratorio for mezzo-soprano, boy alto, narrators, mixed chorus, boys' chorus and orchestra, text by Samuil Marshak (1950). fp Moscow, 19 December 1950

Vocal

Four Songs, texts by Lermontov, Prokofiev, Pushkin and traditional (1903)

Ancient, Gnarled Oaks (Mastitïye, vetvistïye, dubï), text by A. Maykov (1906–7)

Two Poems for voice and piano, Op. 9: *There Are Other Planets*, text by Konstantin Balmont; *La Barque démarrée*, text by A. Apukhtin (1910–11). fp (Balmont text only) St Petersburg, 17 March 1914

The Ugly Duckling (Gadkiy utenok), Op. 18, text by Hans Christian Andersen, adapted by Nina Meshcherskaya, later orchestrated by Sergey Prokofiev (1914). fp Petrograd, 17 January 1915

Five Poems, Op. 23, texts by Balmont, Gorynasky, Gippius, Verin and Agnivtsev (1915). fp (selection only) Petrograd, 27 November 1916

Five Songs to Poems by Anna Akhmatova, Op. 27 (1916). fp Moscow, 5 February 1917

Five Songs without Words, Op. 35, for voice and piano (1920). fp New York, 27 March 1921. No. 2 also exists in a version for voice and orchestra (1920?) (see also Cinq Mélodies in Chamber)

Five Songs to Poems by Konstantin Balmont, Op. 36 (1921). fp Milan, May 1922

Two Songs from *Lieutenant Kizhe*: 1. *The Little Grey Dove is Cooing*; 2. *Troika*, Op. 60b (1934)

Six Mass Songs, Op. 66: 1. *Partisan Zheleznyak*; 2. *Anyutka*; 3. *The Fatherland Is Growing*; 4. *Through Snow and Fog*; 5. *Beyond the Hill*; 6. *Song of Voroshilov* (1935)

Three Children's Songs, Op. 68: 1. *Chatterbox*; 2. *Sweet Song*; 3. *The Little Pigs* (1936–9). fp (*Chatterbox* only) Moscow, 5 May 1936

Three Romances, Op. 73, words by Alexander Pushkin (1936). fp (broadcast) Moscow, 20 April 1937

Seven Mass Songs for voice and piano, Op. 79 (1939)

Seven Mass Songs for voice and piano, Op. 89 (1941–2). fp (Nos. 3 and 4 only) Nalchik, November 1941

Pro soma ('Broad and Deep the River Flows'), text by Mikhalkov. Incomplete

Chamber/Instrumental

Humoresque Scherzo, Op. 12b, for four bassoons, arrangement of Ten Pieces, Op. 12, No. 9 (1915). fp London, 2 September 1916

Ballade, Op. 15, for cello and piano (1912). fp Moscow, 23 January 1914

Overture on Hebrew Themes, Op. 34, for clarinet, piano and string quartet (1919). fp New York, 26 January 1920 (see also Orchestral)

Cinq Mélodies for violin and piano, Op. 35b, arrangement of Op. 35 (1925)

Quintet in G minor, Op. 39, for oboe, clarinet, violin, viola and double bass, incorporates music from ballet *Trapeze* (1924). fp Moscow, 6 March 1927

String Quartet No. 1 in B minor, Op. 50 (1930). fp Washington, 25 April 1931

Sonata for two violins in C major, Op. 56 (1932). fp Moscow, 27 November 1932

Violin Sonata No. 1 in F minor, Op. 80 (1938–46). fp Moscow, 23 October 1946

String Quartet No. 2 in F major ('Karbardinian' Quartet), Op. 92 (1941). fp Moscow, 5 September 1942

Flute Sonata in D major, Op. 94 (1943). fp Moscow, 7 December 1943. Arranged as Violin Sonata No. 2, Op. 94b (1943–4). fp Moscow, 17 June 1944

Adagio from *Cinderella* for cello and piano, Op. 97b (1944). fp (broadcast) Moscow, 19 April 1944

Sonata for unison violins/solo violin in D major, Op. 115 (1947). fp Moscow, 10 March 1960

Cello Sonata in C major, Op. 119 (1949). fp Moscow, 1 March 1950

Sonata for unaccompanied cello in C sharp minor, Op. 134. Unfinished. fp (fugue only) London, 1 December 1991

Piano

Juvenilia (1896–1909): includes *Indian Galop* in F major (1896), March in C major (1896), Waltz in C major (1896), March in C major for four hands (1897), Polka in G major (1899), Piece with zither (1900), Bagatelle No. 1 for four hands (c. 1901)

Sixty 'Songs' (or 'Ditties') – five series of piano pieces (1902–6): includes No. 32, Vivo in G minor, written for father's fiftieth birthday; No. 39, Allegretto in A minor; No. 47, Minuet in F minor; No. 50, Scherzo; No. 53, Waltz in G minor; No. 54, March in F minor, later developed into March, Op. 12; No. 60, étude-Scherzo in C major

Sonata in B flat (1903–4)

Song without Words in D flat (1907)

Sonata 'No. 2' in F minor (1907). Later reworked as Piano Sonata No. 1, Op. 1

Sonata 'No. 3' in A minor (1907). Later reworked as Piano Sonata No. 3, Op. 28

Sonata 'No. 4' (1907?). Lost

Sonata 'No. 5' (1908). Later reworked as Piano Sonata No. 4, Op. 29

Sonata 'No. 6' (1908–9?). Lost

Sonata No. 1, Op. 1 (1909), revision of first movement of 1907 Sonata 'No. 2'. fp Moscow, 21 February 1910

Four Études, Op. 2 (1909). fp (three only) Moscow, 21 February 1910

Four Pieces, Op. 3: *Story, Badinage, March, Phantom* (1907–8; revised 1911). fp St Petersburg, 28 March 1911

Four Pieces, Op. 4: *Reminiscence, Élan, Despair, Suggestion diabolique* (1908; revised 1910–12). fp St Petersburg, 18 December 1911

Toccata in D minor, Op. 11 (1912). fp Petrograd, 27 November 1916

Ten Pieces, Op. 12 (1906–13). fp (three only) Moscow, 23 January 1914. No. 9 arranged as Humoresque Scherzo for four bassoons, Op. 12b (1915)

Sonata No. 2 in D minor, Op. 14 (1912). fp Moscow, 23 January 1914

Five *Sarcasms*, Op. 17 (1912–14). fp Petrograd, 27 November 1916

Visions fugitives (Mimoletnosti), Op. 22 (1915–17). fp Petrograd, 15 April 1918

Sonata No. 3 in A minor, Op. 28, 'From Old Notebooks' (1917), reworking of 1907 Sonata 'No. 3'. fp Petrograd, 15 April 1918

Sonata No. 4 in C minor, Op. 29, 'From Old Notebooks' (1917), after Sonata 'No. 5' and Symphony in E minor. fp Petrograd, 17 April 1918 (see also Andante, Op. 29b, in Orchestral)

Old Grandmother's Tales (Skazki staroy babushki), Op. 31 (1918). fp New York, 7 January 1919

Four Pieces, Op. 32: *Danza, Menuetto, Gavotte, Valse* (1918). fp New York, 30 March 1919

Sonata No. 5 in C major, Op. 38 (1923). fp Paris, 9 March 1924

Choses en soi (Things in Themselves, Veshchi v sebe), Op. 45: i. Allegro moderato; ii. Moderato scherzando (1928). fp New York, 6 January 1930

Six Transcriptions for piano, Op. 52, from Opp. 46, 35, 50, 48 (1930–1). fp Moscow, 27 May 1932

Two Sonatinas, Op. 54 (1931–2). fp (broadcast, No. 2 only) London, 17 April 1932

Three Pieces, Op. 59: *Promenade, Paysage, Sonatina Pastorale* (1933–4). fp Moscow, 1935

Thoughts (Mïsli, Pensées), Op. 62, for piano (1933–4). fp Moscow, 13 November 1936

Dumka (1933?)

Music for Children, Op. 65, twelve easy pieces for piano (1935). fp Moscow, 11 April 1936

Romeo and Juliet, Op. 75, ten pieces for piano (1937). fp Moscow, 1937

Gavotte, arrangement from incidental music for *Hamlet* (1938). fp (broadcast) Moscow, 22 November 1939

Sonata No. 6 in A major, Op. 82 (1939–40). fp Moscow, 8 April 1940

Sonata No. 7 in B flat, Op. 83 (1939–42). fp Moscow, 18 January 1943

Sonata No. 8 in B flat major, Op. 84 (1939–44). fp Moscow, 30 December 1944

Three Pieces, Op. 95, from *Cinderella* (1942)

Three Pieces, Op. 96, arrangements from *War and Peace* and *Lermontov* (1941–2)

Ten Pieces, Op. 97, from *Cinderella* (1943)

Six Pieces, Op. 102, from *Cinderella* (1944)

Sonata No. 9 in C major, Op. 103 (1945–7). fp Moscow, 21 April 1951

Sonata No. 5 in C major, Op. 135, second version (1952–3). fp Alma-Ata, 2 February 1954

Sonata No. 10 in C minor, Op. 137 (1953). Unfinished

Arrangements

Buxtehude: Organ Prelude and Fugue in D minor, arranged for piano (1920)

Schubert: Waltzes by Schubert, arranged as a suite for piano (1920). Revised as a suite for two pianos (1923)

Five Popular Songs of Kazakhstan (1927)

'O, no John!', English folk song arranged for voice and orchestra (1944)

Twelve Russian Folk Songs, Op. 104 (1944). fp Moscow, 25 March 1945

Two Duets, Op. 106, arrangements of Russian folk songs for tenor and bass with piano (1945)

Further Reading

Surprisingly, for someone who led such an eventful life, Prokofiev has been the subject of only one first-rate biography: Michel Dorigné's great tome is at present, unfortunately, only available in French. The most substantial English-language biography, by Harlow Robinson, is no longer in print and in any case is sadly riddled with inaccuracies, and so should be approached with caution. The two most reliable biographies published in English are, by default, those by Israel Nestyev and David Gutman, though caveats are outlined for each in their respective entries. At the time of writing, David Nice is undertaking a major monograph on the composer – it is to be sincerely hoped that his work, which follows abortive attempts by Malcolm Brown and the late Christopher Palmer, reaches completion.

Blok, V. (ed.) *Prokofiev – Materials. Articles. Interviews* (Moscow, Progress Publishers, 1978)
Includes an enlightening essay by the Soviet biographer, Israel Nestyev, about his working relationship with Prokofiev; publishes Prokofiev's working notes for a speech given to the Composers' Union in 1936.

Buckle, R. *Diaghilev* (London, Weidenfeld & Nicolson Ltd, 1979)
The most reliable biography of Diaghilev and his circle available.

Dorigné, M. *Serge Prokofiev* (Paris, Fayard, 1994)
The most scholarly and by far the most musically literate monograph on Prokofiev published, available in French only.

Duke, V. *Passport to Paris* (Boston/Toronto, Little, Brown and Company, 1955)
Includes vivid and affectionate reminiscences of Prokofiev and the friends Duke and he shared.

Gutman, D. *Prokofiev* (London, Omnibus Press, 1990)
A digest of various writings on Prokofiev presented within a continuous narrative mainly about Soviet politics and culture; despite some sharp insights into the music, Prokofiev is a somewhat shadowy figure in Gutman's narrative.

Moreux, S. 'Prokofieff – An Intimate Portrait', *Tempo*, No. 20 (1949)
A vivid and affectionate portrait of Prokofiev in the early 1930s, including his confession of profound homesickness.

Nabokov, N. *Old Friends, New Music* (London, Hamish Hamilton, 1951)
Includes a more acid portrait of Prokofiev than Vernon Duke's, but just as revealing.

Nestyev, I. *Prokofiev*, translated by Florence Jonas, foreword by Nicolas Slonimsky (London, Oxford University Press, 1961)
A biography worth reading since – at least initially – it was prepared with Prokofiev's assistance. But it is notoriously biased politically, and handicapped by Nestyev's free airing of Soviet prejudices in the chapters dealing with the 1920s and early 30s; his account of Prokofiev's last five years, due to political pressures, verges on the fictitious.

Prokofiev, S. *Prokofiev by Prokofiev – A Composer's Memoir*, translated by Guy Daniels, edited by David H. Appel (New York, Doubleday, 1979)
There are some intriguing and vivid recollections, plus extensive quotations from letters to and from Prokofiev; the text should be treated with caution, though, as it was written decades after events and mostly under adverse conditions: some events, as a result, are conflated or chronologically dislocated. The English translation is at times stilted and not always reliable.

— *Selected Letters of Sergei Prokofiev*, translated and edited by Harlow Robinson (Boston, Northeastern University Press, 1998)
A new edition of letters between Prokofiev and his Russian colleagues, many published in English for the first time.

— *Soviet Diary 1927 and Other Writings*, translated and edited by Oleg Prokofiev and Christopher Palmer (London, Faber, 1991)
A candid record of Prokofiev's first 'return' to the USSR, particularly revealing about his relationship with friends and colleagues from his St Petersburg years.

Radzinsky, E. *Stalin* (London, Hodder & Stoughton, 1996)
A substantial but racy account of Stalin's life and thought; alone among Stalin's biographers, Radzinsky goes into some detail about the dictator's impact on Soviet culture.

Robinson, H. *Sergei Prokofiev – A Biography* (London, Robert Hale, 1987)
The most detailed English-language biography, containing substantial chunks of original research and balanced political insight, but mixed with some unaccountable lapses in reliability.

Schwarz, B. *Music and Musical Life in Soviet Russia 1917–70* (London, Barrie & Jenkins, 1972)
This remains perhaps the best informed, and certainly most readable, single volume on Soviet music.

Seroff, V. *Sergei Prokofiev – A Soviet Tragedy* (New York, Funk & Wagnalls, 1968)
A readable, if partisan, biography that was a valuable corrective to Nestyev's rosy view of Prokofiev's final years in the USSR.

Shlifstein, S. (ed.) *Prokofiev – Autobiography. Articles. Reminiscences*, translated by Rose Prokofieva (Moscow, Foreign Languages Publishing House, 1956)
Includes essays by Kabalevsky, Lina Prokofieva, Rostropovich, etc.

Volkov, S. *St Petersburg – A Cultural History* (London, Sinclair-Stevenson, 1996)
Invaluable for its vivid portrayal of the rich cultural life of St Petersburg throughout this century.

Werth, A. *Musical Uproar in Moscow* (London, Turnstile Press, 1949)
A deservedly famous contemporary account by a British journalist of Zhdanov's savaging of Soviet composers in 1948. Allowing for the writer's lack of in-depth knowledge of the subject, it is a lucid and vivid account of the events and arguments raised at that time.

Wilson, E. *Shostakovich – A Life Remembered* (London, Faber, 1994)
An invaluable anthology that vividly paints the vicissitudes of Soviet cultural life and includes reminiscences about Prokofiev and several other leading Soviet musicians.

Selective Discography

The aim of the following list is to give a broad spectrum of what is available of all Prokofiev's major works with minimal duplication; while it has not always been possible to avoid recommending recordings that sound little better than play-throughs (such as Järvi's *Symphonic Song* on Chandos, the only recording ever made of that work), recordings have been selected for presenting outstanding or at least sympathetic performances in good sound. Some superb recordings have, unaccountably, been removed from circulation, even within two years of their initial release. Hence, regrettably, the need to list more 'currently unavailable' releases than is usual in this series.

For a musician whose reputation (and certainly living) was initially made through his piano playing, Prokofiev, sadly, made very few recordings. Apart from a polished account of his Third Piano Concerto and a few other pieces, there are some not altogether reliable Duo-Art piano roll recordings, which are a poor reflection of the pianist that can be heard on the few 78s he made.

Leading interpreters of Prokofiev include the pianist Sviatoslav Richter and the conductors Gennady Rozhdestvensky and Valery Gergiev, almost all of whose recordings can be recommended. Any that were made in the former USSR, however, particularly those taken from radio broadcasts, are often in barely adequate or even poor sound; furthermore, they are often crudely edited.

Mention should also be made of a number of Melodiya recordings yet to surface in BMG's ongoing project of making quality transfers onto CD. Neither *Semyon Kotko*, stolidly but reliably recorded in the early 1960s by Zhukov, nor *Story of a Real Man*, recorded in a heavily edited (by Mira Mendelson-Prokofieva) version conducted by Ermler in 1961, has ever been transferred onto CD. Many other recordings, previously made available in the West in CD format by Olympia, Chant du Monde and other companies, have been withdrawn because of Melodiya's exclusive agreement with BMG: I have none the less listed those recordings which I consider any serious collector of Prokofiev's music will want to look out for, either in libraries or in second-hand record shops.

Historic

Prokofiev Plays Prokofiev
Piano Concerto No. 3
Solo Piano Works
Sergey Prokofiev (piano); London Symphony Orchestra conducted by Piero Coppola
PEARL GEMM CD 9470

Prokofiev Plays Prokofiev (Duo-Art Piano Rolls)
Toccata
Pieces from Op. 12
'Love for Three Oranges' Intermezzo
Old Grandmother's Tales
Sergey Prokofiev (duo-art piano); with works by Mussorgsky, Glazunov, Myaskovsky, Skryabin and Rimsky-Korsakov
LASERLIGHT DIGITAL 14 203

Rostropovich: The Russian Years 1950–74
Cello Sonata (world première)
Symphony-Concerto
Cello Concertino
Adagio and Waltz-Coda, from Cinderella
March, from The Love for Three Oranges
Mstislav Rostropovich (cello), Sviatoslav Richter (piano); with works by Britten, Shostakovich, Boris Chaikovsky, Kabalevsky, etc.
EMI CZS 5 72016 2 (13 CD set)

Opera

Maddalena
Elena Ivanova, Alexey Martynov, Sergey Yakovenko,
Natalya Koptanova, Victor Rumyantsev, male members
of the USSR Ministry of Culture Chamber Choir,
USSR Ministry of Culture Symphony Orchestra
conducted by Gennady Rozhdestvensky
MELODIYA SUCD 10-00053 (currently unavailable)

The Gambler
Kirov Opera conducted by Valery Gergiev
PHILIPS 454 559–2 (due to be released)

The Love for Three Oranges (in French)
Gabriel Bacquier, Jean-Luc Viala, Hélène Perraguin,
Vincent Le Texier, Georges Gautier, Didier Henry,
Michèle Lagrange, Catherine Dubosc, Jules Bastin,
Choeurs et Orchestre de l'Opéra de Lyon conducted by
Kent Nagano
VIRGIN VCD7 59566-2

The Fiery Angel
Sergey Leiferkus, Galina Gorchakova, Kirov Chorus
and Orchestra, St Petersburg conducted by Valery
Gergiev
PHILIPS 446 078-2

Betrothal in a Monastery
Larissa Diadkova, Nikolay Gassiev, Sergey Alexashkin,
Anna Netrebko, Marianna Tarassova; Kirov Chorus and
Orchestra, St Petersburg conducted by Valery Gergiev
PHILIPS 462 107-2

War and Peace
Galina Vishnevskaya, Lajas Miller, Wieslaw Ochman,
Nicolay Gedda, Nikola Ghiuselev, Choeurs de Radio
France, Orchestre National de France conducted by
Mstislav Rostropovich
ERATO 2292-45331-2

War and Peace
A. Gergalov, Y. Prokina, G. Gregoriam, O. Borodina,
I. Bogachova, Y. Marusin, N. Okhotnikov, Kirov
Chorus and Orchestra, St Petersburg conducted by
Valery Gergiev
PHILIPS 434 097-2

Ballet

Chout
USSR Ministry of Culture Symphony Orchestra
conducted by Gennady Rozhdestvensky
OLYMPIA OCD 126 (currently unavailable)

Chout – concert suite
Grand Symphony Orchestra of Radio and Television
conducted by Gennady Rozhdestvensky; with
Autumnal Sketch and Waltz Suite
RUSSIAN REVELATION RV 10046

Le Pas d'acier
On the Dnieper
USSR Ministry of Culture Symphony Orchestra
conducted by Gennady Rozhdestvensky
OLYMPIA OCD 103 (currently unavailable)

The Prodigal Son
Scottish National Orchestra conducted by Neeme Järvi;
with Divertimento, Andante, Op. 29b and *Symphonic
Song*
CHANDOS CHAN 8728

Romeo and Juliet
London Symphony Orchestra conducted by André
Previn
EMI CZS5 68607-2

Cinderella
Russian National Orchestra conducted by Mikhail
Pletnev; with *Summer Night*
DEUTSCHE GRAMMOPHON 445 830-2

The Stone Flower
Bolshoi Theatre Orchestra conducted by Gennady
Rozhdestvensky
RUSSIAN DISC RC CD 11 022

Theatre and Film

Lieutenant Kizhe
Alexander Nevsky – cantata
Chicago Symphony Orchestra conducted by Claudio
Abbado; with *Scythian Suite*
DEUTSCHE GRAMMOPHON 447 419-2

Eugene Onegin
Timothy West, Samuel West, Niamh Cusack, Dominic
Mafham, Helena McCarthy, Terrence Hardiman,
Sinfonia 21 conducted by Sir Edward Downes
CHANDOS CHAN 9318/9

Alexander Nevsky – complete score
Evgenia Gorohovskaya, Chorus of St Petersburg
Teleradio Company, Chamber Chorus of St Petersburg
and St Petersburg Chorus Capella 'LIK', St Petersburg
Philharmonic Orchestra conducted by Yury
Temirkanov
RCA VICTOR RED SEAL 09026 61926 2

Ivan the Terrible (arranged Christopher Palmer)
L. Finnie, N. Storozhev, Philharmonia Choir,
Philharmonia Orchestra conducted by Neeme Järvi
CHANDOS CHAN 8977

Ivan the Terrible (arranged M. Lankester)
T. Sinyavskaya, S. Leiferkus, C. Plummer, New London
Children's Choir, London Symphony Chorus, London
Symphony Orchestra conducted by Mstislav
Rostropovich; with *Alexander Nevsky – cantata*
SONY S2K 48387 (currently unavailable)

Vocal/Choral

The Ugly Duckling
Zara Dolukhanova (mezzo-soprano), Berta Kozel
(piano); with Three Romances, five of twelve Russian
folk songs and various other songs
RUSSIAN DISC RD CD 11 341

Five Songs to Poems of Anna Akhmatova
Galina Vishnevskaya (soprano), Mstislav Rostropovich
(piano), Russian State Symphony Orchestra conducted
by Igor Markevitch; with songs by Tchaikovsky and
Mussorgsky
PHILIPS 446 212-2 (limited availability)

Seven, They Are Seven
Zdravitsa
(*Seven, They Are Seven*) Elnikov, Moscow Radio
Orchestra and Chorus conducted by Gennady
Rozhdestvensky, (*Zdravitsa*) USSR Radio Orchestra and
Chorus conducted by Evgeny Svetlanov; with *Alexander
Nevsky*
CHANT DU MONDE LDC 278389 (currently unavailable)

Seven, They Are Seven
Jaroslav Kachel, Prague Philharmonic Choir, Czech
Philharmonic Orchestra conducted by Karel Ancerl;
with Piano Concerto No. 1, *Scythian Suite* and
Symphony No. 1
PRAGA PR254 004

Cantata for the Twentieth Anniversary of October
Gennady Rozhdestvensky (speaker), Philharmonia
Chorus and Orchestra conducted by Neeme Järvi; with
excerpts from *The Stone Flower*
CHANDOS CHAN 9095

Cantata for the Twentieth Anniversary of October
(without Stalin movements)
Moscow Philharmonic Orchestra and Chorus
conducted by Kirill Kondrashin
MELODIYA (currently unavailable)

Alexander Nevsky – cantata
(see under Theatre and Film scores)

Orchestral

Autumnal Sketch
London Symphony Orchestra conducted by Vladimir
Ashkenazy
DECCA 448 273-2DF2

Piano Concertos Nos. 1–5
Michel Béroff, Gewandhaus-Orchester Leipzig
conducted by Kurt Masur; with *Overture on Hebrew
Themes* and *Visions fugitives*
EMI CMS 762542-2

Piano Concertos Nos. 1–5
Vladimir Ashkenazy, London Symphony Orchestra
conducted by André Previn
DECCA DOUBLES 425 570-2DM2

Violin Concertos Nos. 1 and 2
Gil Shaham, London Symphony Orchestra conducted
by André Previn; with Sonata for solo violin
DEUTSCHE GRAMMOPHON 447 758-2

Violin Concertos Nos. 1 and 2
Itzhak Perlman, BBC Symphony Orchestra conducted
by Gennady Rozhdestvensky
EMI CDC7 47025-2

Symphonies Nos. 1–7
Scythian Suite
Russian Overture
London Symphony Orchestra, London Philharmonic
Orchestra conducted by Walter Weller
DECCA 430 782-2

Symphony No. 1
Sinfonietta, Op. 48
Orchestre de Chambre de Lausanne conducted by
Alberto Zedda; with works by Debussy and Milhaud
VIRGIN CLASSICS CUV5 61206 2

Symphony No. 2
Dreams
Autumnal Sketch
Symphony No. 1, 'Classical'
National Symphony Orchestra of Ukraine conducted
by Theodore Kuchar
NAXOS 8.553053

Symphony No. 3
Symphony No. 4 (original version)
Scottish National Orchestra conducted by Neeme Järvi
CHANDOS CHAN 8401

Cello Concerto in E minor
János Starker, Philharmonia Orchestra conducted by
Walter Susskind; with works by Boccherini, Dvořák,
Fauré, Dohnányi and Milhaud
EMI CZS 5 68745 2

Peter and the Wolf
Symphony No. 1, 'Classical'
The Love for Three Oranges suite
Lieutenant Kizhe suite
(*Peter and the Wolf*, 'Classical' Symphony) Ralph
Richardson, London Symphony Orchestra conducted
by Sir Malcolm Sargent, (*The Love for Three Oranges
suite*) London Philharmonic Orchestra conducted by
Walter Weller, (*Lieutenant Kizhe*) Paris Conservatoire
Orchestra conducted by Sir Adrian Boult
DECCA 433 612-2

Peter and the Wolf
March in B flat major
Overture on Hebrew Themes
Symphony No. 1, 'Classical'
Sting, The Chamber Orchestra of Europe conducted by
Claudio Abbado
DEUTSCHE GRAMMOPHON 429 396-2

Russian Overture
Symphony No. 1
Symphony No. 5
(*Russian Overture*) London Philharmonic Orchestra
conducted by Walter Weller, (Symphonies Nos. 1 and 5)
London Symphony Orchestra conducted by Walter
Weller (see also complete symphonies, Decca)
BELART 461 320-2

Semyon Kotko – symphonic suite
Symphony No. 5
Grand Symphony Orchestra of Radio and Television
conducted by Gennady Rozhdestvensky
RUSSIAN REVELATION RV 10041

Symphony No. 6
Leningrad Philharmonic Orchestra conducted by
Evgeny Mravinsky; with Symphony No. 5
PRAGA PR250 014

Symphony-Concerto
Violin Concerto No. 1
Mstislav Rostropovich (cello), London Symphony
Orchestra conducted by Seiji Ozawa; Anne-Sophie
Mutter (violin), National Symphony Orchestra
conducted by Mstislav Rostropovich
ERATO 2292 45708-2 (currently unavailable)

Symphony No. 7
Symphony No. 3
Ukraine National Symphony Orchestra conducted by
Theodore Kuchar
NAXOS 8.553054

Chamber/Instrumental

Quintet, Op. 39
Ensemble Walter Boeykens; with *Overture on Hebrew
Themes* and works by Kókai and Aram Khachaturian
HARMONIA MUNDI HMA 1901419

String Quartets Nos. 1 and 2
The American Quartet
OLYMPIA OCD 340

Violin Sonatas Nos. 1 and 2
Cinq Mélodies
Mayumi Fujikawa (violin), Craig Sheppard (piano)
ASV DCA 667

Cello Sonata
(see Rostropovich: The Russian Years, in Historic)

Piano: juvenilia

'Song' No. 28: Presto in C major
'Song' No. 41: Allegretto in C minor
'Song' No. 50: Scherzo
Allegro in D minor
Lento in D minor
Tarentella
Frederic Chiu; with *Old Grandmother's Tales, Music for
Children*, Ten Pieces, Op. 12
HARMONIA MUNDI HMU 907190

'Song' No. 32: Vivo in G minor
'Song' No. 39: Allegretto in A minor
Frederic Chiu; with *Visions fugitives*, Toccata, Four
Pieces, Op. 3, Four Pieces, Op. 4, Three Pieces, Op. 96,
Sarcasms
HARMONIA MUNDI HMU 907169

'Song' No. 47: Minuet in F minor
'Song' No. 53: Waltz in G minor
'Song' No. 54: March in F minor
Étude-Scherzo in C major
Boris Berman; with Allegretto, Sonata No. 5 (original
version), Sonata No. 6, Sonata No. 10 (fragment),
Toccata, Gavotte from 'Classical' Symphony
CHANDOS CHAN 9361

Piano: mature works

Piano Sonatas Nos. 1 and 8
Four Pieces, Op. 3
Old Grandmother's Tales
Three Pieces Op. 59
Oleg Marshev
DANACORD DACOCD 392

Piano Sonatas Nos. 2 and 4
Four Pieces, Op. 4
Song without Words
Things in Themselves
Children's Music, Op. 65
Oleg Marshev
DANACORD CACOCD 394

Piano Sonata No. 3
Four Pieces, Op. 32
Oleg Marshev; with Prokofiev's Ten Pieces, Op. 12,
Thoughts, March, Op. 89, Sonata No. 5 (revised version)
DANACORD CACOCD 393

Visions fugitives
Nikolay Demidenko (piano); with music by Skryabin
CONIFER CDCF 204

Piano Sonata No. 5 – original version
Piano Sonatas Nos. 2, 3, and 9
Yefim Bronfman
SONY CLASSICAL SK 53273

Piano Sonatas Nos. 6 and 7
Dumka
Visions fugitives
Oleg Marshev
DANACORD DACOCD 391

Piano Sonata No. 7
Sviatoslav Richter; with music by Skryabin and
Myaskovsky
MELODIYA/BMG 74321 294702

Piano Sonata No. 8
Visions fugitives, Nos. 3, 6 and 9
Sviatoslav Richter; Warsaw National Philharmonic
Orchestra conducted by Witold Rowicki; with Piano
Concerto No. 5
DEUTSCHE GRAMMOPHON 449 744-2

Three Pieces, Op. 96
Frederic Chiu; with juvenilia (see separate entry above)
HARMONIA MUNDI HMU 907169

Index

Page numbers in italics refer to picture captions.

Photographic Acknowledgements

AKG Photo, London: 39, 130
Corbis-Bettmann/UPI: 30, 46,
   79, 117, 158, 183
The Hulton Getty Picture
   Collection, London: 17, 43, 53,
   62, 99
The Lebrecht Collection, London:
   13, 16, 142, 154 (reproduced with
   permission of the Prokofiev
   Estate), 174, 181
Novosti, London: 9, 18, 48, 50, 51,
   63l, 72, 109, 122, 152, 153, 163,
   167, 177, 190, 191, 194, 196, 198,
   205, 207
The Prokofiev Estate: 2, 12, 37, 58,
   63r, 65, 69, 70, 75, 77, 78, 80, 81,
   83, 85, 91, 92, 94, 95, 100, 101,
   103, 104, 108, 113, 115, 126, 136,
   137, 139, 143, 146, 185, 209, 211
Society for Co-operation in
   Russian Soviet Studies: 161, 169,
   189
Theatre Museum, London: 105
Natalia Savkina, *Prokofiev*,
   Paniniana Publications Inc.,
   New Jersey (1984): 23
Nina Krivosheyna, *Four Thirds of
   our Life*, YMCA Press, Paris
   (1984) 35

Text Acknowledgements

We are grateful for the permission
to quote from the following
sources:

R. Buckle, *Diaghilev* (London,
   Weidenfeld & Nicolson Ltd,
   1979)
I. Nestyev, *Prokofiev*, translated by
   Florence Jonas (London, Oxford
   University Press, 1961)
S. Prokofiev, *Soviet Diary 1927 and
   Other Writings*, translated and
   edited by Oleg Prokofiev and
   Christopher Palmer (London,
   Faber & Faber, 1991)
S. Prokofiev, *Prokofiev by
   Prokofiev*, edited by David H.
   Appel, © 1979 by Doubleday, a
   division of Bantam Doubleday
   Dell Publishing Group, Inc.
H. Robinson, *Sergey Prokofiev – A
   Biography* (London, Robert
   Hale, 1987), permission kindly
   given by the author
B. Schwarz, *Music and Musical Life
   in Soviet Russia 1917–1970*
   (London, Barrie & Jenkins,
   1972)
A. Schopenhauer, *The World As
   Will and Representation*,
   translated by E. F. J. Payne (New
   York, Dover Publications Inc.,
   1966)